Citizens, Political Communication, and Interest Groups

Recent titles in the
PRAEGER SERIES IN POLITICAL COMMUNICATION
Robert E. Denton, Jr., *General Editor*

Citizens, Political Communication, and Interest Groups

Environmental Organizations in Canada and the United States

John C. Pierce, Mary Ann E. Steger,
Brent S. Steel, and Nicholas P. Lovrich

Praeger Series in Political Communication

PRAEGER

Westport, Connecticut
London

Library of Congress Cataloging-in-Publication Data

Citizens, political communication, and interest groups : environmental
organizations in Canada and the United States / John C. Pierce . . .
[et al.].
  p. cm. — (Praeger series in political communication, ISSN 1062-5623)
Includes bibliographical references and index.
ISBN 0-275-93579-5 (alk. paper)
  1. Environmental policy—United States—Citizen participation.
2. Pressure groups—United States. 3. Political culture—United
States. 4. Environmental policy—Canada—Citizen participation.
5. Pressure groups—Canada. 6. Political culture—Canada.
I. Pierce, John C. II. Series.
HC110.E5C57 1992
363.7′057′0973—dc20   92-15686

British Library Cataloguing in Publication Data is available.

Library of Congress Catalog Card Number: 92-15686
ISBN: 0-275-93579-5
ISSN: 1062-5623

First published in 1992

Praeger Publishers, 88 Post Road West, Westport, CT 06881
An imprint of Greenwood Publishing Group, Inc.

Printed in the United States of America

(∞)™

The paper used in this book complies with the
Permanent Paper Standard issued by the National
Information Standards Organization (Z39.48-1984).

10 9 8 7 6 5 4 3 2 1

Contents

Figure and Tables

Series Foreword

Those of us from the discipline of communication studies have long believed that communication is prior to all other fields of inquiry. In several other forums I have argued that the essence of politics is "talk" or human interaction.[1] Such interaction may be formal or informal, verbal or nonverbal, public or private, but it is always persuasive, forcing us consciously or unconsciously to interpret, to evaluate, and to act. Communication is the vehicle for human action.

From this perspective, it is not surprising that Aristotle recognized the natural kinship of politics and communication in his writings *Politics* and *Rhetoric*. In the former, he establishes that humans are "political beings [who] alone of the animals [are] furnished with the faculty of language."[2] And in the latter, he begins his systematic analysis of discourse by proclaiming that "rhetorical study, in its strict sense, is concerned with the modes of persuasion."[3] Thus, it was recognized over 2300 years ago that politics and communication go hand in hand because they are essential parts of human nature.

Back in 1981, Dan Nimmo and Keith Sanders proclaimed that political communication was an emerging field.[4] Although its origin, as noted, dates back centuries, a self-consciously cross-disciplinary focus began in the late 1950s. Thousands of books and articles later, colleges and universities offer a variety of graduate and undergraduate coursework in the area in such diverse departments as communication, mass communication, journalism, political science, and sociology.[5] In Nimmo's and Sanders's early assessment, the key areas of inquiry included rhetorical analysis, propaganda analysis, attitude change studies, voting studies, government and the news media, functional and systems analyses, technological changes, media technologies, campaign techniques, and research techniques.[6] In a survey of the state of the field in 1983, the same authors and Lynda Kaid found additional, more specific areas of concern such as the presidency, political polls, public opinion, debates, and advertising, to name a few.[7] Since the first study, they also noted a shift away from the rather strict behavioral approach.

Today, Dan Nimmo and David Swanson assert that "political communication has developed some identity as a more or less distinct domain of scholarly work."[8] The scope and concerns of the area have further expanded to include critical theories and cultural studies. While there is no precise definition, method, or disciplinary home of the area of inquiry, its primary domain is the role, processes, and effects of communication within the context of politics broadly defined.

In 1985, the editors of *Political Communication Yearbook: 1984* noted that "more things are happening in the study, teaching, and practice of political communication than can be captured within the space limitations of the relatively few publications available."[9] In addition, they argued that the backgrounds of "those involved in the field [are] so varied and pluralist in outlook and approach, . . . it [is] a mistake to adhere slavishly to any set format in shaping the content."[10] And more recently, Swanson and Nimmo called for "ways of overcoming the unhappy consequences of fragmentation within a framework that respects, encourages, and benefits from diverse scholarly commitments, agendas, and approaches."[11]

In agreement with these assessments of the area and with gentle encouragement, Praeger established in 1988 the series entitled "Praeger Studies in Political Communication." The series is open to all qualitative and quantitative methodologies as well as to contemporary and historical studies. The key to characterizing the studies in the series is the focus on communication variables or activities within a political context or dimension. Scholars from the disciplines of communication, history, political science, and sociology have participated in the series. To date, there are nearly fifty titles in the series.

This volume is a rich study of political communication with several dimensions. First, it is an informative analysis of the role and impact of interest groups in democratic politics. The authors provide an overview and critique of the traditional pluralistic interest group perspective of democratic politics in a postindustrial society.

This book is also a study about the formation of public policy focusing on a technical and scientific environmental concern, acid rain. Although many issues confronting public life are becoming more and more complex, the need for public awareness and involvement in governmental decisions is critical if we are to maintain a truly vibrant and pluralistic democracy. Thus, the authors provide insight into the dilemma of how to maximize public interest and involvement in the formation of complex and very technical public policy.

This study is also a valuable cross-national investigation of political communication. Although Canada and the United States share a common border and a common environmental concern about acid rain, they differ in cultural heritages and political institutions. The authors' analyses provide an opportunity to identify and assess the general patterns of interest group activities and contextual influences and constraints across national boundaries. Such analyses contribute to the development of system-level conceptions of political communication.

Finally, this is an empirical study. Over 4,000 environmental group members and citizens were surveyed to generate several impressive datasets that provide the basis for the cross-cultural and public policy analyses.

The authors of this landmark study demonstrate the value and importance of interest groups in modern, technologically complex democracies. Ultimately, they argue that the key to interest group activity is the communication of policy-relevant technical knowledge and information. Perhaps because the stakes are even higher, citizens today demand greater access to information and opportunities for participation in the formation of public policy.

I am, without shame or modesty, a fan of the series. The joy of serving as its editor is in participating in the dialogue of the field of political communication and in reading the contributors' works. I invite you to join me.

Robert E. Denton, Jr.

NOTES

1. See Robert E. Denton, Jr., *The symbolic dimensions of the American presidency* (Prospect Heights, IL: Waveland Press, 1982); Robert E. Denton, Jr., and Gary Woodward, *Political Communication in America* (New York: Praeger, 1985, 2nd edition, 1990); Robert E. Denton, Jr., and Dan Hahn, *Presidential communication* (New York: Praeger, 1986); and Robert E. Denton, Jr., *The primetime presidency of Ronald Reagan* (New York: Praeger, 1988).

2. Aristotle, *The politics of Aristotle,* trans. Ernest Barker (New York: Oxford University Press, 1970), p. 5.

3. Aristotle, *Rhetoric,* trans. Rhys Roberts (New York: The Modern Library, 1954), p. 22.

4. Dan Nimmo and Keith Sanders, "Introduction: The Emergence of Political Communication as a Field," in Dan Nimmo and Keith Sanders, eds., *Handbook of political communication* (Beverly Hills, CA: Sage, 1981), pp. 11–36.

5. Ibid., p. 15.

6. Ibid., pp. 17–27.

7. Keith Sanders, Lynda Kaid, and Dan Nimmo, eds., *Political communication yearbook: 1984* (Carbondale, IL: Southern Illinois University, 1985), pp. 283–308.

8. Dan Nimmo and David Swanson, ''The Field of Political Communication: Beyond the Voter Persuasion Paradigm,'' in David Swanson and Dan Nimmo, eds., *New directions in political communication* (Beverly Hills, CA: Sage, 1990), p. 8.

9. Sanders, Kaid, and Nimmo, *Political communication yearbook*, p. xiv.

10. Ibid., p. xiv.

11. Nimmo and Swanson, ''The Field of Political Communication,'' p. 11.

Acknowledgments

This book represents a collective effort among the four authors, certainly, but it was a collaboration supported by a much wider array of persons and organizations. First, appreciation must be expressed for the generosity of the Canadian government, provided in the form of a grant from the Canadian Embassy in Washington, D.C., under their faculty research grant program. Resources from this grant partially supported the collection of the survey data reported here.

Additional support for the research field work and subsequent analysis of findings was provided by the several universities involved—Washington State University, Oakland University, Northern Arizona University, and Oregon State University. The authors benefited both from general university resources and from the useful suggestions and constructive criticisms of colleagues. In addition, a number of students also were critical to the success of one or another aspect of the work reported here, with special thanks being owed in this regard to Blair Stieber, Barbara Reskin, Lynette Lee-Sammons, and Craig Curtis.

In the preparation of the book manuscript, the enduring thanks of the authors are due to three exceptional individuals—Ruth Self, Linda Moore, and Carolyn Hood—whose patience, diligence, and problem-solving skills were indispensable to the book's completion. From the earliest drafts of field instruments to the final production of camera-ready figures and tables, their good cheer and remarkable abilities made the work pleasurable and satisfying.

While many persons and organizations shared in the tasks of collecting information and analyzing that information for some appropriate insights, the authors alone bear the responsibility for what is said here.

Neither the Canadian government nor the four universities in question should be held responsible for the observations made and the conclusions drawn; any errors of omission or commission, any questionable assumptions or misinterpretations of evidence are the sole responsibility of the authors.

Citizens, Political Communication, and Interest Groups

Chapter One

Information, Individuals, and Interest Groups

This book grows out of a long-term concern with the conditions under which democratic citizenries are able to influence complex issues of public policy in contemporary postindustrial societies. In particular, we are interested in the means by which individuals are able to acquire, process, and apply policy-relevant information in the pursuit of individual or shared interests. This searching for information on the part of individuals is especially critical when the policy issues in question are of a technical or scientific nature and, as a consequence, present themselves as being highly complex and difficult to assess (Pierce and Lovrich 1986; Pierce et al. 1989). The research reported in this work focuses on the ways in which interest groups may assist citizens in democratic countries to cope effectively with such complex issues of contemporary public policy.

This potential role of interest groups is examined in the context of environmental policy inasmuch as this area of public affairs commonly features issues of significant complexity from a scientific and technical perspective. While environmental policy issues have become increasingly complex over time as new knowledge about human effects upon the natural ecology becomes available, the environmental policy arena is nonetheless one in which there has been persistent pressure for expanding public involvement in the management of environmental affairs. Finally, environmental politics is a policy arena in which interest group activity has been a major feature of political conflict.

The decision to investigate the information component of interest group roles in democratic politics in a cross-national context was made in order to identify any effects that differing political cultures and distinctive political institutions might manifest. Canada and the United States have been said to differ substantially in their respective political cultures, and in the specific character of their respective political institutions as well. While perhaps differing in these important ways, Canada and the United States, however, share a common elevated concern about environmental issues generally, and about a specific shared environmental issue—acid rain—that provides the substantive focus of this work (Wetstone 1987). This combination of similarities in policy concerns and differences in political heritage provides an opportunity both to identify the general patterns of interest group activities (with respect to information gathering and the use of that knowledge to educate citizens and influence public officials) and to assess the contextual constraints that might obtain on those patterns.

As background for the empirical work presented in this book, this chapter begins with a brief overview of the traditional pluralistic interest group perspective on democratic politics and a review of the major critiques of that perspective. The discussion then addresses the particular demands placed on interest groups as a consequence of the technical information quandary common to postindustrial democracies (Pierce and Lovrich 1986). The paradox giving rise to this quandary reflects the fact that while many issues on the public agenda are increasingly complex and scientifically complicated in character (e.g., ozone depletion, recombinant DNA, global warming, hazardous waste disposal), the demand for public involvement in governmental decisions concerning these matters is growing at the same time (Graham 1987). The rationale for the Canadian–American contrast in the study of this paradoxical phenomenon then is presented, focusing on the divergent cultural heritages, the distinctive political institutional arrangements, and the shared socioeconomic dynamics obtaining in these two postindustrial democracies. Finally, the chapter outlines several hypotheses growing out of the combination of concerns stemming from group theory, the postindustrial information and participation quandary, and the cross-cultural differences separating Canada and the United States.

THE INTEREST GROUP PERSPECTIVE

The pluralist perspective on twentieth century democracies has underscored the critical role of interest groups for the effective representation of diverse constituencies in complex and heterogeneous societies (Ziegler 1964). In particular, the interest group theories of Arthur Bentley (1908), Peter Odegard (1928), Pendleton Herring (1940), David Truman (1951), Earl Latham (1952), and Bernard Crick (1959) largely reflected the character of American politics of the first half of this century. The politics of that period primarily entailed conflict and competition rooted in economic interests, with the status quo being challenged by the social welfare agenda of newly emerging political and economic classes (Bailey 1950). Pluralist interest group theory suggested that, in this advanced capitalistic economic context, citizens with common individual interests or shared stakes in political outcomes would be inclined to come together to pool their political resources and to exert influence on the political process in a way that would be far more effective than the pursuit of atomistic individual activity (Beer 1958). Organizations representing a wide range of these shared interests would act on their members' behalf in communicating with public officials and policymakers (Ehrmann 1960). Thus, in tandem with formal electoral processes, individual citizens could continue to exert meaningful and satisfying political influence via their interest-based organizational affiliations even in the difficult context of the mass society produced by industrial democracy (Dahl 1967).

Beginning largely in the 1960s, this traditional interest group view of Western democracies generally (and the United States in particular) was challenged widely (Bauer et al. 1963; McConnell 1966). The critique of interest group pluralist theory appeared on a variety of fronts. Some critics disputed the most fundamental assumptions of interest group theory. Mancur Olson, for example, demonstrated via formal economic theory that under certain common conditions rational individuals will not join organizations that promote their particular shared interests (1965). In those frequent cases in which individuals would receive the benefit of the group's activity and the individual's nonparticipation would not diminish significantly the capacity of the group to achieve its goal, it is "rational" for that individual to abstain from participation (Mitchell 1971).

In the same vein, others have argued that the political goals of the organization, presumably based on the shared interest of the individual members, are frequently not the primary reasons that individuals join interest groups (Clark and Wilson 1961). Potential group members often respond to "solidary" incentives related to the social and psychological benefits derived from group membership. In many cases, people may be induced to join because of material benefits provided by the group that are unrelated to the group's goal, but that may be available exclusively to group members (Salisbury 1969; Grupp 1971). James Q. Wilson similarly has argued that the distinctive mix or structure of the incentives offered by groups to prospective or existing members has a major effect on other important characteristics of political organizations (1962). For example, organizations concentrating on material incentive structures to attract members (e.g., producer associations) will mobilize different sorts of resources and employ different political strategies and tactics than will those organizations with agreement on the group's political goals (e.g., contemporary right-to-life groups) as the primary source of membership.

Traditional interest group pluralism also has been criticized for its intermingling of normative and empirical perspectives. That is, descriptions of the importance of interest groups in the operation of the American democracy were taken by some to mean that democratic political systems operate best under such conditions (Zolberg 1966, pp. 93–127). Because the "natural" formation of groups results in interest representation, some observers explicitly concluded that virtually all such interests would be represented and thus that democracy would be best served in an environment that fostered widespread group activity (Almond and Verba 1963; Almond and Powell 1966). Indeed, interest "aggregation" and "articulation" were identified in political theory as essential functions that must be performed by certain "structures" in a political system for that system to process political demands effectively (Macridis 1961; Easton 1965).

Interest group theorists of the pluralist school also were accused of glossing over unequal opportunities and capacities for organizing and expressing political demands (Galbraith 1952; Schattschneider 1960). The pluralist system was seen by a number of scholars as unfairly restrictive, permeable only by powerful individuals and groups possessing scarce financial resources to expend in political organization and direct influence of decision makers (Bachrach 1967; Bachrach and Baratz 1970). In particular, interest group democracy was said, in effect, to disenfranchise the poor, minorities, and others lacking the economic capacity to organize well, lacking the political legitimacy of establishment interests, and lacking the history of political access that guaranteed the opportunity to be heard (Eckstein 1963; Lowi 1969). Even the traditional economic interest group configuration (e.g., business, labor, agriculture) was seen to be less relevant than before to the then-current conflicts over major policy issues. Positions on the "social issues" of crime, race, and life-style mores and on the political actions associated with the protest against the war in Vietnam seemed unrelated to traditional group allegiances, much less to the long-standing partisan attachments of those groups (Rothman 1960; White and Sjoberg 1972).

The allegedly outmoded nature of traditional interest group liberalism was reinforced by what appeared to be the newly dominant forms of political activity in evidence in many industrial democracies (Barnes et al. 1979). These forms of political influence seemed to make irrelevant the long-standing patterns of behavior and access exhibited by the traditional interest groups (Peterson 1990). Civil disobedience, protest marches, boycotts, and class action law suits took the center stage in the public drama of politics, shoving to the wings the old-style interest group politics (Wills 1972). Moreover, public law and judicial decisions more and more frequently mandated formalized mechanisms of public involvement in heretofore closed areas of public policy in which special interests and government agencies could reach cozy accommodations outside of public view (Kweit and Kweit 1981). Citizen advisory committees, public hearing requirements, new-found legal standing in the courts, and heightened use of the initiative and referendum appeared to shift the focus of interest-based political activity to new forums and new types of political competition (Vogel 1981; Loomis 1983).

At the same time that newly emphasized forms of political expression were challenging traditional interest groups, there also appeared two relatively new forms of political organization—the public interest group (McFarland 1976) and the single issue interest group (Butler and Ranney 1981). To be sure, the public interest group and the single-interest group were not entirely "new"; however, their rapid proliferation did stand in stark contrast to the traditional interest group system based primarily on shared economic interests. The *public interest group* was defined as a group with goals that, when met, would result in benefits distributed to all citizens regardless of their participation (or lack thereof) in the political activity leading to the achievement of that goal (McFarland 1983). Environmental interest groups represent a prime example of public interest groups; others include such organizations as Common Cause, the League of Women Voters, and the American Civil Liberties Union. *Single-interest groups* are those formed around a particular position on such a single specific issue as abortion, school prayer, or the death penalty (Tatalovich and Daynes 1988). That issue alone becomes the sole criterion by which other citizens, organizations, candidates, and parties are to be judged. Such commitment to the salience of a single issue seriously dampened the political environment for traditional interest groups that characteristically emphasized multiple issues considered across time, issues among which compromise and negotiation could be used as the dominant modes of group member interaction (Verba 1965).

The formidable barrage of attacks made on the theory of traditional interest group pluralism has been sketched only briefly here. Even so, it is apparent that this critique reflected a full spectrum of theoretical, normative, empirical, and political inroads into what had been at one time the dominant analytical paradigm of political science, one that purported to explain a broad range of individual, organizational, and institutional behavior in the United States and other democratic nations (La Palombara 1960).

INTEREST GROUPS AND
THE POSTINDUSTRIAL QUANDARY

Against this broad backdrop, the thesis of this book is that interest groups remain very important in the modern, highly technological, sociologically "postindustrial" political world of contemporary Western democracies. Important to note, however, is the likelihood that the focus of interest groups' responses to the needs of the contemporary democratic citizen may have changed substantially in a way helpful to addressing the postindustrial quandary. The argument proposed here is that key to much contemporary interest group activity is the communication of policy-relevant technical knowledge and information. To be sure, scholars long have argued that the communication of information is integral to the political success of interest groups and their leaders (Garceau 1941). However, that information tended to be restricted largely to the groups' political position and to the substantive implications of policy options for the shared interests of the groups' members (Hagan 1958). In the current scientifically charged and technologically complex policy context, however, the information needs of individuals who share the group's concerns have expanded beyond those conventional forms.

The changing character of the policy context is of particular consequence in an environment in which interest group activism has become newly intensified (Bennett and Sharpe 1984; Zald and McCarthy 1987). Many observers suggest that the postindustrial changes of the last three decades responsible for giving rise to numerous difficult technical and scientific policy issues also have had other significant societal consequences. One of those noteworthy consequences is broadly thought to be a substantial change in the fundamental values of many citizens who have gained greatly from a prolonged period of prosperity and security (Inglehart 1971, 1977, 1990). Individuals maturing in a period of prosperity and security, feeling free to affirm values of self-expression, aesthetics, and affiliation, are argued to turn to the political world in ways that are different from those of their elders. Not only do such "postmaterialists" focus on a distinctive set of policy questions, but they also are more inclined than their materialistic elders to claim the inherent right to influence the outcomes of the political processes addressing those questions (Dalton 1988).

The claim of the right of general publics to exercise influence over such contentious issues as nuclear energy or genetic engineering, often with highly technical and scientific content, clearly is not without counterclaims from those who see a deep danger in popular participation in such policy forums. That threat is believed to be rooted in several sources. General public preferences, as well as the organized interests representing particular segments of the public, are viewed as likely to be deficient on multiple counts.

First, public preferences are said to be based too often on inappropriate values. In some cases, those values are thought to be too concerned with material gratification, and in other cases they are viewed as insufficiently concerned with economic development (Huntington 1974, 1975).

From either perspective, however, the point is the same—the public is too often wrong-headed and/or too easily misled and should steer clear of direct involvement in those areas of the policy process that should be governed by experience and appropriate technocratic expertise. Second, even if citizens were to possess appropriate values and predispositions, it is clear to some of their critics that they are informed insufficiently to make wise choices about how to convert those values into public policy (MacKuen 1990).

Why is it, then, that we argue that interest groups have the potential to perform a significant role for democratic citizenries in policy areas prototypical of postindustrial politics? To answer that question, it is necessary to establish the conceptual context underlying the public's need to employ some means by which to address the quandary we ascribe to postindustrial politics (Pierce and Lovrich 1986). A schematic outline of that process is shown in Figure 1.1.

POSTINDUSTRIAL SOCIETY

The observation that the past 40 years have witnessed fundamental changes in the economics, social relationships, and politics of industrial nations has become virtually commonplace (Marcuse 1970; Yankelovich 1982; Kassiola 1990). The period before World War II had been dominated by "traditional" political issues stemming from the economics of the worldwide depression and the international politics produced by instability in Europe and Asia. Social welfare policy and the need to ensure domestic and international security dominated the concerns of citizens and the political agendas of Western democracies. This preoccupation with social welfare domestic policy and international security issues continued into the early postwar decades. In the United States, for example, elections were fought and won or lost on such questions as the nation's proper posture toward communism or the obligation of the federal government to guarantee a minimal standard of living for its citizens (Galbraith 1958).

In hindsight, it has become clear that even while social welfare economics and national security dominated the political agendas of many nations in the postwar period, the seeds of change in that political landscape already had been sown. The increasing economic affluence of many Western democracies diminished for their mass publics the relative importance of social welfare concerns (Lasch 1972; Gappert 1979). Likewise, the fading memories of the threats of world war and the seeming vulnerability of the "Marxist menace" also allowed democratic citizenries to shift their concerns either to new issues or away from politics entirely.

The unprecedented affluence and lasting security were concurrent

Figure 1.1
The Development of Postindustrial Society

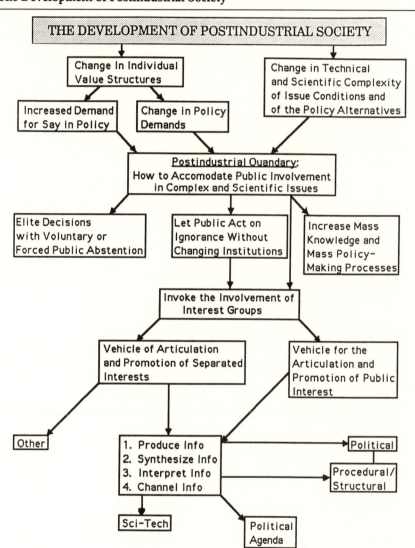

with—and largely the result of—some rather fundamental changes in the structure of economic and social systems in a number of Western democracies. Those changes have been described by Everett Ladd and Charles Hadley (1978) thusly:

The post-industrial order centers decisively around the precipitants and consequences of several interrelated developments: affluence; advanced technological development; the central importance of knowledge, national communication processes, the growing prominence and independence of the culture; new occupational structures, and with them new life styles and expectations, which is to say new social classes and new centers of power. (p. 184)

Central to the operation of postindustrial society for most scholars concerned with this construct has been the heightened role of modern technology: "Technology is creating the Post-Industrial society just as it created the industrial society" (Inglehart, 1977, p. 8).

Technology has facilitated the development of affluence; it has created new kinds of knowledge as sources of power and influence; it has become the core of both national and international communication processes, revolutionizing the speed and quality of information transmission; technology has become an integral part of the postindustrial culture and provides it with its independence from many traditional political and social institutions; technology has created new occupational structures and the need for expertise to fill positions in that structure; and, technology has created new centers of power and new resources for traditional power brokers (Galbraith 1967). It is the high degree of permeation of society by advanced technology and the changes that development has wrought that most clearly distinguishes postindustrial society from industrial society (Roszak 1972; Heisler 1974; Touraine 1971; Tsurutani 1977).

Postindustrial society and its attributes have had significant consequences for the nature of public policy challenges to be faced—such as environmental pollution, urban sprawl, biomedical discoveries for prolonging life—and in the kinds of policy claims made by activists among postindustrial citizens (Nelkin and Tancredi 1989). The impact of postindustrial society on the public policy agenda of democratic politics has been manifested in an important way in the alteration of the distribution of value orientations among citizens in postindustrial countries (Lafferty and Knutsen 1985; Inglehart 1990).

VALUE CHANGE

The proposition that postindustrial society has produced significant value shifts of a particular sort among important elements of mass publics has been documented most effectively by Ronald Inglehart (1990). Inglehart and his associates, in turn, have based their theory of value change on Maslow's widely known concept of a fixed hierarchy of individual needs motivating human behavior (1954).

Abraham Maslow has argued that people universally respond to a hierarchy of psychological needs, with the satisfaction of the most basic fundamental needs being the first object of an individual's efforts. These most basic needs felt by people everywhere are for safety and physical security. It is theorized that once such needs are satisfied, people will come to focus on the "higher-level" needs of affiliation and belonging-ness. At the apex of the need hierarchy are needs for personal growth or self-actualization, understood as such ends as the opportunity to express one's feelings about important political and social questions and to achieve one's own "full potential" as a human being (Maslow 1971).

When lower-order needs are threatened or the means of satisfying them are in short supply, people will forego efforts to achieve higher-order needs. According to Maslowian theory, then, what one values—the values he or she articulates—reflects the state of one's own needs. Individuals value those things that will help them satisfy the need most in ascendance. For example, individuals who are economically and physically secure are likely to have different values than those who must worry about their safety or their capacity to provide sufficient shelter and nourishment. Likewise, individuals who are secure and eco-nomically advantaged and well connected in their social affiliations then are "free" to exhibit values reflecting the highest need level of self-actualization.

Postindustrial society, then, produces a political impact through this hypothesized need hierarchy. Because postindustrial society is charac-terized by widespread affluence and prolonged security, fewer people are forced to focus primarily on the satisfaction of security and material needs—quite unlike the environment of the prewar and wartime peri-ods. Reflecting the Maslowian hierarchy concept, Inglehart has labeled as "materialist" those values that reflect the lower-order needs of indus-trial economy, and "postmaterial" those higher-order values that char-acterize people enjoying the benefits of the relatively affluent, secure postindustrial era.

An important aspect of Inglehart's concept of "culture shift" in which materialistic values are supplanted progressively by postindustrial val-ues reflecting higher-order needs in postindustrial societies is that there is a time lag phenomenon. According to Inglehart, an individual's value preferences are most likely to reflect the state of need satisfaction at the time of one's greatest sensitivity to socialization, namely, one's youth and early adulthood (Jennings 1989). Thus, one's personal values will tend to become "crystalized" as a reflection of conditions existing at the time during which one comes of age publicly and socially. Conse-quently, different generations will exhibit different values to the extent that during their time of socialization the character of environment-produced need satisfaction also differed. Inglehart's theory would pre-dict, then, that individuals socialized under the conditions of postindus-trial society will be more likely to exhibit postmaterial values than will individuals socialized in earlier times.

What are these particular values that characterize postmaterialist citizens of contemporary postindustrial societies? Inglehart has made the argument that two major components of postmaterial values exist that clearly reflect concern for higher-order needs. The two components reflecting the need for self-actualization are, first, giving a high value to having more say in determining the course of public policy and, second, having a secure right to express one's views about issues of public policy without fear of punishment (Inglehart 1990, p. 132). It is argued further that, in addition, such postmaterial values are associated with a syndrome of related concerns with particular kinds of policies and issues—namely those pertaining to:

- environmental protection
- gender/civil rights
- permissiveness in life-style decisions
- peace (antimilitarism)

Inglehart's conceptualization of value change (or culture shift) has held center stage on the comparative research agenda of scholars studying postindustrial effects on mass publics. It is important to note, however, that there are competing views on the nature of the value changes occurring in postindustrial societies, as well as on the consequences of such changes for democratic politics and the course of public policy.

Some scholars concur that widespread value change has occurred, but argue that the single dimension of the shift from materialist to postmaterialist values is not the best way of characterizing that change. For example, Scott Flanagan has argued that the most important value changes have been multidimensional, and that both Inglehart's instrument of measurement and his conceptualization of culture shift are flawed seriously (Flanagan 1982). Flanagan suggests that there are "two distinct kinds of value change taking place in the advanced industrial democracies" and he argues that Inglehart has "obscured this distinction by collapsing indicators of both into a single scale" (1987, p. 1303). Flanagan suggests that there is not only a "materialist–nonmaterialist" value dimension, but that there also has emerged an independent "authoritarian–libertarian" value dimension symbolized by the equally nonmaterialist "New Left" and "New Right."

Within the nonmaterialist (i.e., "new politics") dimension, those falling on the libertarian side support "the new left issue agenda, including liberalizing abortion, women's liberation, gay rights and the new morality issues." But, "on the other side of this value cleavage, the authoritarians endorse the New Right agenda, which includes right-to-life, anti–women's liberation, creationism, antipornography, and support for traditional moral and religious values" (Flanagan 1987, p. 1306).

According to Flanagan, the New Right "is as much nonmaterialist as the New Left" (1987, p. 1308). Inglehart, in stark contrast, maintains that the New Right and neoconservatism represent nothing more than a reaction by materialists against modernity. Inglehart argues specifically that neoconservatism is "a socio-cultural reaction to value change and cultural liberalization which cuts across traditional social class and party lines" (Minkenberg and Inglehart 1989, pp. 101–102).

Other critics of Inglehart share Flanagan's view of value change, suggesting that postindustrial society has unleashed both left-wing and right-wing versions of "new politics" and that Inglehart's indicator confuses or obscures these changes. Savage (1985), for example, argues that the left–right dimension and postmaterialism are distinct scales and that left-wing and right-wing postmaterialism both are evident in advanced industrial society. Other research conducted by Bakvis and Nevitte (1987) in Canada found that postmaterialists tend to be multidimensional as opposed to uniformly tolerant; they suggest that "postindustrial man may not be as liberal and democratic as generally supposed" (p. 357).

In short, Inglehart's work has focused attention on one type of value change evident in mass publics in the United States, western Europe, and Japan, and he has attributed that change to the advent of postindustrial society in these contemporary democratic nations. While a number of scholars have disagreed with Inglehart's conceptualization of that change, for the most part they do not discount the belief that *some* important value change has occurred and continues to take place. What is critical for our interest, though, is that both Inglehart's postmaterial values concept and Flanagan's idea of increasing "liberation" from conventional restraints on personal choice have led to two major effects upon politics and the role of interest groups in structuring the political debate: (1) heightened demand for having a say in policy outcomes on the part of individuals with the prototypical value configurations and (2) the articulation of relatively novel policy demands on the political system by new politics-oriented people, which often features a high degree of technical and scientific content affecting complex value trade-offs (e.g., environmental protection vs. jobs in the spotted owl and old-growth forests case; provision of life support technology vs. the right to die; development of safer nuclear energy plants vs. use of alternative energy sources).

ISSUE CHANGE

The value changes that have been documented among citizens in a number of postindustrial democracies take on special implications in the context of the contemporary nature of the postindustrial political agenda. As noted above, that agenda is partly a consequence of individual value changes that have produced public concerns with the satisfaction of higher-level needs. At the same time, however, postindustrialism's core components themselves have created political, economic, and social conditions that both generate certain kinds of new issues and alter the dimensions of traditional policy questions. These new issues or issue dimensions tend to possess some attributes that make rather problematic the preference for enhancing the involvement of the public in public affairs, which is also characteristic of postindustrial democracies.

NEW ISSUES

The technological developments that both lead to and stem from postindustrial society in some cases have become issues of public policy dispute. For example, the worldwide interpersonal and intrasocietal communications revolution (from written word to voice transmission to voice and picture transmission to satellite and laser imagery) has had as its backbone technological change (Dizard 1985). These changes in the ability to communicate allow a much more broadly based distribution of a multitude of types of information. At the same time, however, some social commentators have argued that these changes also serve to create the potential for enhanced dependency and information control by those who command access to and operate the communications technology in question (Miles and Gershung 1986). Similarly, revolutionary change has occurred in plant and animal biotechnology. Humans now possess the potential to alter at will the genetic structures of many plant and animal species. Such genetic changes have the potential to increase our agricultural productivity, to make organisms more resistant to disease, to make plants more tolerant of drought, or to provide humans with new medicines better able to deal with such common threats to our health as cancer or heart disease.

While the list of potential benefits is long, few of these genetic-material-altering undertakings are without controversy. The capacity to make benevolent change also implies the potential either for the production of unintended consequences or even for malevolent uses of this new power over life. The novelty of the issues being confronted and the complexity of their diverse components combine with individual uncertainty and limited knowledge to give rise to volatile perceptions of risk associated with such technology-induced change (Douglas and Wildavsky 1983).

NEW DIMENSIONS

Postindustrial change has neither fully supplanted nor left untouched the traditional issues of public policy. As noted in the section, "Value Change," shifts in values have elevated some issues into new promi-

nence on the political agenda. At the same time, moreover, the technological foundations of postindustrialism have added new content to
some public policy disputes of long-standing significance. The environmental policy arena upon which this book focuses is perhaps the prototypical example of technology-induced policy dynamics. To be sure, the
environmental policy arena received some degree of attention prior to
the advent of the postindustrial society; but, as the consequence of the
value shift, particularly among youthful cohorts, this policy arena has
received particularly heavy attention in postindustrial democratic nations (Dunlap 1989). It is fair to say that both the pace and extent of
technological change in postindustrial society served to inject new
sources of conflict, uncertainty, and perceptions of risk into considerations of environmental health and ecological well-being for many citizens of postindustrial societies (Hays 1987). Environmental policy conflict moved beyond polite discussion of the relative worth of wilderness
preservation, multiple use of public lands, or unfettered development
of natural resources. In the place of such discussions, many new, largely
technology-driven issues emerged, such as discovering safe means of
hazardous waste disposal, assessment of the damage caused by acid
rain deposition, calculation of the need for wetlands preservation, engineering the biodegradability of products and packaging, and determining the need for renewable energy source development. As Caulfield
has noted: "The conservation movement did not have to face the problem of air and water pollution, toxic and hazardous wastes, and chemi-
cal poisoning. Until the late 1960s these problems largely were not perceived by professionals or the public as general problems" (1989, p. 52).

THE QUANDARY

The postindustrial quandary is posed by the intersection of the two
major streams just described: (1) individual level value change leading
to changes in policy demands and enhanced claims for influence on
policy outcomes and (2) technological and scientific content being im-
parted to old issues and new policy conflict around technologies and
their impact, both of which are direct consequences of postindustrial
societies' heavy reliance on continuous scientific discovery and constant
technological advancement. Elsewhere, this "technical information
quandary" has been described in the following way: "How can the
democratic ideal of public control be made consistent with the realities
of a society dominated by technically complex policy questions?" (Pierce
and Lovrich 1983, p. 1). To be sure, a long history of debate exists over
the degree to which the mass public possesses the consistent capacity
to make sufficiently well-informed judgments about important issues of
public policy over the long term. It is our contention that this long-

standing issue concerning the capacity for sustained self-governance is brought even more fully to our attention by contemporary demands for greater public involvement coincident with heightened policy complexity; both forceful and persisting public demands for participation and a growing complexity of public policy issues are fundamental aspects of postindustrial societies.

The collision of the forces favoring greater public involvement and forces that make public policy issues evermore difficult to understand serves to strike at the very heart of questions of political power (Medcalf and Dolbeare 1985). Indeed, while the phrase "knowledge is power" is perhaps a cliche, cliches sometimes ring true. What brings a special caste to postindustrial power questions is the importance of knowledge and information that would allow mass publics to participate effectively in policy formation. Consequently, the principal focus of this book is on the question of whether interest groups assist both self-interested and public-interested citizens to deal with these difficult policy questions. Before we explore this potential role for contemporary interest groups more carefully, though, it is necessary to sketch out a brief overview of some alternative solutions offered to the policy complexity versus high desire for citizen participation quandary of contemporary postindustrial politics. Our discussion focuses upon common assumptions made about the public's level of knowledge and illustrates the importance of those assumptions for determining the public's rightful role in the policy process.

RESPONSES TO THE QUANDARY

Status Quo

One possible response to the quandary is to affirm the status quo, even while admitting that the public in large part fails to hold significant stores of policy-relevant scientific and technical information. This view reflects the belief that the holding of scientific and technical knowledge is largely irrelevant to the public's general capacity to produce sound policy. What the public really needs to know is its own value preferences, and in turn to reflect those values in its choices of elected officials and initiatives or referenda (Key 1966). Public involvement on policy, in this view, most appropriately would come into play to define the major priorities of government attention and reflect citizen assessments of the capacity of their governmental system and of science and technology to implement those priorities. If the public is decidedly cynical about either official goals or the capacity of government to implement its policies, governmental efforts are likely doomed to failure. Prohibition would represent a historical example of such failure, and perhaps the "war on drugs'' represents a more contemporary manifestation of this phenomenon (Schmidtz 1991, pp. 33–52). Citizen cynicism itself is not necessarily based on sound information, nor does it need to be. That cynicism can be rooted in the history of policy failure and successes and the extrapolation—whether proper or not—of those outcomes to likely future policy outcomes within the same genre of undertakings. The important concern throughout is that the public's values are incorporated into the policy outcome. The willingness of the public to support specific policy designed to achieve those values likely will be based primarily upon the history of proximate policy success, and only secondarily on the specific scientific and technological issues at stake (Krimsky 1984).

Another, more cynical version of the status quo position would suggest that no change is necessary since the processes of public influence are primarily symbolic in any case (Edelman 1964; Boorstin 1971). Why worry about public knowledge when the public's role in policy formation is only pro forma, and rightly so from this perspective (Rossini and Porter 1984).

Elite Guarantees

A second reaction to the quandary is to restrict the public's access to the policy process greatly. The proponents of this position suggest that it is largely a waste of time to attempt to educate the public in the complexities of modern-day policy issues. The public is either inherently incapable or unalterably unwilling to improve its low state of knowledge. It follows that the appropriate course of action is to accept that unalterable fact and move on to more expertise-based "technocratic" solutions (DeSario and Langton 1984). Moreover, the nature of some issues facing contemporary societies is so pressing and complex that public officials cannot endure the inefficiencies of a fully democratic and deliberative policy process. For such contemporary problems as the AIDS epidemic, the protection of endangered species, or the drawing down of reservoirs to compensate for drought conditions, the immediacy of problems faced does not permit sufficient time for the consensus-building processes of democratic government to discover an agreeable middle ground approach. In some cases, moreover, the middle ground may even be the worst possible approach (Olson 1981).

The answer, then, is to restrict participation greatly in certain policy areas to those individuals with the requisite store of appropriate knowledge. The question of how those elites possessing such knowledge are to be identified, of course, has a number of answers. In many cases, that elite is thought to be composed of those individuals with formal training in the substantive area affected by the policy. For example, in the nuclear policy area, the experts or elites making policy would be individuals with the highest-standing expertise in nuclear physics or nuclear engineering. Likewise, decisions about the use of forest resources would be left to those with the requisite formal training and experience in forestry (Benveniste 1972).

Advocates of another version of elite reservation of power distrust scientific experts almost as much as they distrust the public. Rather than an elite of expertise, it is an elite of political position that is said to occupy the Delphian vantage. True policy-relevant knowledge, in this view, comes neither from the short-term, self-interested motivation of individual citizens nor from the narrow scientific/technical training of experts. Neither the public nor the experts, it is said, have the breadth of perspective necessary to understand the full policy context (Cook 1985). That context relates to the long-term social and political dimensions of policy decisions and to their consequences for other policy areas outside the immediate context. Whether elected or appointed, these elites must have clear control over policy outcomes in more technical and scientific areas because "they are too important to be left to the experts" and "far too difficult to be left to the public" (Mazur 1981; Wamsley et al. 1987).

Public Rehabilitation

A third perspective is based on assumptions about the fundamental capacity of the public to learn and to apply that learning to public policy processes. The response to the quandary should not be to reject the public and restrict its role, but rather to embrace the public and encourage greater instructive participation (Hadden 1989). That embrace should (1) enhance the public's access to policy-relevant knowledge and (2) facilitate the acquisition and application of that knowledge in open policy formation processes (Barber 1984).

The first element assumes that the public, or significant portions of it, has the capacity to acquire and process a significant amount of policy-relevant knowledge. In democratic societies, then, it is the public's right to choose whether or not to partake of that communion joining politics and the body of scientific knowledge (von Hippel and Primack 1972). Given that public prerogative, it is the responsibility of others in the process to provide both the opportunity for learning and the channel for converting that knowledge into influence via an open process (Carroll 1971). With that knowledge and those channels, citizens have the opportunity either to serve their own self-interest or to promote the public welfare as they understand it and to maximize the policy benefits to their own value preferences. In reflection of these beliefs concerning the public's rightful role in public policy-making in science and technology issues, much existing statutory and regulating law contains requirements that public policy formation and implementation processes be structured to facilitate public involvement (Berry 1981). While the environmental policy area may have the greatest number of these formal requirements, they surface across a wide variety of policy areas. Indeed, to some extent the more technical and complex the policy area the greater has been the pressure for formalized public involvement mechanisms (Gruber 1987, pp. 121–148). That pressure, at the same time, may well have been in response to countervailing forces striving to inhibit public influence in those same realms of public policy (Rosenbaum 1978).

Another of the continuing critiques of the public involvement-oriented approach to policy-making in such areas of high science and technology content is that even if the public has the general capacity for informed involvement, there are far too many issue areas and policy questions requiring such involvement for this form of citizen participation to be practical. Critics argue that even if the dutiful and well-intentioned citizen has the potential for meeting the demands of the most extreme requirements for participation, "demand overload" will take its toll on citizens in short order and public involvement programs will prove ineffective as a consequence of lack of sustained public interest (Huntington 1981). The advocates of the public involvement approach agree that the number of technical and scientific policy questions to be considered is indeed beyond the time and cognitive carrying capacity of the individual citizen, however dutiful. They argue that citizens who command the capacity to understand such issues, given the time, also possess the capacity to make informed judgments about effective substitute means of achieving the same value-based, self-interested, or public interest-oriented policy outcomes (Dahl 1989, Part 4; Farber and Frickey 1991, pp. 132–144). It is to perhaps the most frequently identified substitute mechanism that we now turn—namely, issue-specific interest groups.

Interest Groups

In a number of ways, interest groups can be suggested as an effective solution to the paradox of the technical information quandary of contemporary postindustrial democracies. The argument presented here is that interest groups provide an effective and economical means by which individuals may have their information needs met. The costs of obtaining public policy-relevant information take both economic and cognitive forms. Issue-specific interest groups may serve citizen needs for information as they pursue their own interests and/or their visions of the "public interest." The provision of this information may contribute both to the general welfare of citizens and to the achievement of a sense of efficacy and societal connectedness of some citizens. In addition, the group's provision of information to individual members may satisfy some such nonpurposive goal (connected neither to public nor private interests) as the desire for information for its own sake.

The societal role of such interest groups with respect to serving the information needs of individuals obviously is not without its own group-serving dimensions. The group clearly must attract members and financial resources, and it engages in a complex exchange relationship with individuals for their affiliation (Salisbury 1969). If information is felt to be an important need of potential members, a group's ability to offer that information as a benefit of affiliation constitutes a powerful weapon in building its organizational base. Such groups also must compete effectively in the world of legislative and bureaucratic politics, and in a policy area with complex technological and scientific issues in which the command of specialized knowledge clearly represents a political strength.

We have framed this issue largely in the context of the proliferation of issues bearing heavy scientific and technical contents. It should be understood, however, that the full scope of information being discussed is much broader than simply that contained in the policy substance itself. A variety of kinds of information are important both to the group and to the potential group member. It is not necessary to elaborate these types of information in great detail here, but it is important to note them briefly. Information about timing and the political agenda—issues currently (or about to be) confronted in the policy process—is critical to the citizen's capacity to support the pursuit of either self-interest or the public interest as she or he might know it. If citizens are uninformed about when issues affecting them are on the table, it is unlikely that they will act to protect or advance effectively their own stake in the outcome of the policy process. The interest group, because of its focus of attention on the policy process and because of its access to and familiarity with that process, usually is able to signal its members when critical issues or critical events in the policy process are about to transpire.

A second important type of nontechnical/scientific information to be considered is *procedural information*, which concerns how policy decisions are made and where they take place. Procedural information defines who has the power to structure policy outcomes and by what criteria those outcomes are determined. In most cases, citizens, either individually or collectively, will act ineffectively if they are ignorant of the vital pressure points in the political system. Moreover, citizens will be well-served in applying that pressure only if they are privy to the types of concerns to which decision makers will respond in addressing their pleas. Again, interest groups have the resources and the policy process access to identify effectively the needed knowledge. It is true, of course, that significant variation exists across groups with respect to their degree of understanding of the process and in their extent of access to the critical pressure points in the policy process. In this regard, Helen Ingram and Dean Mann have noted that: "Strategies of environmental groups can best be understood as attempts to gain access to governmental decision-making rather than attempts to differentiate themselves in order to have relatively better positions in competition for members and contributors, or to build support" (1989, p. 143).

Finally, information about the politics of a policy area also represents a critical group asset. By "politics" is meant the array of actors (groups, individuals, firms, institutions) potentially affected by a policy outcome, the interests and positions or stakes those actors have in those outcomes, and the probabilities of various outcomes occurring as a result of that array. Organizations with high levels of this political information will be much more effective than groups lacking such important knowledge.

ASSESSING THE ROLE OF GROUPS

The argument for recognizing the positive role of groups in the contemporary setting is fairly straightforward. Policy issues produced by postindustrial society frequently are complicated by the need for knowledge about numerous new technologies and some scientific discoveries. That complexity exacerbates the problems of providing for citizen influence in the policy process and ensuring popular control in democratic polities generally. Other changes brought on by postindustrial society, nonetheless, heighten the senses of many contemporary citizens that they ought to exercise rights of direct involvement in public policies affecting their quality of life. A variety of responses to this apparent paradox in the governance of modern democratic societies have been proposed. Interest groups are a traditional vehicle for public influence, but their potential for addressing this paradox has been relatively ignored in the study of politics in postindustrial societies. Our argument is that interest groups can and do assist citizens in postindustrial democracies in dealing with the difficulties posed by issues entailing a high degree of scientific and technical content. This group activity focuses to a considerable degree on the development and dissemination of policy-relevant information. We suggest that it is economical for individuals to turn to groups for such information, and that it is economical and wise for groups to provide it to members inasmuch as it serves as a powerful incentive for affiliation.

To be sure, a good deal of recent scholarly literature on interest groups does recognize information as a significant incentive for group membership. However, the parallel literature concerning knowledge and information distribution processes in contemporary democratic societies accords interest groups scant attention given their likely importance to the political process. The goal of this book is to try to join these two strands of research and scholarship on the contemporary policy process.

The currents of postindustrial change, as well as their many unanticipated consequences, sweep across a broad range of contemporary nations. Fully understanding the potential information role of interest groups requires moving beyond the context of a single nation into a cross-national mode of analysis. The question then becomes framed in the following form: Does the role of interest groups in responding to the technical information quandary depend on the political culture in which postindustrial change has occurred? Thus, we turn to a consideration of how this possibility may play out in Canada and the United States.

THE CANADIAN AND AMERICAN CONTEXTS

Canada and the United States are both postindustrial democracies with a largely common European philosophical legacy. Even so, the two nations are broadly believed to possess rather distinct political cultures and governmental structures (see Gibbins and Nevitte 1985; Horowitz 1966; Presthus 1974; Lipset 1985; Lipset 1990). These differences have implications both for interest group activity and for the character of attitudes about the environment. Even though in some ways Canadian society is thought to be more group oriented than American society, Canadian politics is no more pluralistic and relatively less configured by competition among distinct interests than is the politics of the United States (Merelman 1991; Presthus 1973). In addition, it also is argued widely that the Canadian political culture produces a conceptualization of the environment in which humans and their natural surroundings are intertwined more closely than is the case among Americans (Atwood 1972).

The Political Culture Dimension

The Canadian political culture is broadly thought to be more organic and collectivistic in nature than its American counterpart, while the American political culture is seen as reflecting a Lockean individualistic conception of society (Lipset 1985, 1990). It has been argued that the Canadian public exhibits relatively "deferential patterns of authority" and is characterized by a "quasi-participative condition insofar as the citizen's role in politics is concerned" (Presthus 1974, p. 6). In sharp contrast, the American political culture is said to reflect a strongly individualistic conception of society in which public policy is shaped by pervasive, strongly held values that stress the free enterprise system (Dolbeare 1982).

The Canadian national identity is reflected in a number of distinctive cultural institutions. There is a general fear, especially evident in the arguments surrounding the free trade issue, that this identity will be swallowed up by the United States as Canada increasingly becomes tied closely in economic affairs to its neighbor to the south (Chacko 1987). At a 1986 conference on the theme "Cultural Sovereignty: Myth or Reality?" the discussion among conferees tended to focus on the free trade agreement and the cultural and arts institutions of Canada. The participants—representatives of government, the media, and the academic community—examined this question: "If there is ever increasing Canadian economic dependence on the United States through free trade, to what extent can Canada realistically maintain its cultural sovereignty?" (Chacko 1987, p. xviii). Cultural sovereignty is crucial because indigenous cultural activities contribute importantly to a sense of Canadian identity and social cohesion (Globerman 1987).

Noted Canadian writer Margaret Atwood (1972, 1984) makes the argument that the literary symbol that is at the heart of this Canadian identity is that of "survival"; in contrast, the American symbol is that of the "frontier." She defines the obstacles to survival as physical and spiritual: "In later writers the obstacles tend to become both harder to identify and more internal; they are no longer obstacles to physical survival but obstacles to what we may call spiritual survival" (1972, p. 33). This leads to a representation of "Canada as a . . . victim, or an 'oppressed minority' or 'exploited'" (p. 86). Although Atwood is looking at unifying themes in the literature of the two countries, the exploitation and victim status seem critical to more general cultural dimensions and may have implications for the two countries' views of the environment and of the character of their respective politics.

Just as the national identities of Canada and the United States are thought widely to differ, so too is it possible to point to studies that document significant differences in the mass political beliefs of these two nations (see Horowitz 1966; Presthus 1974; Lipset 1985; Gibbins and Nevitte 1985). It has been argued that Canadians at both elite and mass levels are more supportive of state intervention and less individualistic than Americans (Pross 1975; Lipset 1985; Manga and Broyles 1986). These differences also have been associated with comparisons of the geography and demography of Canada and the United States: "Canada controls an area, which larger than her southern neighbor's, is much less hospitable to human habitation in terms of climate and resources. Her geographical extent and weaker population base have induced direct government involvement'' (Lipset 1985, p. 112). Canadian author and *Toronto Star* correspondent Richard Gwyn (1987) summarizes these differences thusly:

[O]ur different political cultures cause society to pursue progress in quite different ways. . . . Americans view collective progress with extreme skepticism; collective power or state power is constrained by the division of powers and by the cardinal importance of the courts . . . in Canada, individual progress is regarded with extreme skepticism. . . . Yet, we take the possibility of collective progress for granted. (p. 271–272)

While we might cite diverse interpretations of contemporary patterns of beliefs and values in both Canada and the United States, it should be sufficient to note that some potentially significant differences between Canadians and Americans likely do exist. Much of the work in subsequent chapters of this book reflects on the extent to which these differences are present in survey data collected among our samples of interest group members and citizens in Michigan and Ontario. These American/Canadian differences are especially important because (1) they are said to affect quite directly the character of interest group politics, (2) they are said to be manifest in differing conceptions of government's obligation to protect and respect the environment, and (3) there is some indication of change in those attributes in the direction of greater convergence of the two cultures.

We have noted that both Canada and the United States are postindustrial democracies. As such, they are subject to many of the same social, economic, political, and technological forces. In the face of historically divergent political cultures and institutions, the question then arises as to whether there is occurring an inevitable convergence of the two systems featuring a diminishment of their historical distinctiveness. The possibility of cultural convergence as a postindustrial by-product has been of special concern to Canadians. Indeed, the recent free trade agreement with the United States was fought out on the turf of cultural autonomy for the Canadians.

Consistent with the convergence thesis, scholars observing the development of new forms of interest group activity in Canadian politics have begun to express concerns that an American-style interest group complex increasingly is supplanting conventional partisan and institutional channels of policy-making. For A. Paul Pross (1986), sectorial and administrative interests have arisen and begun to act in ways to alter the patterns of Canadian politics profoundly; for S.J.R. Noel (1976), the evolution of bureaucratic clientelism has a similar effect on how Canadian politics operates; for John Meisel (1979), the decline of Canadian political parties can be blamed in large measure on the advent of a strong interest group subsystem in Canadian society; and, for Khayyam Paltiel, unless "creative politics" can be practiced by leading politicians, it will not be possible to "galvanize the Canadian political process in a direction which would permit the disciplining of the interest groups which currently threaten the stability and legitimacy of liberal democracy in Canada" (1982, p. 210).

Yet, Seymour Martin Lipset, perhaps the most widely read and highly regarded student of Canadian–American comparative politics, in considering the issue of convergence has argued that: "The United States and Canada remain two nations formed around sharply different organizing principles. Their basic myths vary considerably, and national ethics and structures are in large part determined by such images" (1990, p. 225).

A major purpose of the study presented in this book is to determine if those differences in ethics, image, and culture noted by Lipset persist with respect to the way citizens of these two postindustrial nations make use of interest groups to cope with the technical information quandary. Is it possible that the political realities of postindustrial society force a new type of common response to the desire for democratic influence in the form of a new type of reliance upon interest groups? Such is the challenge of this book, to answer this and related questions on the contemporary role of interest groups in postindustrial democracies.

The Environmental Policy-Making Dimension

It is critical to remain sensitive to the possibility that any culture-based differences that exist will be acted out in Ontario and Michigan, settings that reflect the centralized versus fragmented nature of their respective national-level political systems. In Ontario, power is centralized in the majority party (or coalition) government, which acts through the premier and the cabinet and controls the legislative assembly. Two cabinet ministers are concerned with environmental issues—the minister of the environment and the minister of natural resources—and both maintain control over policy-making in their respective areas. The chief administrative officers in these ministries, however, are deputy ministers appointed by the premier. The Environmental Assessment Board is a major actor in the provincial environmental policy process, but the decisions made by the board can be overruled by the cabinet. In Michigan, power over environmental policy is dispersed among a wide array of both elected and appointed officials, including the governor, the Senate and House of the Michigan legislature, the Joint Committee on Administrative Rules (which must sign off on any proposed administrative rule), the Air Quality Control Commission (a body appointed by the governor that issues permits and notices of noncompliance to industry), and the Michigan Department of Natural Resources.

Cross-national differences in the structure of the policy process and in government institutions are likely to affect group access as well as influence the strategies and tactics groups use in their dealings with decision makers and in their efforts to communicate information to their members and the public (Bruce 1989). The fragmented structure of the American system allows for access at many points, at both national and state levels of government. In the more hierarchically organized Canadian system, access is quite restricted. Reflecting these fundamental differences, Christopher Leman (1980) found in his comparative study of welfare reform in Canada and the United States that the

two countries differed sharply in the extent to which outsiders had access to knowledge and power in welfare debates. U.S. experts, media, and interests participated actively in debates on welfare policy, unlike their Canadian counterparts. . . . While U.S. policy-making circles were remarkably porous to the entry of outside participants, Canadian circles seemed hermetically sealed. (p. 158)

Consequently, in the Canadian policy-making system, interest groups must adapt to a process of elite accommodation (Presthus 1974) while their American counterparts operate in a more open and competitive system.

The Natural Environment Dimension

The differences in the political cultures of Canada and the United States—collectivist, quasi-participative, and organic versus individualistic, participative, and pluralistic, respectively—also are broadly thought to be reflected in the respective views of the natural environment held by Canadians and Americans.

Recall Margaret Atwood's focus on survival as characterizing Canadians' posture toward the environment. The very severe Canadian weather, as well as its forbidding mountain ranges and vast expanses of territory, represent true natural obstacles to this Canadian concern for survival. These obstacles are argued to lead to a recognition of and respect for the power and danger of natural phenomena, making of nature a formidable force to be survived (Atwood 1972). Such a hostile climate might well increase awareness of and respect for the importance of the environment generally. The more temperate climate of the United States may well lead to taking nature for granted; nature is something to conquer, as represented in the notion of the frontier theme of so much American literature and popular culture.

While a variety of interpretations of contemporary patterns of beliefs and values in both Canada and the United States could be cited, suffice it to note once more that some potentially significant differences between Canadians and Americans likely do exist. Moreover, these differences may affect attitudes toward the environment in general, and influence citizens' views concerning both countries' attempts to define and deal with the problem of acid rain deposition in particular. For example, the respect Canadians have for the physical power of nature might combine with the collectivist view of society thought to characterize the Canadian political culture to produce higher levels of support for environmental protection than is the case for Americans. This difference would be especially likely if environmental beliefs stress the integration of people and nature similar to the "spaceship earth" idea found in contemporary conceptions of environmentalism.

A recognition of the interconnectedness of all things is the basis for a belief system—labeled the *new environmental paradigm* (NEP) (see Dunlap and Van Liere 1978)—that is central to contemporary environmentalism. Individuals who support this belief system are distinguished from the rest of society by these characteristics:

High valuation of nature, their sense of empathy, which generalizes to compassion toward other species . . . their desire to carefully plan and act so as to avoid risks to humans and nature, their recognition that there are limits to growth to which humans must adapt. (Milbrath 1984, p. 21)

Canadians are expected to support this set of environmental beliefs to a greater degree than Americans; this difference in support would reflect the distinctiveness of each nation's national identity and political beliefs and values.

The combination of differing interest group systems and differing views of the environment ought to result in distinct patterns in Canada and the United States with regard to environmental group behavior. One may find differences in the reasons people form groups, in the ways they look at other groups, and in the way the groups structure their information gathering activities. Those differences then may have implications for the way interest groups assist citizens in coping with the technical information quandary.

The Interest Group Politics Dimension

As noted in this chapter, the relative importance of interest group phenomena in American politics long has been recognized. Alex de Tocqueville's discussion of "political associations" in the America of the 1830s ranks among the most important early commentaries offered from a comparative perspective (1948). James Bryce, on the basis of his prolonged diplomatic service in America as a representative of the British Crown, made similar note of the relative abundance and substantive importance of organized interests in American politics at the turn of the century (1887). In addition, numerous more contemporary scholars such as Theodore Lowi (1976), Mancur Olson (1982), and Samuel Huntington (1981) all have drawn attention to the potential dangers to democracy and social adaptability of a hyperpluralistic society. For some scholars, this adoption of a conception of politics emphasizing the virtues of individual self-interested advocacy of claims through voluntary organization is part and parcel of American exceptionalism. Whether it be the influence of the liberal tradition of Louis Hartz (1955) or the happy consequences of a nonkaleidoscopic history bestowed upon a people blessed with mild climate, fertile soil, and great wealth of natural resources (Boorstin 1973), for many scholars the nature of interest group politics in the United States can be understood as a fundamental reflection of its political culture and institutional proclivities.

What can be said about Canada in this regard? The traditional view of groups in Canadian society and politics provides contrasting images at two different levels of focus. Some of the more widely noted observers of the two countries suggest that at the level of fundamental political culture, the Canadians hold much more positive feelings about the role of groups than do Americans. For example, Seymour Martin Lipset recently wrote that:

My central argument is that the two countries differ in their basic organizing principles. Canada has been and is a more class-aware, elitist, law-abiding, statist, collectivity-oriented and *particularistic (group-oriented)* society than the United States. (1990, p. 8; italics added)

Similarly, Robert Presthus has commented that while

Canada's political culture includes a generally affirmative perspective of interest groups based largely upon a corporatist theory of society and a mildly positive appreciation of government's role and legitimacy, neither government nor interest groups have enjoyed a similar legitimacy in the United States. (1973, p. 4)

In a recent work, Merelman agrees that "in Canada, the culture of political participation is dominantly group-oriented" while in "the United States the culture of political participation is fluid, egalitarian, and individualistic" (1991, p. 11).

Somewhat paradoxically, the dominant view that groups are much more accepted as a part of political culture in Canada than in the United States does not lead to a concurrent belief that they actually are any more important in Canadian political life than they are in the political life of the United States. Indeed, for quite some time scholars of Canadian politics were relatively unconcerned with the role of interest groups. As A. Paul Pross noted in the mid-1970s:

Scholars frequently complain that very few studies of Canadian pressure groups exist. . . . One writer has linked this to a common tendency amongst the general public to argue that pressure groups do not operate in Canada. To him, the rather thin literature is symptomatic of an attempt "to sublimate a process that seems functionally essential in any political system." (Pross 1975, p. 3)

Other scholars concur with Pross that pressure groups are quite important in Canadian politics (e.g., Presthus 1973, 1974), contrary to the long-standing perception to the opposite. In fact, in a later work, Pross argues that the perhaps less evident activity of pressure groups in the early post–World War II period gave way to "an explosion of pressure group formation and participation, much of it stemming from the expansion of government" (1986, p. 63). As an introduction to that work, Pross postulated that pressure groups "have indeed proliferated and their influence has swollen" (1986, p. 3).

While in many people's views both Canada and the United States are characterized by considerable pressure group activity, it is not clear that the matter rests. Merelman recently has suggested that group conflict is essential to democratic politics (1991), which he calls "conflictive democratic participation." But, Merelman argues,

the cultural raw materials for conflictive democratic participation exist in Canada, but Canadian culture is too insecure and well-mannered to produce broad political action . . . by comparison, in the United States, people "know" that America is unique. The irony is that being American means eschewing conflictive democratic participation. In neither society, therefore, does culture fully realize conflictive democratic participation. (1991, p. 135)

THE AMERICAN AND CANADIAN CONTEXTS IN BRIEF

So what perceptions do we have and what conclusions do we draw? We have both historical and contemporary beliefs that groups are important to democratic political systems. We have two different political cultures, one more group oriented (Canadian) and one more individualistic (American). We have political arenas in which one traditionally has had more evident political interest group conflict (American) than the other (Canadian). We have the perception that the two countries are now more similar than in the past in the level of group activity, with the rapid expansion of that activity occurring in one of these nations (Canada). We have contrasting perceptions of whether that relatively comparable level of group conflict is sufficient to ensure educative and efficacious democratic politics. Finally, we have the question of whether the postindustrial, high information policy area of the environment produces patterns consistent with all of this. In order to try to sort out this web of perceptions and impressions, we have developed some tentative hypotheses to be addressed in the book. We turn now to those hypotheses.

HYPOTHESES GUIDING THE STUDY OF CANADIAN AND AMERICAN ENVIRONMENTAL INTEREST GROUPS

The remainder of this book begins by investigating whether the hypothesized cultural differences show up in the data we have collected among Canadian and American citizens and environmental groups. We then move to a consideration of whether those differences—either hypothesized by others or present in our own survey and interview data— are revealed in the patterns of group membership and perceptions of groups in the two societies. Then the analysis addresses the questions of why people join environmental interest groups, and whether those reasons differ between the two countries in ways that reflect their different cultures. Finally, we examine the interest groups themselves—their structure, their activity, and their relative focus on information in their relationships with their members and with their respective political decision makers. The rest of this chapter constructs these implicit hypotheses more explicitly.

Hypothesis 1

Canadian beliefs, values, and attitudes will reflect a political culture more organic, collectivist, particularistic, and corporatist than will those of Americans.

This hypothesis obviously grows out of the discussion and referenced literature of this first chapter. One of the critical issues to be confronted is whether there is any evidence to suggest that the historical differences in the two political cultures are converging in the youngest cohorts. The common consequences of postindustrial society may serve to erase historical cultural differences. Thus, Chapter 2 explores the cross-national similarities and differences in a number of values and beliefs; that chapter also examines the extent to which any differences persist under controls for individual attributes that themselves may intervene in or contribute to cultural change attributable to postindustrial society.

Hypothesis 2

Canadians will exhibit greater overall trust of interest groups than Americans, while Americans will demonstrate greater differentiation in their level of trust of different types of interest groups.

We expect Canadians to be more positive toward interest groups generally because of the broadly held perception that Canadian culture is more particularistic—organic, corporatist, and group based. In contrast, among Americans, society tends to be viewed more as a collection of individuals than as a composition made up of numerous groups. Americans will tend to support or trust particular interest groups because they advance individual interests—albeit in a collective format—and therefore Americans will be more likely than Canadians to differentiate among groups, and that differentiation is more likely to be based on self-interest. Canadians will differentiate less among groups because groups per se have prima facie legitimacy. Thus, Chapter 3 examines differences between Canadians and Americans regarding the trustworthiness of interest group information. It also looks at the degree to which the evaluations of interest groups are reflective of an individual's political beliefs and values. We again look at cohort differences in these patterns in order to assess whether there is any evidence of convergence in cultures among the younger age groups.

Hypothesis 3

Individual incentives will explain greater variation in interest group participation in the United States than in Canada. Moreover, Americans will be more likely to join interest groups for purposive and information-gathering reasons than the Canadians, while the Canadians will be more likely to join for solidary reasons.

The individual rather than group basis of American political culture will lead Americans to be more likely to join groups in order to promote individual political interests. Americans are more likely than Canadians to see interest groups as means to advance individual political goals rather than as legitimate and natural elements of the political process and social system. Thus, the political goals (purposive) and the instrumental information that helps achieve them will prove to be more important among Americans than among their Canadian counterparts. Chapter 4 addresses these and related questions dealing with incentives to interest group participation in Canada and the United States. The focus is on the relative role of information as an incentive to interest group membership, given the potential role of interest groups in mitigating the information deficit in technical and scientific issues. More specifically, Chapter 4 examines the degree to which the purposive and informational incentives jointly occur among citizens in the two countries. Given the discussions in this chapter, in particular the individual, self-interested basis of the American political culture, we expect more Americans than Canadians to respond to the combination of informational and purposive incentives to group membership.

Hypothesis 4

American environmental interest groups will be more likely than Canadian environmental interest groups to focus on policy-relevant information in their relationships with members and in their interactions with policymakers.

Organizations, just as individuals, must operate within the given characteristics of their own particular political culture. Interest groups in the American political culture are broadly seen as products of the individualistic character of their political environment; as such, they are more likely to focus on policy-relevant information as a means of achieving purposive political ends than their Canadian counterparts. Because Canadian interest groups grow out of a corporatist, particularist political culture in which long-established shared identities and goals have been established with policymakers, the task of policy-relevant information dissemination is less critical to group success in Canada than in the United States. Consequently, it seems reasonable to suspect that the development and dissemination of policy-relevant information would be less important to Canadian interest group activity than would strategies and tactics aimed at clarifying and identifying the preexisting shared goals and values. Chapters 5 and 6 explore the cross-national differences in the information activities of environmental interest groups.

CONCLUSION

Postindustrial society poses fundamental questions for modern democracies, especially when they are confronted with complex and difficult policy questions brought on by frequent scientific discovery and rapidly changing technology. How are citizens to reassure themselves that they influence the answers to those policy questions, especially when they have prima facie evidence that they suffer severe information deficits? We suggest in this chapter that interest groups provide one potential vehicle for democratic citizenries to deal with the technical information quandary. Yet, it is quite apparent that the interest group answer to this dilemma is likely to depend on the cultural and institutional context within which it is proferred. We have chosen Canada and the United States as our divergent cultural contexts for studying the extent to which interest group action might be facilitating informed, effective, and satisfying democratic participation in environmental politics by mass publics. After describing the mechanics of our study, Chapter 2 addresses with empirical evidence some of the hypothesized differences in political culture as exhibited in the beliefs and behavior of citizens and environmental activists in the state of Michigan and the Province of Ontario.

Chapter Two

The Political Culture Context

A major theme of Chapter 1 was that prevailing conceptions of the American and Canadian political cultures hold these two nations to be quite distinct in their respective views of politics and society. In brief, the Canadian political culture is seen as being characterized properly as collectivist, organic, and holistic in nature. When given expression through a parliamentary system, that culture has produced an interest group system that has been relatively nonparticipative and nonconflictive, characterized by a high level of cooperation with and even cooptation by governmental and partisan elites. In contrast, the American political culture tends to be seen as pluralistic and highly competitive, with interest groups unabashedly seeking to advance their aggregated individual interests in a markedly decentralized governmental and electoral context. More recently, though, some scholars have argued that the common forces of postindustrial change and economic interdependence are producing convergence in the political cultures of Canada and the United States, and greater similarity in the operation of their respective systems of interest group politics.

The question of convergence or divergence of the Canadian and American political cultures and their interest groups' attributes is critical to an adequate understanding of the role interest groups might play in response to the technical information quandary. Interest groups that operate in a pluralistic, competitive environment may tend to respond differently to their members' and potential members' needs for information to deal with the collection of complex, technical, and scientific issues facing the citizens of contemporary postindustrial democracies.

This chapter provides an empirical basis upon which to draw some conclusions about the cultural context of interest group activity in the contemporary Canadian and American settings as observed in the province of Ontario and in the state of Michigan. We confront these issues in a comparison of the viewpoints expressed by both Canadian and American citizens and by environmental activists in Canada and the United States. In our analysis, we investigate a number of fundamental value dimensions and probe a set of environmental orientations that reflect the cultural differences broadly believed to characterize the two countries. One of the primary foci of our attention will be age-related differences among Canadians and Americans. If cultural convergence is in fact occurring, it may be reflected in systematic variations across generational cohorts. More specifically, younger cohorts may exhibit greater cross-national similarity than older cohorts. To the degree that distinct national political cultures are manifested differently in public attitudes and values, to the same extent they then may cause interest groups to play different roles in dealing with the technical information quandary.

DATA SOURCES

The empirical data pertinent to questions of the character of Canadian and American political cultures come from several independent studies. In 1985–1986, separate mail surveys of the public and members of environmental organizations were conducted in Ontario and Michigan. These two jurisdictions are contiguous geographically, both have experienced a common environmental problem in the form of significant acid rain deposition, and both are rather similar in population size and degrees of urban density.[1] The acid rain issue was of primary public interest during the period of the surveys described here. Findings regarding the similarities and differences among American and Canadian respondents have been reported in some detail elsewhere (Steger et al. 1988; Pierce et al. 1988). For the survey of the publics, two samples of approximately 1000 citizens each were drawn from telephone directories from all cities with populations of 25,000 or greater in Michigan and in Ontario. Citizens from cities falling in each population size category were chosen randomly in proportion to the state/provincial population found in each of these size categories.[2] In the Ontario sample of the public, 897 questionnaires were distributed to bona fide residents and 600 questionnaires were returned, producing a response rate of 66.9%. In Michigan, the response rate was 54.5%—873 questionnaires were delivered, of which 476 were returned.

Sample lists of environmental activists were developed by contacting directors of environmental organizations in Ontario and Michigan. Directors of organizations with large memberships were asked to send questionnaires to their members; 9 Canadian-based and 14 Michigan-based groups sent from 10 to 100 questionnaires to their respective members. In addition, single questionnaires were mailed to 124 Ontario groups and 400 individuals who were part of the Michigan Clean Air Campaign. Approximately 600 questionnaires were distributed to the environmental activists in Ontario, and 554 were completed (a response rate of 92%); approximately 1000 questionnaires were distributed to environmental activists in Michigan, and 684 were completed (a response rate of 68%).

In 1987, survey questionnaires again were sent to 98 environmental organizations in the Canadian province of Ontario and to 71 environmental organizations in the state of Michigan. From this initial contact, 63 Ontario groups and 43 Michigan groups distributed survey questionnaires at random both to a sample of members or contributors (at least 10 per group) and to their respective officers, which included staff and/or members of the board of directors (at least 3 per group). The participation rate for contacted groups was 63% in Ontario and 61% in Michigan. The number of questionnaires sent to participating organizations was 819 in Ontario and 645 in Michigan; of these, 498 questionnaires were returned from the Canadian province and 385 from the American state. These outcomes represent a response rate of 61% in Ontario and 60% in Michigan.

Finally, during the spring and summer of 1988, mail surveys were sent to random samples of the public in Toronto and Detroit. The approximate population of Toronto consolidated is 3,427,000 and that of Detroit Standard Metropolitan Statistical Area (SMSA) is roughly 4,353,000. After conducting two large pretests of the survey instrument in Toronto and Detroit during April and May 1988, a final version of the survey was sent to 1300 randomly selected citizens in both research sites. Household names and addresses were drawn from municipal telephone directories. Three waves of the survey and a final reminder card were sent to encourage responses. All inaccurate addresses were replaced with valid addresses from a backup pool of randomly selected subjects to insure a large sample in both locations. The final response rate for Toronto was 69.9%, and for Detroit it was 69.1%.

Together, these several data sets provide a broad basis upon which to draw for making comparisons of significant elements of the political cultures of Canada and the United States. To be sure, these data have a significant limitation; namely, we are comparing patterns of attitudes and value orientations produced in a single, albeit relatively comparable, geographic region of each country. This comparison disguises the fact that both Canada and the United States are quite heterogeneous in culture. Consequently, this comparison oversimplifies the complex regional and sectorial differences that most certainly characterize American/Canadian political culture differences. These observations notwith-standing, as major heartland metropolitan areas, the study locales of the field research reported here do offer the potential of providing significant insight into the question of cultural effects in the comparative analysis of Canadian and American political behavior. As a modified type of "similar systems" design, the analytical approach adopted in these studies provides the opportunity to focus upon the likely residual effects of "national context" in the comparison of political behavior relative to interest groups (Przeworski and Teune 1970, pp. 32–34; Dogan and Pelassy 1990).

DIMENSIONS OF POLITICAL CULTURE

The first question to be confronted is that of the relevant dimensions along which the two countries should be compared (Granberg and Holmberg 1988, pp. 10–15). Political cultures are thought to contain some common core attitude dimensions along which any set of countries can be arrayed (Almond and Verba 1963). For some scholars, of course, the idiographic nature of nations and random effects of chance should cause students of political life to focus attention on unique or exceptional aspects of the political life of any one country or one world region; such is the belief of many single country specialists and regional studies scholars. In the case of Canadian and American comparisons, the contrasting of two nations with political cultures that bear at least superficial similarity (e.g., high regard for constitutionalism, respect of private property and civil liberties, preference for federalism and local self-governance), the task of finding the distinctive trees of interest in the thick forest of commonality grows in complexity.

The apparent outward similarities of two democratic systems may mask important underlying differences in the affective and phenomenological foundations upon which these similar processes are built. Likewise, the more obvious differences in the formal governmental structure and electoral systems (e.g., parliamentary versus presidential government, multiparty versus two-party systems) may mask highly similar informal systems of political negotiation, campaigning, and decision making. A number of both older and more recent comparative empirical analyses of Canada and the United States do provide considerable guidance as to where scholars might search for those potential differences in political culture (Crawford and Curtis 1979; Nevitte et al. 1991). These studies tend to underscore the urgency of assessing the extent to which historically-based cultural differences may be diminishing in the era of transnational postindustrialism, the expansion of global communication systems, and greatly reduced world trade barriers (Thurow 1983).

One important commonly presumed difference between the Canadian and American political cultures is thought to revolve around distinctive views as to how social and political life should be conceptualized. For some Canadian scholars this difference entails a certain claim to superiority of the Canadian approach to many social issues and governmental responsibilities. In this vein, Westell has remarked recently that: "The Canadian sense of national identity and purpose has rested largely on the belief that it has a system of government and a set of goals and values different from, and in some respects better than, those of the United States" (1991, p. 263). As we noted in Chapter 1, Canadian political culture is widely thought to reflect an organic, holistic, and collectivistic conception of society. The American political culture, in contrast, is said to reflect an individualistic and pluralistic conception of politics and society, with a focus on open competition among diverse interests as a preferable approach to setting public policy to that of prescribing a single conception of the common good (Baer et al. 1991). In the following sections, we look at the degree to which some of these expected political culture differences appear in our survey data.

Political Values

Chapter 1 noted that one of the central dimensions of cross-national comparison in recent years has been the degree to which countries and their citizens exhibit postindustrial attributes. At the individual level, such research typically focuses on the extent to which the citizens of various nations express postindustrial values. Ronald Inglehart has taken the lead in defining those values, labeling a particular syndrome of values as "postmaterial" (1977). Postmaterial values emphasize "belonging, self-expression, and the quality of life" and are founded in "the unprecedented levels of economic and physical security that prevailed during the postwar era" (Inglehart 1990, p. 66). These values are distinguished from those that give "top priority to physical sustenance and safety" and that Inglehart refers to as "material" values. The particular values an individual expresses are said to be a product of "the socioeconomic environment; one places the greatest subjective value on those things in relatively short supply." According to Inglehart, the extent to which conditions of plenty or conditions of insecurity obtained "during one's preadult years" (the time of greatest crystalization of socialization effects) determine the degree of fixation upon materialist or postmaterialist values (Inglehart 1990, p. 68).

Since the advent of postindustrial society has been both a richly researched topic and a common experience among Western democratic nations, it becomes a quintessential aspect of the test of cultural convergence in the Canadian–American context. If the political cultures of Canada and the United States are different in substantial ways, then a contemporary comparison of these two cultures should reveal continued distinctiveness despite the transnational cultural changes attributable to the postindustrial qualities of the post–World War II era. Such a comparison is influenced, of course, by the degree to which the postindustrial value syndrome differs from the "dominant social paradigm" (Dunlap and VanLiere 1978, 1984). Canadian society, with its more organic, holistic, collectivist political culture, might be more open than American society to the higher-order needs reflected in postmaterial values. In contrast, the United States, with its traditional focus on economic individualism and self-interested pluralistic politics, might be slower to embrace the sociotropic values of postindustrial politics. Based on these observations, a general hypothesis might be inferred that the incidence of "postmaterialists" would be more frequent in Canada than in the United States, even if the United States is seen as the prototypical postindustrial state.

It should be noted again (see Chapter 1) that movement along the materialist–postmaterialist dimension has not been accepted universally as the most critical aspect of value change attributable to the advent of postindustrial society. Recall that Flanagan has argued, for example, that important value change has occurred along an authoritarian–libertarian dimension, with the postindustrial value syndrome taking on more of the libertarian flavor (i.e., more freedom from authority and convention in the exercise of personal life choices) (1987). Thus, the degree to which Canadians and Americans studied here differ in values also will be investigated in regard to the continuum of authoritarian–libertarian values set forth by Scott Flanagan.

Postmaterialism. Inglehart's measure of postmaterial values takes two forms. The original index is a fairly simple set of statements from which individuals are asked to select their two most preferred goals. These goals include:

A. Maintain order in the nation
B. Give people more say in the decisions of government
C. Fight rising prices
D. Protect freedom of speech

People selecting Goals A and C are labeled materialists, while those choosing B and D are postmaterialists. In subsequent versions, Inglehart augmented the original index with additional statements relating to economic growth, strong defense, more say at work, environmental beautification, stable economy, fighting crime, friendlier society, and a society in which ideas are important (Inglehart 1990, pp. 74–75). The enhanced index is summative, "a continuum having numerous intermediate categories'' (p. 75). Our data were collected via mail surveys, in which space is at a premium. Consequently, we employed the original, short version of the measure of postmaterial values.

Table 2.1 displays the distribution of postmaterial value types obtained in two of our surveys. The first set includes the data from the 1985–1986 surveys of the public and environmental group members in Michigan and Ontario. The second set of findings is drawn from the 1988 surveys of general publics in metropolitan Detroit and Toronto.

Table 2.1
Distribution of Postmaterial Value Types (in Ontario and Michigan)

1985-1986 Study: Ontario and Michigan

	ONTARIO Public	MICHIGAN Public	ONTARIO Activists	MICHIGAN Activists
Value Types				
Materialist	13.5%	26.4%	3.2%	5.2%
Mixed	64.4%	63.0%	43.1%	49.0%
Postmaterialist	22.1%	10.7%	53.7%	45.7%
TOTAL	100%	101%	100%	99.9%
	(N = 548)	(N = 413)	(N = 378)	(N = 516)

1988 Study: Metropolitan Toronto and Detroit

Value Types	TORONTO Public	DETROIT Public
Materialist	16.9%	20.1%
Mixed	64.2%	62.7%
Postmaterialist	18.9%	17.2%
TOTAL	100%	100%
	(N = 871)	(N = 860)

The two studies provide slightly different results, but the differences likely reflect the differing urban/rural mix in the 1985–1986 and 1988 surveys. In the statewide samples, citizens in the Michigan public are twice as likely to be materialist as are those in the Ontario public (26.4% vs. 13.5%). Conversely, the Ontario public is twice as likely to be post-materialist as is the Michigan public (22.1% vs. 10.7%). In the metropolitan Detroit and Toronto public study, however, much smaller differences surface, albeit in the same direction. The most likely reason for the differences in results would be that the nonmetropolitan areas of Ontario are more postmaterialist than are the nonmetropolitan areas of Michigan, perhaps as a consequence of differing traditional dominant social paradigms in Canada and the United States. It is reasonable to assume, of course, that value convergence is most likely to occur in urban centers where the effects of postindustrial society are most intense; in more rural areas, in contrast, traditional cultural differences tend to persist for relatively long periods (Honadle 1982; Seroka 1986).

We return to the 1985–1986 acid rain study results to examine directly the empirical connection between rural–urban location and postmaterial value preferences. In that survey, respondents were asked to indicate the size of the town or city in which they were raised. In keeping with Inglehart's emphasis upon the effects of preadult socialization experiences, the character of the location of one's upbringing is presumed to constitute an important test of the salience of the rural–urban distinction. Table 2.2 presents the distribution of materialist, mixed, and postmaterial value types among the Canadian and American publics arrayed across a continuum of levels of population density of hometown origins. Within categories of the same level of population density, some rather significant cross-national differences are found.

The most striking Canadian–American difference is found between Canadians and Americans raised on farms, in the country, or in villages; 37% of the Canadians in that category profess postmaterialist values as compared to only 3% of the Americans. This pattern would seem quite reasonable if it can be assumed that (1) the traditional and historic American and Canadian political cultures are most likely to be found among individuals raised in rural areas and (2) the postmaterial value structure is more consistent with the traditional Canadian political culture than with the traditional American political culture. Among Canadians and Americans raised in cities ranging from 50,000 to 99,999, the proportion of postmaterialists is nearly equal, but materialist Americans far outnumber materialist Canadians. In the largest cities, the proportion of postmaterialists drops off somewhat in both countries, and the proportion of American materialists declines considerably.

In a recent analysis of value change in Canada, the United States, and Mexico, Neil Nevitte and his associates have shown that "the young

Table 2.2
Size of City in which Raised and Postmaterial Value Preferences (among Canadian and American Citizens)

| | City Size of Place Raised | | | | | | | |
| | Small | | Medium | | Larger | | Large | |
Postmaterialist Value Types	U.S.	Can	U.S.	Can	U.S.	Can	U.S.	Can
Materialist	41%	8%	30%	11%	40%	12%	17%	18%
Mixed	56%	55%	57%	66%	33%	64%	74%	68%
Postmaterialist	3%	37%	14%	23%	27%	24%	8%	14%
TOTAL	100%	100%	101%	100%	100%	100%	99%	100%
N	(64)	(97)	(111)	(111)	(45)	(81)	(195)	(254)

Small = 1, 2, 3 = farm, country, village
Medium = 4, 5, 6 = 2,500-49,999
Larger = 7 = 50,000-99,999
Large = 8 = 100,000 +

1985-1986   Acid Rain Study

are less likely than the old to emphasize materialist values in all three countries'' (1991, p. 9). In both Canada and the United States, ''materialists outnumber postmaterialists'' among the oldest cohort, but the relative positions of these value types are reversed in the youngest cohort (1991, p. 10). Our data confront the question of value-orientation change across generations with somewhat of a twist. While our samples are more narrowly based than those of Nevitte and his associates, we do have the ability to make comparisons similar to theirs among citizens and environmental organization activists in Ontario and Michigan. One key question we can ask is: Are the age differences in value preferences evident in the general population also present among environmental group members? Convergence may be accelerated or divergence may be masked among activist populations in policy areas where that activism is stimulated by the postmaterial values in question. This seems a likely possibility in environmental politics. Table 2.3 shows the results of an analysis of the relationship between value preferences and age among both citizens and environmental group activists in Ontario and Michigan.

In Michigan, among the public respondents there is a regular decline in the percentage of postmaterialists with increasing age. Four times as many persons in the youngest age category are postmaterialist as in the oldest age group. In Ontario, the findings are similar; there are higher proportions of postmaterialists among the younger citizens than among the older-age groups. However, the age group differences are neither as great nor as consistent as in the Michigan sample. In neither the Canadian nor the American setting does the postmaterial portion of the youngest cohort reach even a third of the sample.

The activist portion of Table 2.3 indicates that no more than 8% (oldest American activists) of any cohort is materialist, and that no fewer than 42% (middle-age Americans) is postmaterialist. Overall, age cohort effects among activists do not appear in either Michigan or Ontario. While in the general public age (and, by implication, cohort) makes some difference in the holding of postmaterial values for Canadians and Americans, what is perhaps more noteworthy here is that the activists in both countries differ so much from their respective publics in their commitment to postmaterialist values. In comparing the activists of the two nations, one difference surfaces in the percentage of postmaterialists in the youngest cohort. Younger Canadian activists are somewhat more likely to profess postmaterialist values than are the youngest American activists (55% vs. 43%).

The environmental policy arena is one in which postmaterial values and postindustrial politics clearly are present as a stimulus to political involvement on the part of mass publics (Milbrath 1984, 1989). Especially in the United States, environmental politics attracts postmaterial-

Table 2.3
**Relationship of Age Cohort to Postmaterial Value Preferences among
Canadian and American Publics and Activists**

Public

Age Cohorts

Postmaterialist Value Types	Young*		Middle		Older	
	U.S.	Can	U.S.	Can	U.S.	Can
Materialist	24%	11%	31%	15%	26%	18%
Mixed	57%	61%	57%	71%	69%	60%
Postmaterialist	19%	28%	12%	15%	5%	22%
TOTAL	100%	100%	100%	101%	100%	100%
N	(129)	(191)	(110)	(183)	(178)	(180)

Activists

Postmaterialist Value Types	Young		Middle		Older	
	U.S.	Can	U.S.	Can	U.S.	Can
Materialist	4%	3%	7%	2%	8%	4%
Mixed	53%	42%	51%	53%	48%	48%
Postmaterialist	43%	55%	42%	45%	45%	48%
TOTAL	100%	100%	100%	100%	101%	100%
N	(199)	(229)	(285)	(145)	(130)	(75)

* *Young = born in 1951 or later*   *1985-1986 Acid Rain Study*
  Middle = born in 1935 to 1950
  Old = born before 1935

ists from all age groups. While the younger cohort is disproportionately more likely to be postmaterialist than older cohorts in Michigan, the older postmaterialists are more likely to be drawn into the political arena than their younger compatriots (43% postmaterialists among activists vs. 19% among citizens in the youngest cohort as compared to equivalent figures of 45% postmaterial vs. only 5% postmaterial among the oldest groups of activists and citizens, respectively).

The activist portion of the statewide study provides another interesting contrast. To be sure, there are slightly more postmaterialists among the Ontario activists than among the Michigan activists (54% vs. 46%). However, the distinctive difference is between the two activist groups and their respective public samples. About half of each activist sample possesses postmaterialist values. The value of having more say in government clearly distinguishes ordinary citizens from activists in both countries. It seems clear that value convergence may be most in evidence among the activist segments of the United States and Canada.

Authoritarian–Libertarian Values. Scott Flanagan has been the primary proponent of an alternative conceptualization of value change in postindustrial societies in recent decades. Flanagan suggests that:

The core of the debate revolves around my argument that there are two distinct kinds of value change taking place in the advanced industrial democracies and that Inglehart has obscured this distinction by collapsing indicators of both into a single scale. My argument has been that these two kinds of change are not only conceptually distinct but are explained by different causal phenomena and exhibit different patterns of relationships with key demographic and political variables. (1987, pp. 1303–1304)

Our introduction of the Flanagan position here is not to resolve the debate with Inglehart; that discussion is presented in a separate forum (Steel et al. 1992). Rather, we want to use the Flanagan perspective as a way to expand the range of cross-national cultural contrasts drawn in this analysis.

Flanagan suggests that a libertarian–authoritarian dimension is critical to understanding value change in postindustrial societies and charting its consequences. Indeed, he argues that this dimension itself can internally divide the materialists or the postmaterialists of Inglehart. Thus, "it is important, therefore, to reach an independent determination of a respondent's position on these value dimensions" (1987, p. 1306). Table 2.4 contrasts the Detroit and Toronto samples on the individual items in Flanagan's libertarian–authoritarian scale.

In most cases, the differences between Detroit and Toronto publics are in the direction of greater support for the libertarian position among the Canadian respondents. Moreover, the largest differences are in the direction of the greater support of libertarian values expressed among the Toronto citizens. For example, Canadians in these samples are more likely to indicate that there currently is too much emphasis on national defense, too little sexual freedom, too much respect for authority, too much emphasis on removing pornography from the public marketplace, and too much emphasis on teaching children good manners and obedience. Americans from Detroit are more likely than their Canadian counterparts to say that there is too little personal freedom and too much emphasis on loyalty to one's country.

Table 2.4
**Detroit and Toronto Public Responses to Flanagan's Libertarian–
Authoritarian Scale Items**

% Too little	DETROIT	TORONTO	Percent Difference
Increasing benefits for the disadvantaged	57.8	63.1	+5.3
Protecting homosexuals from discrimination	27.8	35.8	+8.0
Personal freedom	61.4	50.6	-10.8
Seeking personal fulfillment	32.0	34.1	+2.1
Being open-minded to new ideas	77.1	73.3	-3.8
Sexual freedom and abortion	25.1	40.7	+15.6
Improving the environment and quality of life	88.9	88.0	-.09

% Too much	DETROIT	TORONTO	Percent Difference
Patriotism and loyalty to one's country	26.2	15.8	-10.4
Providing for strong defense forces	40.8	71.6	+30.8
Respect for authority	17.8	31.7	+13.9
Preserving traditional morals/values	20.1	23.8	+3.7
Following custom and the expectations of one's neighbors	42.9	50.8	+7.9
Removing pornography from the marketplace	25.2	37.3	+12.1
Having deep religious faith	22.2	28.0	+5.8
Teaching children good manners and obedience	0.6	11.5	+10.9

The somewhat greater support for libertarian orientations among Toronto residents seems a bit contrary to expectations, given the greater
degree of consensual political forms and stronger sense of deference to
official authority and rules thought to exist among Canadians. It may be
that the traditional cultural differences separating Canada and the
United States are captured more fully by the measure of postmaterial

values than Flanagan's libertarian–authoritarian scale. At the same time, it should be noted that postmaterial values are related to support for libertarian orientations. As the findings in Tables 2.5 and 2.6 indicate, postmaterialists generally give more support to libertarian values than do those with either mixed or materialist values. Indeed, the libertarian value index score mean difference between postmaterialists and materialists is greater among Toronto residents than among Detroit citizens (see Table 2.6).

To this point, we have seen that the overall value distributions on the postmaterial measure are relatively similar in the two countries, although the 1985 study does show a slightly greater proportion of postmaterialists in Ontario than in Michigan. This cross-national difference is consistent with the common view that Canada is a more collectivistic, holistic, and organic society than the United States. It is also the case that the Canadian public gives greater support to libertarian values than does the American public. While the two value sets are related, the question remains whether postmaterialists and materialists in Canada and the United States have similar or dissimilar connections to the libertarian items. The answer is shown in Table 2.7, which gives the Canadian–American difference in the support for each libertarian value item within postmaterial value types.

Cross-national differences in support for libertarian values remain in evidence when controlling for postmaterial value type. Indeed, the largest country differences generally are found between Canadian and American respondents who share postmaterial values. It is clear that fundamental value-based cultural differences exist between the two countries, differences for which the postmaterial value dimension apparently fails to account fully. To be sure, we have argued that the traditional Canadian political culture appears more consistent with postmaterial values than does the traditional American political culture. The collectivistic, organic, holistic components of Canadian political culture seem more sympathetic to the other-regardingness of postmaterial values than do the individualistic, competitive, pluralistic elements of American political life. However, on the basis of these two studies, Canada and the United States seem rather similar in their distributions of postmaterial, mixed, and materialist value orientations. While the political culture differences between Canada and the United States do not translate into markedly different aggregate levels of value types on the Inglehart scale, it is clear that such value orientation differences *do* make for noteworthy differences between the way American and Canadian postmaterialists size up their individual political worlds.

Flanagan has argued that "What I call libertarian and what Inglehart and others label postmaterialist items are essentially identical" (1987, p. 1304); he has also argued that "regardless of how we choose to identify

Table 2.5
Distribution of Authoritarian–Libertarian Value Orientations by Inglehart's Postmaterialist Value Types

	Metro-Detroit				Metro-Toronto			
% Too Little	MAT	MIXED	POST	(D)*	MAT	MIXED	POST	(D)*
Increasing benefits for the disadvantaged	45.3	55.1	79.8	(34.5)	46.0	63.3	76.7	(30.7)
Protecting homosexuals from discrimination	18.6	27.4	41.5	(22.9)	32.0	33.7	47.1	(15.1)
Personal freedom	36.6	62.3	70.7	(34.1)	41.3	47.3	69.2	(27.9)
Seeking personal fulfillment	24.0	34.8	34.4	(10.4)	32.7	31.1	45.9	(13.2)
Being open-minded to new ideas	63.3	83.0	70.1	(6.8)	78.6	68.6	84.3	(5.7)
Sexual freedom and abortion	18.0	27.0	25.9	(7.9)	25.3	34.1	47.3	(22.0)
Improving the environment and quality of life	82.5	88.3	93.1	(10.6)	88.0	86.4	93.0	(5.0)
% Too much	MAT	MIXED	POST	(D)	MAT	MIXED	POST	(D)
Patriotism and loyalty to one's country	0.5	25.5	45.5	(45.0)	0.4	10.8	41.9	(41.5)
Providing for strong defense forces	2.6	39.5	58.7	(56.1)	41.5	78.1	81.8	(40.3)
Respect for authority	0.5	17.9	32.5	(32.0)	0.6	29.3	62.8	(62.2)
Preserving traditional morals/values	0.3	20.4	33.1	(32.8)	10.7	20.9	45.9	(35.2)
Having deep religious faith	0.5	17.9	51.9	(51.4)	16.7	21.2	61.6	(44.9)
Teaching children good manners and obedience	0.5	0.6	0.8	(0.3)	0.8	5.1	36.6	(35.8)
Additive scale mean =	4.0	6.1	7.4		4.8	5.6	9.6	
median =	4.0	6.0	7.0		5.0	6.0	9.0	
N =	173	539	148		147	559	165	

* Difference between postmaterialists and materialists

Table 2.6
Mean Libertarian Index Score among Materialist, Mixed, and Postmaterialist Value Types (Toronto and Detroit)

Postmaterialist Value Types	DETROIT			TORONTO		
	Materialist	_Mixed_	_Postmaterialist_	_Materialist_	_Mixed_	_Postmaterialist_
$\overline{X}$*	4.0	6.1	7.4	4.8	5.6	9.6
N	(173)	(539)	(148)	(147)	(559)	(165)

* The entry in each cell is the average score on the 0-15 liberty-authority index.

Table 2.7
Cross-National Differences in Libertarian Values within Postmaterialist
Value Types

	Postmaterialist Value Types[a]		
Flanagan Libertarian- Authoritarian-Scale Items	*Materialist*	*Mixed*	*Postmaterialist*
1. *Disadvantaged*	+ 0.7	+ 8.2	- 3.1
2. *Homosexuals*	+13.4	+ 4.6	+ 5.4
3. *Personal Freedom*	+ 4.7	-15.0	- 1.5
4. *Personal Fulfillment*	+ 8.7	- 3.7	+15.5
5. *New Ideas*	+15.5	-14.4	+14.2
6. *Sexual Freedom*	+ 7.3	+ 7.1	+21.4
7. *Environment*	+ 5.5	-14.4	+14.2
8. *Patriotism*	- 0.1	-14.7	- 3.5
9. *Strong Defense*	+38.9	+39.6	+23.1
10. *Authority*	+ 0.1	+11.4	+30.3
11. *Morals/Values*	+10.4	+ 0.5	+12.8
12. *Customs*	+ 0.1	+ 4.2	+34.2
13. *Pornography*	+20.1	+ 1.7	+43.8
14. *Religious Faith*	+16.2	+ 3.3	+ 9.7
15. *Good Manners*	+ 0.3	+ 4.5	+35.8
Index average[b]	+ 0.8	- 0.5	+ 2.2

[a]   The entry in each cell is the difference between the Canadian and American respondents providing the libertarian response within each postmaterial value type.

[b]   This figure is the difference in the average score on the libertarian additive index within each postmaterial value type.

these items, we are measuring essentially the same set of values'' (1987, p. 1304). Our observations here suggest that Flanagan's libertarian index may be considerably more sensitive to the effects of Canadian–American cultural differences, and more revealing of the impact of recent value change in those countries than is the abbreviated form of the postmaterial value indicator used in our surveys. Value change in Canada may have focused on libertarian dimensions of culture, with Canada's traditional culture being more consistent with the direction of cultural change than is the American culture. In short, our argument would be that libertarianism equals postmaterialism equals greater compatibility with traditional Canadian culture, leading to more responsiveness to value change on the part of Canadian society. The apparent discontinuity in the findings produced by the two value measures is thus more a consequence of the peculiarities of the two measures and their differing specific foci rather than any fundamental substantive difference in their conceptual content.

At this point in the analysis, then, convergence in political cultures does not seem to be in evidence in the overall distribution of political values in the neighboring Canadian and American jurisdictions of Ontario and Michigan. At an aggregate level, it appears that the net effect of the advent of postindustrial society in this area of Canada and the United States has been to reinforce the preexisting divergence of political cultures. Without time-series data, of course, it is impossible to trace the effects of change with any great degree of certainty. We can make, however, some rough estimates of change effects by looking at value differences across cohort or age categories. With age comparisons drawn at one time point, it is not possible to tell if differences across cohorts are due to socialization effects or aging effects. That is, while we might observe that older people have systematically different values than younger people, we would not know whether the older people always have had their current values or whether they acquired them as they aged. Likewise, the younger cohort may continue to adhere to its current values or it might change its values as it matures (Pierce, Beatty, and Hagner 1982). Within those constraints, the results presented in Table 2.8 are nonetheless instructive. That table presents the average libertarian index score for each age group for the three Inglehart value types (materialist, mixed, and postmaterialist) in Toronto and in Detroit.

The findings reported in Table 2.8 suggest that both in Canada and the United States, age cohort influences the level of support for libertarian values, even when controlling for postmaterial values. The results indicate that the younger cohort is not only more likely than other age cohorts to profess postmaterial values, but it also is inclined to support those libertarian values that Flanagan has argued are a direct product of the postindustrial age. It is also clear that there is an interaction between values and age such that the highest libertarian values are found among the youngest postmaterialists; this finding occurs both in the Detroit and Toronto settings. A relationship between postmaterial values and libertarian values also is present such that within each age cohort both in Canada and the United States postmaterialist respondents have higher mean libertarian value scores than do their materialist compatriots.

Table 2.8
Mean Libertarian Index Score by Postmaterialist Value Type, Age Cohort, and Nationality*

Postmaterialist Value Types	DETROIT		
	Young	Middle	Older
Materialist	5.3	4.5	3.1
Mixed	7.3	6.4	3.9
Postmaterialist	9.2	6.1	4.5

Postmaterialist Value Types	DETROIT		
	Young	Middle	Older
Materialist	8.0	5.3	4.6
Mixed	6.9	5.8	4.8
Postmaterialist	10.7	9.8	7.7

The entry in each cell is the mean score on the libertarian index.

* Young equals 18 to 30
 Middle equals 31-45
 Old equals 46 +

Table 2.9 presents cross-national differences in mean levels of support for libertarian values when controlling for both age cohort and postmaterialist–materialist values. Among both materialists and postmaterialists, Canadians have higher average scores on the Flanagan libertarian values index in every age cohort. Controlling for postmaterial values does not eliminate the cross-national differences in libertarian values. Cross-national differences among the mixed value cohorts are indeed "mixed" as well as being smaller in magnitude than is the case for postmaterialists and materialists.

Some interesting effects of age cohort on cross-national convergence on libertarian values appear in the comparison of Canadian and Ameri-

Table 2.9
Cross-National Differences in Mean Libertarian Score by Postmaterialist
Value Type and Age Cohort*

Postmaterialist Value Types	AGE COHORT		
	Young	*Middle*	*Older*
Materialist	+2.7	+ .8	+1.5
Mixed	- .4	- .6	+ .9
Postmaterialist	+1.5	+3.7	+3.2

* A plus means a higher Canadian score; a minus indicates a higher American score on the Flanagan libertarian index.

can materialists and postmaterialists. Among materialists, the differences between Canadians and Americans in libertarian value index scores are greater in the younger groups than in the older cohort. In contrast, among the postmaterialists, the differences between Canadians and Americans on the libertarian index are greater in the older two cohorts. These results suggest that cross-national convergence in libertarian values exists among those who are both the most likely to have been exposed to common environmental influences and who share postmaterialist values. In *both* the United States and Canada, the highest libertarian scores are found among younger postmaterialists.

From these results, it is clear that among significant subsets of the populations of the Canadian and American study sites a perceptible convergence of values is occurring. While the subtle value changes occurring among the general citizenries of Canada and the United States may be noteworthy, the convergence of values is in very strong evidence among organizational activists. It must be noted, of course, that such convergence is rather concentrated among the young and among postmaterialists. From these findings it is also apparent, however, that long-standing cultural differences will continue to persist among a large segment of both Canadian and American society, very likely serving to influence the way interest groups operate within the Canadian and American political settings.

Environmental Orientations and Political Culture

The relevant dimensions of political culture that might affect the information function of environmental interest groups include more elements than merely the most basic political values of Canadian and American citizens. Political culture also includes the entire range of widely shared political beliefs and behavioral predispositions that might constrain the range of interest group behavior. It is possible that Canadian and American publics and activists may differ on more specific beliefs and behavior even as they share common fundamental political values. It also is possible that differences in political beliefs and behavioral predispositions between the two countries may be greater among citizens than among group activists. Table 2.10 presents a summary of mean values for the new environmental paradigm (NEP),[3] eight general public policy process orientations,[4] and three orientations specific to acid rain entailing the estimation of the risk of damage to the ecology and human health of acid rain, the relative seriousness of acid rain as compared to other issues of current concern, and the level of government action that should be taken to prevent further acid rain deposition.[5]

As the results set forth in Table 2.10 reveal, statistically significant differences are found between citizens and activists in Canada and the United States on a number of the general public policy process orientations and attitudes specific to acid rain. Indeed, the overall pattern of the differences is consistent with the Canadian–American cultural differences broadly believed to separate Canada and the United States. Among both citizens and activists, Canadians exhibit greater support for the NEP and express greater distrust of science and technology. In addition, both the Canadian public and activist samples are more extreme in their strength of preservationist identification than are their American counterparts. Canadians perceive less conflict to be present among their decision-making elites than do Americans, and they give more support to government regulation than do their American citizen and activist counterparts. Ironically, while Canadian citizens and activists express slightly greater regard for the value of citizen participation, they actually participate somewhat less than do Americans. This result is consistent with the view of Canadian political culture as being low in participation even while strongly affirming the value of that participation (Merelman 1991, p. 135).

With respect to the more specific policy-relevant dimensions of the

Table 2.10

Comparison of Mean Values in Ontario and Michigan for Various Environmental Orientations

ENVIRONMENTAL ORIENTATIONS	ONTARIO Public (n=600) Mean	MICHIGAN Public (n=476) Mean	t-value	ONTARIO Activists (n=447) Mean	MICHIGAN Activists (n=556) Mean	t-value
Support for the NEP	24.24	23.29	3.69***	26.62	25.75	3.89***
GENERAL ORIENTATIONS:						
Distrust of Science and Technology	7.93	7.43	3.19***	9.34	8.48	4.81***
Political Ideology+	2.98	3.06	-1.50	2.32	2.62	-4.77***
Perceived Policy Influence	6.15	6.97	-6.26***	7.64	7.40	1.82
Support for Citizen Participation	5.03	4.84	2.08*	6.24	5.95	4.23***
Level of Political Participation	1.49	1.68	-2.08*	4.18	4.35	-1.72
Preservationist Identification	3.47	3.33	3.06**	3.89	3.78	2.68**
Cooperation or Conflict Among Policy Elites++	4.26	4.68	-3.99***	4.05	5.32	-12.76***
Support for Government Regulation+++	1.42	1.67	-4.82***	1.27	1.54	-5.82***
SPECIFIC ORIENTATIONS:						
Seriousness of Acid Rain Problem	5.65	4.85	9.55***	6.16	5.61	7.93***
Harmful Effects of Acid Rain Deposition	45.93	43.41	5.23***	46.66	46.61	0.14
Support for Moratorium on Acid Rain-Causing Activities	5.37	4.60	6.91***	6.07	5.62	6.46***

*p≤.05; **p≤.01; ***p≤.001; + higher value=conservative; ++ higher value=conflict; +++ higher value=lack of support.

two political cultures, Table 2.10 also sets forth findings on attitudes and beliefs pertaining to acid rain. Canadian citizens are more likely than American citizens to see acid rain as a serious problem, to ascribe harmful effects to acid rain deposition, and to call for a moratorium on acid-rain-causing activities. Save for the attribution of harmful effects to acid rain deposition, similar differences exist between the Canadian and American activists. On this finding, one would expect the common educative quality of interest group membership in the United States and Canada and the shared motivation leading to group affiliation in those countries to combine to produce comparable levels of information about the effects of acid rain.

The higher level of support for the NEP among Canadians is of particular interest to the issue of the political culture differences hypothesized between Canada and the United States. The NEP measure itself reflects the "spaceship earth" conception of an interdependent, holistic understanding of the connections between humans and the natural, physical environment. Not only does the NEP accord humans and other living organisms equivalent status, but it also underscores the practical importance of regarding their fates as jointly held. This seems to fit more closely the dominant Canadian world view than it does the American mindset. At the most aggregate level, then, the hypothesized cultural differences separating Canada and the United States exist with regard to the NEP.

Returning to the issue of cultural convergence and divergence, it is useful to determine whether these differences in NEP remain after controlling for the effects of postmaterial values and age cohort. That is, if postmaterial values represent the central focus for cross-national cultural convergence, Canadians and Americans who share those values also should exhibit similarities on other cultural dimensions believed to separate them. In addition, if Inglehart's conception of the origin of postmaterialist values is correct, value convergence most likely would occur among those younger generations subject to similar socialization stimuli and to similar economic and international milieu characteristic of postindustrial society. Consequently, one would expect younger cohorts within each postmaterialist value type to exhibit greater cross-national similarity in support of the NEP than would older cohorts. Thus, Table 2.11 displays the mean NEP index scores, controlling for nationality, postmaterial value type, and age cohort.

Nationality, postmaterial value type, and age cohort each demonstrate independent effects on support for the NEP. On the whole, support for the NEP is greater among Canadians than among Americans, greater among postmaterialists than among those with mixed or material values, and greater among younger cohorts than among older-age groups. Support for the NEP also is structured to some degree by inter-

Table 2.11
Mean New Environmental Paradigm Scores by Nationality, Postmaterialist Value Type, and Age Cohort

Age Cohorts		Postmaterialist Value Types*		
Young				
		Materialist	*Mixed*	*Postmaterialist*
	Canada	26.9	24.3	26.8
	U.S.	21.8	23.1	24.8
Middle				
	Canada	25.4	24.3	24.1
	U.S.	22.9	24.9	26.0
Old				
	Canada	20.7	24.5	24.4
	U.S.	21.3	23.5	21.1

Significance

country	$\leq$.001	*country x values*	$\leq$.05	*country x values x age*	$\leq$.01
values	$\leq$.001	*country x age*	$\leq$.05		
age	$\leq$.001	*values x age*	$\leq$.01		

* *The entry in each cell is the average score on the NEP index. A higher value indicates greater average support for the New Environmental Paradigm.*

actions among the value, nationality, and age cohort measures. Among the oldest age group, the only major country difference in support for the NEP exists between the Canadian and American postmaterialists. The older Canadian postmaterialists give greater support to the NEP than do their American counterparts. Such differences are not mirrored among the materialist or mixed value types in these Canadian and American samples.

In fact, among the middle-age group, the pattern observed among older cohorts is reversed; the postmaterialist Americans are higher on the NEP index than their Canadian counterparts. In that same age category, however, materialist Canadians are much more pro-NEP than are materialist Americans. Among the youngest cohort, Canadians give greater NEP support at both the material and the postmaterial value positions than do Americans, with the differences being much greater among materialists. The young American materialists differ little from their middle and older fellow Americans, while younger Canadian materialists are substantially more supportive of the NEP than their older compatriots.

Given these findings, then, what can be said about convergence in the political cultures of Canada and the United States—as it may be exhibited in this analysis of the NEP, postmaterial values, and age cohort? The answer is "yes" to the question of convergence, but not quite in the simple way we might have expected. The greatest support for NEP among the Americans comes from the middle-age cohort postmaterialists, while for Canadians it is found among the youngest postmaterialists and materialists. Consequently, a cross-generational, cross-national convergence seems to be in evidence, with the middle-age cohort Americans and the younger age cohort Canadians coming together. An additional twist to the findings is that postmaterial values play a stronger role in the development of that convergence in the United States than in Canada, perhaps because those values are already somewhat consistent with major elements of the traditional Canadian political culture. The American middle-age group, of course, represents the generation that first exhibited behavior reflecting postindustrial values in the politics of the 1960s and 1970s (Miller and Levitin 1976).

Our conclusion to this point is worth repeating. There is some evidence of convergence, but it seems to be between the postmaterialists of different generations. These findings perhaps arise as a result of (1) the traditional Canadian culture's link to the core concepts of the NEP and (2) the middle-age cohort Americans' particular sensitivity to the composite NEP beliefs as they are linked to that generation's political value socialization in the era of the 1960s.

Other Elements of Political Culture

Conflict and Cooperation. American and Canadian political cultures are thought widely to differ in the nature of their respective perceptions of political conflict. Canadians are believed to view normal politics as entailing a high degree of naturally cooperative efforts on the part of major political figures. Americans, in contrast, are regarded widely as seeing politics as naturally adversarial and conflictful, though occurring within given boundaries and in accord with fixed rules (McClosky and Zaller 1984). The value changes hypothesized to be associated with the advent of postindustrial society suggest more cooperative and collaborative forms of politics. Is there evidence of convergence in this realm of values? Table 2.12 presents the mean level of conflict thought to exist among decision-making elites on the part of Canadians and Americans, again controlling for the effects of age cohort and postmaterial value type.

Overall, Americans and Canadians do differ in their perception of conflict ($p \leq .001$), with Americans generally being more likely to ascribe high levels of conflict to occur among potential leaders responsible for acid rain policy. Postmaterialists are more likely than others to see conflict in environmental policy solutions ($p \leq .05$), and young people are more likely to ascribe high levels of conflict to policy elites than are older generations ($p \leq .01$).

Some mixed findings exist when the analysis becomes more focused

Table 2.12
Mean Perception of Elite Conflict by Nationality, Postmaterialist Value Type, and Age Cohort*

Age Cohorts		Postmaterialist Value Types		
Young		*Materialist*	*Mixed*	*Postmaterialist*
	Canada	4.0	4.3	4.8
	U.S.	4.9	5.3	5.1
Middle				
	Canada	4.2	4.4	5.1
	U.S.	3.7	4.8	5.6
Old				
	Canada	3.9	4.3	4.1
	U.S.	4.5	4.4	3.6

Significance

country	$\leq.001$	*country x values*	ns	*country x values x age*	ns
values	$\leq.05$	*country x age*	$p\leq.05$		
age	$\leq.01$	*values x age*	ns		

* *The entry in each cell is the mean score on the perception of elite cooperation in the solution of acid rain problems. A higher score indicates a greater perception of conflict.*

on subsets of citizens. Among the Americans, postmaterial values have different effects among the middle- and old-age cohorts. In the middle-age group, postmaterial value orientations are associated with perceptions of greater intra-elite conflict while in the oldest age group those citizens professing postmaterial values tend to ascribe less conflict to policy-making elites. Among Canadians, in the two younger age groups (young and middle), values are related to perceived conflict in the same way as among the middle-age group of Americans, namely, postmaterialists are more likely to ascribe conflict to their elites than are other value types. The differences across value types are marginal among the oldest Canadians.

What might account for the postmaterial respondents being more likely to see conflict on the resolution of acid rain problems, especially among those cohorts most likely to be sensitive to value change and its political implications? The young- and middle-age groups of postmaterialists have been in the elite-challenging cohorts of Canada and the United States, pressing for change based on the political implications of their values. Thus, as they attempt to enter policy arenas previously perceived to be closed or, as in the case of acid rain and the environment policy arenas dominated by policy adversaries, conflict may be seen as the more likely mode. Indeed, the group most likely to perceive elite conflict as the likely course is the postmaterial middle-age group of Americans, that cohort socialized in the midst of the "new politics" revolution and forming the core of the environmental movement since the 1970s (Rohrschneider 1991, p. 264).

Government Regulation. The Canadian political culture is also widely thought to be more accepting of government regulation (Paehlke 1991). Such acceptance is consistent with a collectivist, holistic approach to public policy-making. Table 2.13 contains mean scores for a measure of support for greater government regulation in the area of environmental protection. A higher mean score indicates greater *opposition* to government regulation.

As expected, Americans overall tend to express greater opposition to government regulation ($p \leq .001$). In almost every value/age subgroup, the American respondents exhibit equal or greater opposition to government regulation in comparison to their Canadian counterparts. To be sure, in some cases the cross-national differences are small or nearly nonexistent. Perhaps the most significant indicators of the cultural differences are to be found in the upper-left and lower-right corners of the table, namely, the younger cohort materialists and the older cohort postmaterialists. In both cases, American respondents are more opposed to government regulation than are their Canadian age/value counterparts. Indeed, the largest cross-national difference in degree of

Table 2.13
Mean Opposition to Government Regulation by Nationality, Postmaterialist Value Type, and Age Cohort*

Age Cohorts		Postmaterialist Value Types		
Young				
		Materialist	*Mixed*	*Postmaterialist*
	Canada	1.3	1.4	1.5
	U.S.	1.7	1.7	1.8
Middle				
	Canada	1.2	1.7	1.7
	U.S.	1.5	1.8	1.8
Old				
	Canada	1.4	1.2	1.2
	U.S.	1.4	1.7	1.8

Significance

country	$p \leq .001$	*country* x *values*	ns	*country* x *values* x *age* ns	
values	$\leq .05$	*country* x *age*	ns		
age	$\leq .01$	*values* x *age*	ns		

* *The entry in each cell is the mean support for government regulation. A higher value reflects lower support for government regulation.*

opposition to government regulation occurs among the older cohort postmaterialists. In the old-age group, shared political values do little to bridge the cross-national culture gap.

These results should not be viewed as surprising given the fact that the older-age groups rest longer in the canons of the prevailing culture. Among the oldest group, personal mindsets would have developed the most resistance to change away from the long-held and crystallized core values of the traditional culture. Among the middle-age cohort, however, there is virtually no difference between the postmaterial Canadians and the postmaterial Americans.

Distrust of Science and Technology. Beliefs about the role of science and technology constitute a central dimension of environmental policy specifically, and a major element of cultural change generally in the post-industrial world. Science and technology are the handmaidens of a new and better world, the hope for new solutions to the problems of human-kind. At the same time, however, suspicion of science and fear of new technology often do arise from both traditional and modern sources. Traditionalists sometimes view with skepticism the claims of the pro-moters of science and technology, and fear the social and cultural changes that occur in the wake of scientific breakthroughs or technologi-cal developments; they are inclined to see science and technology as contributing to the downfall of the traditional values and beliefs they hold dear. Among postmaterialists, there also are doubts about the rela-tive costs and benefits of science and technology. Science and technol-ogy are viewed at once as sources of elite political and economic control and as too frequently contributing to the sacrifice of environmental values.

The results of an investigation of Canadian and American views on science and technology across value and age dimensions reveal that the diverse sources of distrust of science and technology are equally in evidence in both countries. The results displayed in Table 2.14 indicate that age and postmaterial value types interact in different ways among Canadians and Americans. Among the youngest age cohort the effect of postmaterial values is quite strong for Americans, but only faintly present for Canadians. On the other hand, among the oldest cohort, the effect of these values upon Canadians is strong and among Americans is very weak. Cross-national differences are also present among the middle-age category as well. In this group, postmaterialist values pro-duce distrust for Americans and trust among Canadians. It is quite evident that very different dynamics adhere to science and technology attitudes in Canada and the United States. There is little evidence of any convergence occurring in this area of cultural orientations.

Citizen Participation. Our earlier analysis (Table 2.10) indicated that Canadians give slightly greater support for citizen participation than do Americans. The desire for more involvement in determining what government does is a core element of postmaterial values, and younger cohorts are generally thought to be more desirous of citizen involvement in policy processes than are older-age groups. Do political values and age produce effects that serve to bring Canadian and American views into a closer line of convergence on the issue of citizen involvement? The mean level of support for citizen participation in the several age and value type subgroups is shown in Table 2.15.

Values and age both exhibit significant main effects ($p \leq .001$) on support for citizen participation, but nationality does not. In both coun-tries, the highest level of support for citizen involvement occurs among the middle-age cohort postmaterialists—the "activist" cohort of the 1960s. Likewise, among both Canadians and Americans, the lowest level of support for citizen involvement occurs among the middle-age

Table 2.14
Mean Distrust of Science and Technology by Nationality, Postmaterialist Value Type, and Age Cohort*

Age Cohorts		Postmaterialist Value Types		
Young		*Materialist*	*Mixed*	*Postmaterialist*
	Canada	7.8	7.4	7.5
	U.S.	5.7	7.3	8.4
Middle				
	Canada	9.5	7.3	6.6
	U.S.	6.9	7.5	8.7
Old				
	Canada	7.0	8.5	9.7
	U.S.	7.6	7.4	8.1

Significance

country	p≤.01	country x values	p≤.05	country x values x age	p≤.001
values	≤.05	country x age	ns		
age	≤.001	values x age	p≤.01		

* *The entry in each cell is the average score on the index of distrust for science and technology.*

group materialists. In both countries, the greatest distance in level of support for citizen involvement exists between the middle-age group materialists and the middle-age cohort postmaterialists. While among the older group few value-linked differences are in evidence, younger cohort Americans and Canadians do differ across material and postmaterial value types, with Canadians being the more supportive of citizen involvement in each case.

The irony in these results is that value convergence occurs precisely where one might least expect it. That is, the Americans and Canadians in the oldest age group differ little, while the pure value types in the youngest cohort reveal substantial differences cross-nationally. As was the case with attitudes toward science and technology, the dynamics relating to citizen involvement are quite different in Canada and the United States.

Table 2.15
Mean Support for Citizen Participation in Environmental Policy by Nationality, Postmaterialist Value Type, and Age Cohort*

Age Cohorts		Postmaterialist Value Types		
Young (≤35)		*Materialist*	*Mixed*	*Postmaterialist*
	Canada	5.5	5.5	5.1
	U.S.	4.4	5.6	4.6
Middle (735≤50)				
	Canada	4.4	4.9	5.9
	U.S.	4.1	5.4	6.3
Old (50+)				
	Canada	4.5	4.8	4.9
	U.S.	4.6	4.6	4.9

Significance

country	ns	*country* x *values*	ns	*country* x *values* x *age*	ns
values	≤.001	*country* x *age*	ns		
age	≤.001	*values* x *age*	p≤.001		

* *The entry in each cell is the mean score on support of citizen participation in environmental policy. A higher score reflects higher support for citizen participation.*

CONCLUSION

This chapter addresses the issue of whether cultural differences in the politics of Canada and the United States surface in our public opinion data. The answer is important for understanding the context within which interest groups must operate to help citizens confront the technical information quandary of the postindustrial era. The prevailing views of the respective political cultures of Canada and the United States, if substantiated, would suggest that interest groups would be less effective in Canada than in the United States as intermediary agents in assisting citizens to deal with complex technical and scientific policy areas of public policy.

At the same time, it is necessary to address the issue of cultural convergence, especially within those cohorts increasingly subject to the same economic, political, and informational influences. If cultural convergence is present, it can be expected that the two countries also will come closer in the way they allow for interest group activity.

What have the results reported here shown concerning the nature of contemporary political culture in the United States and Canada? In many ways, the two countries differ in hypothesized directions. At the same time, in the analysis of the factors associated with postmaterial values among Americans and Canadians we found that value convergence appears most likely among the activist segments of the two political cultures. But, when examining libertarian values in conjunction with postmaterialism, there is evidence of a complex pattern of divergence. That is, among *materialists*, the libertarian differences between Canadians and Americans are greatest in the younger age group, but among the *postmaterialists* they are greatest in the older-age cohort. Across these general political values and across other indicators of potential differences in political culture (e.g., perceptions of conflict and cooperation and support for government regulation), there is ample support for our hypothesis. That is, as measured here, Canadian and American interest groups appear to operate in somewhat different cultural contexts as they provide potential ways to confront the technical information quandary. The following chapters will explore the extent to which the differences discovered to this point are translated into the interest group worlds of the two countries.

NOTES

1. According to the U.S. Census for 1980, the total population of Michigan is 9,262,078, and the comparable Ontario figure is 8,715,800. In addition, the province and state have sizable urban populations in cities over 25,000 (4,241,730 in Michigan and 5,920,777 in Ontario), and both contain a large metropolitan center (Detroit and Toronto, respectively). Finally, the economic bases of Ontario and Michigan are roughly similar; each holds a complex of large industrial centers and the economies of both areas possess sizable and growing tertiary sectors.

2. The four population categories used were: (1) 25,000 to 50,000; (2) 50,001 to 100,000; (3) 100,001 to 250,000; and (4) cities with populations of 250,001 or more. The number of respondents selected from the cities in each of the size categories was determined by calculating the proportion of the total provincial/state population in cities of at least 25,000 found in cities in the particular size category. The actual survey respondents were chosen at random from telephone directories. Although samples of 1000 were selected in both Ontario and Michigan, many mailed questionnaires were undeliverable. The following breakdown details the number of survey questionnaires sent to respondents, the number actually delivered, the number returned, and the response rates (the number

returned as a percentage of the number delivered) for the samples selected in Ontario and Michigan for each of the four city population size categories.

Response	Number Mailed	Number Delivered	Number Returned	Rate
Total Sample				
Ont	1,000	897	600	66.9%
MI	1,000	873	476	54.5%
25,000-50,000				
Ont (11.4%)*	114	80	48	60%
MI (19.3%)	193	181	87	48.1%
50,001-100,000				
Ont (19.3%)	193	184	130	70.6%
MI (29.8%)	298	277	153	55.2%
100,001-250,000				
Ont (18%)	180	168	102	61%
MI (22.5%)	225	189	106	56.1%
250,000 plus				
Ont (51.3%)	513	465	320	69%
MI (28.4%	284	226	130	57.5%

*   These figures represent the percentage of the population in cities of at least 25,000 population

3. The indicator representing support for the NEP is based on a short form (six items) of an environmental values inventory developed by Riley Dunlap and Kent VanLiere (1978, 1984). Respondents were asked to indicate agreement or disagreement (5-point Likert scales) on these items: (1) the balance of nature is very delicate and easily upset by human activities; (2) the earth is like a spaceship with only limited room and resources; (3) plants and animals do not exist primarily for human usage; (4) modifying the environment for human use seldom causes serious problems; (5) there are no limits to growth for nations like the United States or Canada; and (6) humankind was created to rule over the rest of nature. The responses were combined into an additive scale.

4. The eight general public policy process orientations investigated included the following: (1) distrust of science and technology; (2) self-declared ideological inclination; (3) perceived level of opportunity provided to citizens for input into government decision making at the federal, state/provincial, and local levels; (4) perception of the value of citizen participation in the environmental policy area; (5) level of participation in natural resource policy-making process; (6) perception of the level of cooperation/conflict occurring among acid rain/air pollution policy elites in Canada and the United States; (7) support for government regulation of industry to prevent acid rain problems; and (8) degree of

support for preservation of nature as against economic exploitation. These several measures took the specific form described briefly below.

On the matter of distrust of science and technology, respondents were asked whether they agreed or disagreed with these three statements: (1) Technology will find a way of solving the problems of shortages in natural resources; (2) People would be better off if they lived a more simple life without so much technology; (3) Future scientific research is more likely to cause problems than to find solutions to problems. A 5-point scale was provided, ranging from "strongly agree" to "strongly disagree." After coding the responses to reflect a distrust of science and technology, the answers were summed in an additive scale.

The measure for self-declared ideological inclination reads as follows: How would you place yourself on the following ideological scale in your country? The response categories in Canada were "very left," "left," "moderate," "right," and "very right." In the United States, the response categories were "very liberal," "liberal," "moderate," "conservative," and "very conservative." On this indicator, lower numbers represent the "very left/liberal" position and higher numbers represent the "very right/conservative" position.

A measure of perceived policy influence was created from the following question: According to what you have read, heard of, or know from your own experiences, how much opportunity does each level of government listed below provide citizens like you to express their views on natural resource and environmental issues? Three levels of government were listed—federal, provincial/state, and city—and respondents were provided with four response categories: "none," "a little," "some," and "a great deal." Responses on these three items were added to form a summary additive measure.

The measure of support for citizen involvement in natural resource policy processes is based on responses to a single item, which reads: In recent years there has been considerable debate over the value of efforts to increase the amount of citizen participation in government policy-making in the environmental area. How would you locate yourself on the following scale regarding these efforts? Respondents were provided with a 7-point scale with the midpoint marked "uncertain" and the respective endpoints marked "these efforts are of no value and add needlessly to the cost of government" and "these efforts are of great value even if they add to the cost of government."

The measure for degree of participation in the environmental policy process is based on the aggregation of responses to six items pertaining to modes of participation available to a citizen in either Canada or the United States. These six items are prefaced with this header: "People participate in various activities to try to influence issues concerning the environment and natural resources. Please indicate below which channels of influence you have used *to affect natural resource policy.* The six channels of potential influence provided were (1) written a letter to a public official, (2) joined a group or organization, (3) contributed money or time to a favored cause, (4) attended a public hearing, (5) signed a petition or initiative, and (6) supported a candidate for public office by active campaigning.

The extent to which respondents perceived cooperation or conflict among policy elites in their country was based on answers to this question: As a general rule, to what extent is there cooperation or conflict in your country between the various elected officials and experts involved in the acid rain/air pollution issue? Respondents were asked to place themselves on a 7-point scale that had endpoints of "cooperation" and "conflict."

Support for government regulation is based on the responses to a single item that reads: Government regulation of industry can reduce the risk of acid rain. Respondents were asked to place themselves on a scale representing their level of agreement or disagreement with this statement; the 5-point scale had endpoints of "strongly agree" and "strongly disagree," and a midpoint of "uncertain."

The measure of preservationist identification was obtained by asking respondents to place themselves on a 5-point scale on which 5 equals strongest preservationist and 1 is the least preservationist.

5. The three policy areas relating to acid rain that were investigated are (1) estimating risks to public health and the ecology of acid rain deposition, (2) the relative seriousness of the acid rain issue, and (3) the extent of government intervention to prevent acid rain problems. The three measures took the following form. First, eight potentially harmful effects of acid rain were listed: respiratory ailments/lung disease, corrosion of buildings or monuments, deforestation, destruction of wildlife, contamination of drinking water, lower agricultural productivity, decimation of freshwater fish stocks, and soil depletion. A 7-point continuum was provided for each effect, with the endpoints labeled "low degree of risk" and "high degree of risk." The responses for the eight potential effects were summed to form an overall index ranging from 8 to 56.

Second, respondents were asked to rate the seriousness of acid rain when compared to other problems facing Ontario and Michigan (such as unemployment, inflation, and crime). Seven response categories were provided ranging from "not serious" to "one of the most serious problems facing North America."

Finally, respondents were asked to respond to the following question: Based upon all you have heard about the issue of acid rain, where would you locate yourself on the following scale? One end of the 7-point scale contained the option of a moratorium on all acid-rain-causing activities while the other end contained the option "continue current practices."

Chapter Three

Trust in Sources of Policy-Relevant Information

As noted in the previous chapters, Canada and the United States are both postindustrial democracies, they share a common adoption of federal governmental forms, and the two nations share a common legal–political legacy. Even so, the two neighboring nations are widely assumed to have distinct political cultures and maintain quite dissimilar governmental practices and institutional structures. It is one thesis of this book that the way in which interest groups operate as sources of political influence and producers and distributors of policy-relevant information may differ in Canada and the United States in ways reflecting these cultural and structural differences.

As Chapter 2 describes, a number of studies comparing the political cultures of Canada and the United States note significant differences in political beliefs and values (see Gibbins and Nevitte 1985; Horowitz 1966; Lipset 1985). By way of review, Canadian political culture is thought to be more organic and collectivist in nature than is American political culture (Lipset 1963; Lipset 1985). American political culture reflects a Lockean individualistic conception of society (Commager 1950, 1977; Hartz 1955; Kluegel and Smith 1986), and public policy in the United States is shaped by pervasive, widely held political values that stress the free enterprise system, individualism, and respect for property rights (Dolbeare and Medcalf 1988; McCloskey and Zaller 1984). Americans, consequently, can be shown to be more insistent on claiming their self-perceived rights—either from government or from other citizens in the form of civil litigation (Hargrove 1967; Kritzer et al. 1990).

The Canadian policy-making system has been characterized as being closed rather than open, with channels of influence primarily organized hierarchically and based to only a limited extent on a pluralistic, competitive approach to decision making (Presthus 1974; Pross 1975). In contrast, the American policy-making system reflects a pluralistic, competitive approach to decision making; the emphasis is on conflict-oriented techniques intended to arouse public opinion (Pross 1975, p. 19; Berry 1989, pp. 240–242; Heinz et al. 1990). In the Canadian political system, a process of elite accommodation is widely thought to take the place of the competitive American version of the public policy process (Noel 1976; Presthus 1974). The Canadian system broadly is presumed to favor elite groups and employ accommodative and consensus-seeking techniques of political communication. Given these putative fundamental differences between the American and Canadian settings, it is plausible to expect that substantial differences will arise in the comparison of Canadian and American citizens and the comparison of Canadian and American environmental group members with respect to their views on interest groups in their respective political systems.

Of particular interest in this chapter is how Americans and Canadians view a broad range of political interests, and how members of comparable interest groups view those same interests. Given our concern with the technical information quandary in postindustrial democracies and the role of interest groups in responding to that quandary, we asked both Canadian and American citizens and environmental interest group members in the two countries to express their level of trust in environmental policy information provided to the policy process by a number of interests.

As hypothesized in Chapter 1, we expect the more organic and collectivist Canadian setting to produce less disparate rankings of trust than the pluralistic and individualistic American setting. That is, the range between the groups receiving the greatest trust and the groups receiving the least trust by any given individual should be less for Canadians than for Americans. In theory, moreover, the Canadian setting should produce overall more trusting attitudes regarding the information disseminated by societal interests and the American setting should produce more skeptical attitudes. For environmental interest group members, it is expected that Canadians will be more inclined to trust in the information provided by "opponents" (e.g., developers, energy companies); for citizens generally, it is expected that Canadians will be more trusting of informational sources across the board as compared to their American counterparts. As a consequence of this lower level of discrimination among informational sources, it is expected that conventional predictors of trust (e.g., ideology, education) will be less effective in predicting levels of trust among Canadians than among Americans.

MEASUREMENTS AND INDICATORS

Environmental group members and citizens were asked to indicate their level of trust in the various information sources listed in Table 3.1. The various sources of natural resource information were categorized into three areas: government sources, expert sources, and private sources. The lead-in heading read: "Many individuals and groups supply information about the environment. We are interested in how much trust you have in the information supplied by each source listed below." For the measurement of the level of trust felt, respondents were provided with a 4-point scale—with the value 1 reflecting "no trust," 2 denoting "not much trust," 3 indicating "some trust," and 4 representing "a great deal of trust." The listing of private-interest-based informational sources included business, hunting and fishing groups, energy companies, developers, labor unions, environmental groups, and citizen groups. The governmental interests included elected officials, the federal government, state/provincial government, and local government. Finally, these "expertise-based" sources of information were listed—technical and scientific experts, college/university educators, and news reporters.

In addition to this central measure, other control variables representing conventional correlates of trust in information were examined. On the basis of previous research on the question of trust of information sources (Lovrich and Pierce 1986; Pierce et al. 1987; Pierce et al. 1988), five background and value-orientation measures are employed as conventional predictors of trust in information sources. Age, gender, education, ideology, postmaterialist values (Inglehart 1990), and new environmental paradigm (NEP) beliefs (Dunlap and VanLiere 1978) all have been shown in previous studies to be related to levels of trust in various sources of information. In general, younger cohorts, women, the highly educated, liberals, postmaterialists, and proenvironmentalist citizens are more inclined to trust information provided by environmentalists and distrust information provided by most other sources—particularly those associated with the private sector (e.g., developers, business, and energy companies, etc.).

The specific measures of the various independent variables are each individual's age (in years), a dummy variable for gender (1 = female, 0 = male), a scale indicating formal educational attainment (from 1 = never attended school to 9 = advanced degree),[1] a scale indicating support for the NEP (from 6 = low level of support to 30 = high level of support),[2] an indicator of subjective political ideology (from 1 = very liberal in the United States or very left in Canada to 5 = very conservative in the United States or very right in Canada,[3]) and a

Table 3.1

Trust in Information on Acid Rain and the Environment: Mean Scores on a Four-Point Scale for Citizens and for Environmental Interest Group Members (in Ontario and Michigan)

	ONTARIO Public (n=600)	MICHIGAN Public (n=476)	Dif.[a]	ONTARIO Activists (n=554)	MICHIGAN Activists (n=684)	Dif.[a]
GOVERNMENTAL SOURCES:						
Elected Officials	2.22	2.33	+ .11	2.34	2.30	- .04
Federal Government	2.63	2.68	+ .05	2.64	2.58	- .06
Prov./State Government	2.66	2.80	+ .14	2.70	2.71	+ .01
Local Government	2.52	2.62	+ .10	2.47	2.39	- .08
EXPERT SOURCES:						
Academic	3.36	3.17	- .19	3.42	3.35	- .07
Science/Technology Experts	3.44	3.33	- .11	3.32	3.40	+ .08
Press	2.87	2.85	- .02	2.88	2.78	- .10
PRIVATE SOURCES:						
Business	2.05	2.34	+ .29	1.99	2.12	+ .13
Hunt & Fish Groups	2.85	2.75	- .10	2.80	2.67	- .13
Energy Companies	2.00	2.13	+ .13	1.87	1.90	+ .03
Developer	1.57	1.77	+ .20	1.68	1.64	- .04
Labor	1.94	1.92	- .02	2.24	1.99	- .25
Environmentalists	3.32	3.27	- .05	3.61	3.47	- .14
Citizen Groups	3.26	3.14	- .12	3.52	3.36	- .16

a Difference between Michigan mean score and Ontario mean score. Mean figures pertain to a 4-point scale ranging from 1 = no trust, 2 = not much trust, 3 = some trust, and 4 = a great deal of trust.

dummy variable assessing postmaterialist value orientations (1 = post-materialist, 0 = other).[4]

OVERALL LEVEL OF TRUST

What can be said of the degree to which our survey data from Ontario and Michigan confirm the presence of a "political culture effect" attributable to a pluralistic and individualistic culture in the United States and an organic and collectivistic culture in Canada? Table 3.1 displays findings regarding the level of trust expressed in each of the 14 sources of information investigated. The expectation raised by the political culture effect is that Canadians will exhibit an overall higher level of trust in the various sources of information than will their American counterparts.

The results reported in Table 3.1 show only limited support for the expectation of greater trust in interest group information on the part of Canadian subjects. Indeed, the overall similarity of results is rather striking. Developers are at the bottom of the public and activist listings of level of trust in information from private interest group sources in both Ontario and Michigan; for all of these same study populations, environmentalists are among the most trusted sources of information. For governmental sources of information, there again appear to be very similar patterns of trust. In the several cases in which a difference between Canadian and American mean responses is in evidence, in five of the eight comparisons the American subjects are more trusting than their Canadian counterparts rather than less trusting as had been expected. With respect to trust in information from parties seen as "experts," both the Ontario and Michigan survey respondents express relatively high levels of trust. In this area, the Canadian subjects indeed did surpass their American counterparts; in five of the six comparisons, the mean scores for Ontario citizens and activists are higher than those of their Michigan counterparts. In terms of differences between citizens and environmental activists in the two settings, the comparisons are again quite similar. In both cases, the activists tend to be marginally less trusting of other economic interests' information than are citizens.

In one important dimension of comparison, however, there is some distinct evidence of a clear American–Canadian difference of the kind predicted by the political culture hypothesis. In assessing the pattern of positive and negative differences between American and Canadian mean values, it is clear that the comparisons between citizens produce one picture—with Americans tending to be more trusting—and comparisons between environmental interest group members produce quite another. Canadian group members are more trusting than their American counterparts. On five of the seven private sources, on three of the four governmental sources, and on two of three expert sources, the Canadian group members tend to be more trusting than their American opposites.

Overall, it would appear that a good deal of similarity of attitudes is in evidence, but the activist responses also show that there is some evidence of a Canadian inclination toward more organic and collectivist orientations toward other societal interests. For citizens, there is little evidence of a greater deference being shown toward official sources, whether they are local, state/provincial, or national government in origin. For environmental group members, however, there is some indication that Canadian activists are more inclined to trust official sources than are their American counterparts. This greater trust among Canadians at the activist, elite level, then, may reflect the putative corporatist, accommodationist nature of elite politics in Canada (Presthus 1973). The relatively more benign view of diverse political interests among interest group activists may grow directly out of the elites' greater stake in the organic, integrated nature of the political culture. By and large, Table 3.1 thus contains some, though rather limited, support for the identification of a "political culture effect" in this area of political behavior, primarily in the realm of interest group activists.

PREDICTING TRUST

What can be said of the ability to predict levels of trust from the knowledge of conventional correlates of faith in sources of information? Recall that it is expected that these variables would be less predictive in the Canadian than in the American setting. Tables 3.2–3.7 show the results of multivariate analyses of trust levels.

Logit models were developed to examine the extent to which the various predictor variables affect trust in environmental information sources. Because the response categories for the dependent variables are restrictive, and due to the fact that the frequency distributions for these measures are rather skewed for most of the information sources, response categories were dichotomized. Respondents reporting that they have "some" or "a great deal" of trust in an information source were given a "1," and those saying they had "none" or "not much" trust were given a "0." For the results from the logit models presented in Tables 3.2–3.7, the coefficient of a particular variable indicates the effect of the variable on the likelihood of trusting a particular source of information (Aldrich and Nelson 1984).

The results from the logit models presented in Table 3.2 assess citizens' level of trust in government information sources. For all models presented, the goodness-of-fit chi-square statistic is not significant, meaning that the specified structure constitutes an acceptable model in the statistical sense.

The findings set forth in Table 3.2 indicate little if any support for the proposition that conventional correlates of trust in government information sources are less predictive of Canadian trust levels than they are for American information trust levels. The predictors in the analysis do equally well in both Ontario and Michigan samples. One noticeable difference between the two samples, however, is the impact of ideology. Subjective ideological orientation does not have a significant effect on government trust levels in Canada, while in the Michigan sample a significant relationship exists for three of the four government sources. American conservatives are significantly less trusting of the information provided by elected officials, the federal government, and state government than are their liberal counterparts. This may well be a product of political culture. Research conducted by Inglehart, Nevitte, and Basanez (1991) has suggested that, while a broader ideological continuum exists in Canada (as reflected in their three major political parties at the national level), when compared to that of the United States, Americans tend to be more ideologically strident in their political orientations within their relatively narrow range of variation.

In order to assess the combined effectiveness of these variables in explaining variation in trust of the government information sources, pseudo-R squares are calculated for each model.[5] On the basis of these summary measures, the correlates of trust appear to work better in the American public sample than in the Canadian public sample. However, for the activist samples, the independent variables have a stronger impact in the Canadian context.

The logit models presented in Table 3.3 investigate the level of trust in governmental information sources for the American and Canadian activist samples. Similar to the models examining citizen trust in government sources, the goodness-of-fit chi-square statistic is not significant for any of the models presented, indicating that the specified structures constitute acceptable models in the statistical sense. Once again, the individual predictor variables do about equally well in the Michigan and Ontario settings, with the Ontario setting appearing to be slightly more favorable. As is evident from Table 3.3, the independent variables employed in these analytical models are more effective in predicting trust in government information sources in Canada than the United States. This finding, of course, is contrary to what was predicted on the basis of hypothesized political culture effects.

The logit models presented in Table 3.4 assess the level of trust in expert sources of environmental information for the public samples. Similar to the previous tables, there is little difference between the American and Canadian public samples concerning the degree to which the various predictor variables affect levels of trust. Significant effects for predicting trust in activist information sources are seen in 12 of the independent variables for the Canadian models and 14 of the indepen-

(text continues on p. 82)

Table 3.2
Logit Estimates for the Predictors of Publics' Trust in Government Information Sources Concerning the Environment

	AGE Coeff. (s.e.)	GENDER Coeff. (s.e.)	EDUC Coeff. (s.e.)	NEP Coeff. (s.e.)	IDEOLOGY Coeff. (s.e.)	POSTMAT Coeff. (s.e.)
			CANADIAN PUBLIC[a]			
GOVERNMENT SOURCES:						
Elected Officials						
$X^2 = 317.14$	-.04**	-.64**	.10	.06	-.22	.39*
$R^2 = .35$	(.009)	(.20)	(.09)	(.07)	(.14)	(.20)
Federal Government						
$X^2 = 218.32$	.04	-.03	.12**	-.42*	-.16	-.29**
$R^2 = .28$	(.04)	(.06)	(.03)	(.20)	(.13)	(.10)
Provincial Government						
$X^2 = 216.56$	-.07*	-.08	-.06*	.36	.18	-.21*
$R^2 = .28$	(.03)	(.10)	(.03)	(.30)	(.20)	(.11)
Local Government						
$X^2 = 101.14$	.02	.11	.01	-.06*	.03	.06
$R^2 = .17$	(.03)	(.08)	(.03)	(.03)	(.03)	(.08)

a Degree of freedom for goodness-of-fit chi square range from 481 to 568. Significance levels are: *$p \leq .05$; **$p \leq .01$

Table 3.2 (continued)

GOVERNMENT SOURCES:	AGE Coeff. (s.e.)	GENDER Coeff. (s.e.)	AMERICAN PUBLIC[a] EDUC Coeff. (s.e.)	NEP Coeff. (s.e.)	IDEOLOGY Coeff. (s.e.)	POSTMAT Coeff. (s.e.)
Elected Officials						
$X^2 = 192.31$	-.02	-.10	.21**	.07	.52**	.08*
$R^2 = .29$	(.02)	(.11)	(.08)	(.07)	(.11)	(.02)
Federal Government						
$X^2 = 206.45$	-.06**	-.03	.03	-.06*	.38**	-.09
$R^2 = .30$	(.001)	(.04)	(.02)	(.06)	(.06)	(.06)
State Government						
$X^2 = 214.62$	.03	-.41**	.10***	.01	.25**	-.02
$R^2 = .31$	(.03)	(.04)	(.02)	(.06)	(.06)	(.06)
Local Government						
$X^2 = 203.91$	-.01**	-.33**	.05	.03	.43	.13
$R^2 = .31$	(.001)	(.06)	(.06)	(.03)	(.38)	(.13)

a Degrees of freedom for goodness-of-fit chi-square range from 442 to 472. Significance levels are: * $p \le .05$; ** $p \le .01$; *** $p \le .001$

Table 3.3
Logit Estimates for the Predictors of Activists' Trust in Government Information Sources Concerning the Environment

GOVERNMENT SOURCES:	CANADIAN ACTIVISTS[a]					
	AGE Coeff. (s.e.)	GENDER Coeff. (s.e.)	EDUC Coeff. (s.e.)	NEP Coeff. (s.e.)	IDEOLOGY Coeff. (s.e.)	POSTMAT Coeff. (s.e.)
Elected Officials						
$X^2 = 418.54$	-.02*	-.80*	.11	.08	.41**	.28*
	(.009)	(.39)	(.09)	(.06)	(.17)	(.30)
$R^2 = .50$						
Federal Government						
$X^2 = 403.91$	-.01	-.28*	.15**	-.05**	.12	-.35**
	(.04)	(.13)	(.04)	(.01)	(.07)	(.13)
$R^2 = .49$						
Provincial Government						
$X^2 = 424.81$	.09*	.43**	.16**	-.03**	.01	.25**
	(.04)	(.13)	(.04)	(.01)	(.06)	(.13)
$R^2 = .51$						
Local Government						
$X^2 = 325.59$	.05	-.24	.11*	-.04*	.07	-.13
	(.05)	(.18)	(.05)	(.02)	(.09)	(.17)
$R^2 = .46$						

[a] Degrees of freedom for goodness-of-fit chi-square range from 399 to 404. Significance levels are: * $p \leq .05$; ** $p \leq .01$.

Table 3.3 (continued)

	AMERICAN ACTIVISTS[a]					
	AGE	GENDER	EDUC	NEP	IDEOLOGY	POSTMAT
GOVERNMENT SOURCES:	Coeff. (s.e.)	Coeff. (s.e.)	Coeff. (s.e.)	Coeff. (s.e.)	Coeff. (s.e.)	Coeff. (s.e.)
Elected Officials						
$X^2 = 217.37$	.02*	-.02	.22*	.01	-.18	-.01
$R^2 = .39$	(.01)	(.23)	(.10)	(.03)	(.14)	(.24)
Federal Government						
$X^2 = 317.85$	.03	-.61**	.15**	-.03**	-.06	.21
$R^2 = .49$	(.05)	(.16)	(.05)	(.01)	(.09)	(.15)
State Government						
$X^2 = 325.28$	-.09*	-.26*	.19*	-.02	-.12	.20
$R^2 = .49$	(.05)	(.14)	(.05)	(.01)	(.08)	(.15)
Local Government						
$X^2 = 248.24$	.01	.60**	.32**	-.09	.14	.11
$R^2 = .43$	(.01)	(.19)	(.07)	(.02)	(.11)	(.19)

a Degrees of freedom for goodness-of-fit chi-square range from 322 to 326. Significance levels are: * $p \leq .05$; ** $p \leq .01$.

Table 3.4
Logit Estimates for the Predictors of Publics' Trust in Expert Information Sources Concerning the Environment

EXPERT SOURCES:	CANADIAN PUBLIC[a]					
	AGE Coeff. (s.e.)	GENDER Coeff. (s.e.)	EDUC Coeff. (s.e.)	NEP Coeff. (s.e.)	IDEOLOGY Coeff. (s.e.)	POSTMAT Coeff. (s.e.)
College/University Educators						
$X^2=204.11$	-.03**	-1.53**	.37**	.04	.01	-.10
$R^2=.25$	(.008)	(.29)	(.06)	(.05)	(.03)	(.11)
Technical and Scientific Experts						
$X^2=314.63$	-.10**	-.67**	-.03	-.38**	-2.25**	-.65**
$R^2=.35$	(.02)	(.20)	(.06)	(.13)	(.38)	(.26)
News Reporters						
$X^2=306.74$	.06**	.56**	.29**	.15	.16	.70*
$R^2=.38$	(.002)	(.21)	(.08)	(.16)	(.17)	(.40)

a Degrees of freedom for goodness-of-fit chi-square range from 538 to 581. Significance levels are: * $p \leq .05$; ** $p \leq .01$.

Table 3.4 (continued)

EXPERT SOURCES:	AGE Coeff. (s.e.)	GENDER Coeff. (s.e.)	AMERICAN PUBLIC[a] EDUC Coeff. (s.e.)	NEP Coeff. (s.e.)	IDEOLOGY Coeff. (s.e.)	POSTMAT Coeff. (s.e.)
College/University Educators						
$X^2=315.63$	-.02**	-.17	.43**	.17	-.21**	.33**
	(.002)	(.11)	(.05)	(.14)	(.06)	(.13)
$R^2=.40$						
Technical and Scientific Experts						
$X^2=346.71$	-.06*	-.41**	.08*	-.23*	.09**	-.13**
	(.03)	(.10)	(.04)	(.13)	(.03)	(.03)
$R^2=.42$						
News Reporters/ Press						
$X^2=318.42$	-.03**	-.47**	.13**	.16**	.18	.11
	(.003)	(.09)	(.04)	(.07)	(.15)	(.06)
$R^2=.41$						

a Degrees of freedom for goodness-of-fit chi-square range from 442 to 472. Significance levels are: * $p \leq .05$; ** $p \leq .01$.

dent variables for the American models. Interestingly, age has a significant and negative relationship for all three expert sources in both countries. Younger respondents are significantly less trusting of academics, technical and scientific experts, and the press than their older counterparts. This age effect is analyzed more thoroughly in the next section of this chapter.

In regard to trust of expert information sources by environmental activists themselves, the findings in Table 3.5 indicate that fewer of the predictor variables have a significant effect than in the public models. Eight of the independent variables in Canada and nine of the independent variables in the United States have significant impacts upon information source trust. This finding, of course, gives no support to what was expected regarding the political culture effect hypothesis.

Tables 3.6 and 3.7 examine public and environmental activist trust in private sources of information concerning the environment. Similar to Tables 3.4 and 3.5 investigating citizen trust in information sources, many (if not most) of the independent variables have a significant impact for both the Canadian and American samples. For the seven models presented for both Michigan and Ontario in Table 3.6, the mean number of variables found to have a statistically significant impact upon information source trust for each Canadian model is 3.86, while for the American models it is 4.30. As with the previous analyses presented for the public samples, there is little clear evidence supporting the political culture hypothesis.

The results presented in Table 3.7 document the impact of the various predictor variables on trust in private sources for the Michigan and Ontario activist samples. Fewer of the predictor variables are related significantly to trust in private sources of information than in the public samples. The mean number of variables found to have a statistically significant impact upon information source trust for the seven Canadian models is 2.57, while for the American models it is 3.14. There are more significant relationships for the American sample when compared to the Canadian sample, as the political culture hypothesis would suggest; however, the cross-national differences in this area certainly are not great.

INTEREST-SPECIFIC TRUST

Another approach to investigating the political culture hypothesis as it applies to interest group politics is to focus more directly on comparisons between the environmental interest group members with respect to their views of other interests as compared to their regard for their own organizations. One way to do this is to analyze the pattern of difference between the level of trust expressed in information provided by environmentalists and that accorded the other specific sources. In such comparisons, given the political culture hypothesis, it would be expected that such differences would be smaller among Canadian environmental group members than among their American counterparts. Table 3.8 contains findings regarding the percentage of Canadian and American environmental activists who register either a 2- or 3-point difference on the 4-point trust scale (lower level of trust) with respect to the degree of trust accorded environmental group information versus information from other groups.

The results reported in Table 3.8 once more offer little support for the hypothesized differences between Canadian and American group activists. With respect to governmental sources, in three of the four cases Ontario environmental activists are more distrusting of other sources of information than are their Michigan counterparts. Similarly, with regard to the private sources of information, we find that in five of seven cases this same pattern of greater comparative distrust among Canadians is observed. In the area of expert sources, both the Michigan and Ontario activists tend to be quite trusting.

Up to this point, the evidence for the collectivist and organic political culture effect hypothesis concerning the evaluation of policy-relevant information is mixed at best. In some respects, the empirical results are consistent with that hypothesis, but in most comparisons the evidence is either inconclusive or contrary to theoretical expectations. One possibility, of course, is that interest group politics in the Canadian polity are changing (e.g., Pross 1986), and that some of the older patterns and some of the newer forms of belief and activity are coexisting in the Ontario setting. One way to investigate this plausible possibility is to compare older and younger environmental group activists with respect to their informational trust characteristics. Table 3.9 presents findings for mean differences between individuals' trust in environmentalist information minus their trust for other sources (e.g., environmentalist trust–business trust) on the 4-point trust scale.

The comparison of younger (39 years or less) and older (51 years or more) environmental group members reveals some very interesting findings. For the Michigan activists, in every case the older members are relatively less trusting of other sources than are their younger colleagues. Whether it be a matter of economic groups or official sources or the expert authorities, younger Michigan activists are uniformly more trusting than their senior associates. A very different pattern is present for the Ontario activists. With respect to the economic interests, in six out of seven cases the younger group members are less trusting than their senior colleagues. Also, it is clear that the oldest third of the Canadian environmental activists is much more trusting of nonenvironmentalist sources than their American counterparts, and that the youngest

(text continues on p. 90)

Table 3.5
Logit Estimates for the Predictors of Activists' Trust in Expert Information Sources Concerning the Environment

CANADIAN ACTIVISTS[a]

EXPERT SOURCES:	AGE Coeff. (s.e.)	GENDER Coeff. (s.e.)	EDUC Coeff. (s.e.)	NEP Coeff. (s.e.)	IDEOLOGY Coeff. (s.e.)	POSTMAT Coeff. (s.e.)
College/University Educators						
	-.01	-.06**	.11**	-.02	.01	-.09
	(.04)	(.11)	(.03)	(.02)	(.06)	(.12)
$X^2 = 209.54$						
$R^2 = .34$						
Technical and Scientific Experts						
	-.03	-.43**	-.09**	.01	.14*	.16
	(.04)	(.11)	(.03)	(.02)	(.06)	(.12)
$X^2 = 405.15$						
$R^2 = .50$						
News Reporters/ Press						
	-.02**	-.27*	.08*	.02	.07	.44**
	(.001)	(.15)	(.04)	(.02)	(.08)	(.15)
$X^2 = 421.86$						
$R^2 = .51$						

[a] Degrees of freedom for goodness-of-fit chi-square range from 399 to 404. Significance levels are: * $p \leq .05$; ** $p \leq .01$.

Table 3.5 (continued)

	AMERICAN ACTIVISTS[a]					
EXPERT SOURCES:	AGE Coeff. (s.e.)	GENDER Coeff. (s.e.)	EDUC Coeff. (s.e.)	NEP Coeff. (s.e.)	IDEOLOGY Coeff. (s.e.)	POSTMAT Coeff. (s.e.)
College/University Educators						
$X^2 = 329.41$	.03	-.34**	.21**	.04**	-.12	.04
$R^2 = .50$	(.05)	(.14)	(.05)	(.01)	(.09)	(.10)
Technical and Scientific Experts						
$X^2 = 238.11$	-.06	.07	.11*	.02	.14	-.30*
$R^2 = .42$	(.05)	(.14)	(.05)	(.02)	(.09)	(.14)
News Reporters/ Press						
$X^2 = 320.65$	.08**	-.04	.15**	-.01	-.22**	-.36**
$R^2 = .49$	(.005)	(.14)	(.05)	(.01)	(.09)	(.15)

[a] Degrees of freedom for goodness-of-fit chi-square range from 332 to 326. Significance levels are: * $p \leq .05$; ** $p \leq .01$.

85

Table 3.6
Logit Estimates for the Predictors of Publics' Trust in Private Information Sources Concerning the Environment

PRIVATE SOURCES:	AGE Coeff. (s.e.)	GENDER Coeff. (s.e.)	CANADIAN PUBLIC[a]			
			EDUC Coeff. (s.e.)	NEP Coeff. (s.e.)	IDEOLOGY Coeff. (s.e.)	POSTMAT Coeff. (s.e.)
Business						
$X^2=306.74$	.02**	-.17	-.16**	.10	.18	-.63**
$R^2=.35$	(.001)	(.17)	(.03)	(.09)	(.14)	(.18)
Hunting & Fishing Groups						
$X^2=317.17$	.01	-.30**	-.40**	-.32	.14	-.64**
$R^2=.35$	(.04)	(.10)	(.08)	(.26)	(.18)	(.12)
Energy Companies						
$X^2=383.42$	.05**	-.39**	.10	-.86**	.26**	-.54**
$R^2=.42$	(.001)	(.16)	(.09)	(.23)	(.04)	(.18)
Developers						
$X^2=371.75$	.16**	-.28**	.41	-.76**	.46**	-.97**
$R^2=.39$	(.04)	(.11)	(.73)	(.10)	(.11)	(.12)
Labor Unions						
$X^2=146.14$	-.03	-.38**	.10	.14	.16	.10
$R^2=.20$	(.02)	(.10)	(.11)	(.18)	(.12)	(.08)
Environmental Groups						
$X^2=366.38$	-.06**	1.64**	.18	.84**	-.96**	1.10**
$R^2=.39$	(.01)	(.43)	(.16)	(.20)	(.31)	(.25)
Citizen Groups						
$X^2=316.45$	-.09**	1.04**	.28**	.69**	-.17	.84**
$R^2=.39$	(.02)	(.31)	(.11)	(.17)	(.14)	(.16)

[a] Degrees of freedom for goodness-of-fit Chi-Square range from 538 to 581. Significance levels are: * $p \leq .05$; ** $p \leq .01$.

Table 3.6 (continued)

PRIVATE SOURCES:	AMERICAN PUBLIC[a]					
	AGE Coeff. (s.e.)	GENDER Coeff. (s.e.)	EDUC Coeff. (s.e.)	NEP Coeff. (s.e.)	IDEOLOGY Coeff. (s.e.)	POSTMAT Coeff. (s.e.)
Business						
X^2=312.68	.02 (.03)	-.28** (.05)	-.06* (.03)	-.34** (.06)	.46** (.09)	-.30* (.07)
R^2=.39						
Hunting & Fishing Groups						
X^2=222.13	.06** (.01)	-.31** (.05)	-.08* (.02)	-.12 (.11)	.04 (.07)	-.17* (.07)
R^2=.32						
Energy Companies						
X^2=323.06	.01** (.001)	-.38** (.06)	-.18** (.03)	-.46** (.11)	.36** (.12)	.05 (.06)
R^2=.41						
Developers						
X^2=322.65	.01** (.002)	-.15* (.07)	-.22** (.03)	-.42** (.13)	.12** (.02)	-.14** (.10)
R^2=.41						
Labor Unions						
X^2=138.32	.03 (.003)	.12 (.11)	.01 (.03)	.06 (.12)	-.11** (.03)	-.09 (.08)
R^2=.23						
Environmental Groups						
X^2=328.74	-.03** (.003)	.11** (.04)	.14** (.03)	.30** (.10)	-.33** (.13)	.38** (.08)
R^2=.41						
Citizen Groups						
X^2=188.12	.01 (.02)	.10** (.02)	.17 (.17)	.14** (.03)	-.16 (.14)	.46** (.11)
R^2=.29						

[a]Degrees of freedom for goodness-of-fit Chi-Square range from 442 to 472. Significance levels are: * $p \leq .05$; ** $p \leq .01$.

Table 3.7

Logit Estimates for the Predictors of Activists' Trust in Private Information Sources Concerning the Environment

PRIVATE SOURCES:	CANADIAN ACTIVISTS[a]					
	AGE Coeff. (s.e.)	GENDER Coeff. (s.e.)	EDUC Coeff. (s.e.)	NEP Coeff. (s.e.)	IDEOLOGY Coeff. (s.e.)	POSTMAT Coeff. (s.e.)
Business						
$X^2 = 249.68$	.03*	-.61**	.06	.10	.33**	-.53
$R^2 = .38$	(.01)	(.36)	(.01)	(.09)	(.08)	(.57)
Hunting & Fishing Groups						
$X^2 = 208.90$	.03	-.16*	-.06	-.02	.10	-.22*
$R^2 = .33$	(.04)	(.10)	(.04)	(.02)	(.60)	(.11)
Energy Companies						
$X^2 = 298.47$	.06**	-2.70	.40*	.11	.70**	-2.32**
$R^2 = .42$	(.02)	(2.33)	(.21)	(.08)	(.30)	(1.01)
Developers						
$X^2 = 228.01$	.17**	1.22	.54	-.31*	.86*	-1.27
$R^2 = .38$	(.07)	(1.76)	(.32)	(.14)	(.43)	(1.72)
Labor Unions						
$X^2 = 207.00$	-.07	-.25	.07	.01	-.55**	-.45*
$R^2 = .33$	(.06)	(.21)	(.06)	(.03)	(.13)	(.22)
Environmental Groups						
$X^2 = 203.36$	-.17*	.11	-.03	.02	-.28**	.03
$R^2 = .33$	(.04)	(.12)	(.04)	(.02)	(.07)	(.13)
Citizen Groups						
$X^2 = 214.49$	-.09**	.10	-.03	.01	-.31**	.16
$R^2 = .34$	(.03)	(.11)	(.03)	(.01)	(.06)	(.11)

aDegrees of freedom for goodness-of-fit chi-square range from 399 to 404. Significance levels are: * $p \le .05$; ** $p \le .01$.

Table 3.7 (continued)

PRIVATE SOURCES:	AGE Coeff. (s.e.)	GENDER Coeff. (s.e.)	EDUC Coeff. (s.e.)	AMERICAN ACTIVISTS[a] NEP Coeff. (s.e.)	IDEOLOGY Coeff. (s.e.)	POSTMAT Coeff. (s.e.)
Business						
$X^2 = 325.89$	.02*	-3.51*	.37**	.04	.56**	.01
$R^2 = .49$	(.01)	(1.93)	(.11)	(.03)	(.23)	(.30)
Hunting & Fishing Groups						
$X^2 = 352.99$	.04	-.45**	-.13**	.01	.30**	-.39**
$R^2 = .51$	(.05)	(.14)	(.04)	(.01)	(.09)	(.15)
Energy Companies						
$X^2 = 123.56$	-.01	-3.26	.28*	-.03	.97**	.56
$R^2 = .27$	(.01)	(3.40)	(.11)	(.03)	(.32)	(.43)
Developers						
$X^2 = 310.80$	.13**	-2.45**	-1.13*	-.03	1.55**	-3.24**
$R^2 = .48$	(.05)	(1.00)	(.54)	(.13)	(.52)	(1.21)
Labor Unions						
$X^2 = 125.58$	-.003	-.25	.05	.02	.07	.81**
$R^2 = .27$	(.007)	(.22)	(.08)	(.02)	(.14)	(.25)
Environmental Groups						
$X^2 = 271.13$	-.001	.51**	.03	.05**	-.21**	.14
$R^2 = .45$	(.005)	(.16)	(.05)	(.01)	(.09)	(.16)
Citizen Groups						
$X^2 = 241.82$	.003	.38**	.08*	.007	-.22**	.06
$R^2 = .42$	(.004)	(.13)	(.04)	(.01)	(.08)	(.14)

[a] Degrees of freedom for goodness-of-fit chi-square range from 322 to 326. Significance levels are: * $p \leq .05$; ** $p \leq .01$.

Table 3.8
Comparison of Environmental Group Members' Level of Trust in Sources of Information Other than Environmental Groups: Percent of Ontario and Michigan Activists Registering 2- or 3-Point (4-Point Scale) Differences of Less Trust

	ONTARIO Activists (n = 554)	MICHIGAN Activists (n = 684)	Dif.[*]
GOVERNMENTAL SOURCES:			
Elected Officials	38.7%	32.1%	+6.6
Federal Government	24.4	26.0	-1.6
Prov/State Government	21.8	16.5	+5.3
Local Government	32.6	32.1	+ .5
EXPERT SOURCES:			
Academic	3.4	4.4	-1.0
Science/Technology Experts	5.1	4.1	+1.0
Press	10.1	11.9	-1.8
PRIVATE SOURCES:			
Business	57.8	46.3	+11.5
Hunt & Fish Groups	19.2	13.6	+5.6
Energy Companies	61.3	57.4	+3.9
Developers	71.5	67.8	+3.7
Labor Unions	40.1	46.6	-6.5
Citizen Groups	5.4	4.4	+1.0

[*] Difference between Ontario and Michigan percentages (Ont.-Mich.).

third is much more like their American counterparts than is the case for older activists. All of these observations would be consistent with the view that, while Canadian and American political cultures may have conditioned the development of quite distinct patterns of interest group behavior in the past, such differences now are diminishing.

Table 3.9
Mean Difference in Trust in Information Provided by Environmentalists versus Information Provided by Other Information Sources: Comparison of Youngest Third and Oldest Third Subgroups among Ontario and Michigan Environmental Group Members

	ONTARIO ACTIVISTS		
	Youngest Third	Oldest Third	Dif.*
Elected Officials	.84	1.07	- .23
Federal Government	.44	.72	- .28
Prov/State Government	.41	.44	- .03
Local Government	.53	.69	- .16
Academic	.16	.20	- .04
Science/Technology Experts	.09	.09	.00
Press	.44	.61	- .17
Business	1.12	.86	+ .26
Hunt & Fish Groups	.45	.60	- .15
Energy Companies	1.10	1.09	+ .01
Developer	1.54	1.40	+ .14
Labor	1.42	1.41	+ .01
	(n = 171)	(n = 178)	
	MICHIGAN ACTIVISTS		
Elected Officials	1.13	1.18	- .05
Federal Government	.79	.99	- .20
Prov/State Government	.55	.89	- .34
Local Government	1.04	1.17	- .13
Academic	.03	.17	- .14
Science/Technology Experts	- .12	.18	- .30
Press	.50	.84	- .34
Business	1.16	1.47	- .31
Hunt & Fish Groups	.44	.81	- .37
Energy Companies	1.41	1.67	- .26
Developer	1.65	2.04	- .39
Labor	1.31	1.76	- .45
	(n = 212)	(n = 224)	

* Difference between youngest and oldest mean trust levels.

CONCLUSION

There seemed to be good reason to expect interest group members and citizens in Canada and the United States to differ in predictable ways with respect to how they view the information provided by organized interests in their respective polities. As Seymour Martin Lipset has observed: ''Regardless of whether one emphasizes structural factors or cultural values, Canada and the United States continue to differ considerably. America reflects the influence of its classically liberal, Whig, individualistic, anti-statist, populist, ideological origins" (1990a, p. 212). As for the neighbors to the north, Canadians "can still be seen as Tory-mercantilist, group-oriented, statist, deferential to authority—a 'socialist monarchy,' to use Robertson Davies' phrase" (1990a, p. 212). For Lipset, the belief is that while "substantial changes in economic productivity, in education, and in rates of upward social mobility" have indeed taken place in Canada, "there has been no consistent decline in the pattern of differences in behavior and values" (1990b, p. 32).

The findings reported here suggest that there is only marginal evidence of a contemporary political culture effect in the informational trust beliefs of Americans and Canadians, and that such differences as may have separated older cohorts of Americans and Canadians are likely being narrowed among younger persons now active in environmental interest groups. The findings in this chapter add credence to those scholars of Canadian politics who have suggested the advent of a more American-like interest group network evolving in Canada (Pross 1986).

Further implications stem from these findings with respect to the potential role of interest groups in both countries in assisting citizens to deal with the technical information quandary. The citizens and the environmental group members responding to our surveys generally respond to information from sources other than environmentalists in much the same manner. While that fact serves to suppress the salience of potential cross-national effects, the nature of their *shared* response of relative attentiveness to many information sources elevates the potential role of interest groups in screening and processing policy-relevant information.

First, significant variations exist across information sources in the level of trust they are accorded by activists and publics. This suggests that both citizens and environmental group activists pay attention to where information originates and that they consciously evaluate those origins differentially. This differential evaluation is the necessary foundation for citizens and environmental activists to screen groups as sources of information that varies considerably in its reliability and its utility.

Second, among both citizens and activists in both Ontario and Michigan, certain types of information sources are seen as deserving of greater credence than are other types. In particular, "expert" sources are accorded more confidence than are the several governmental and the private sources of information. This again suggests that citizens and activists exercise discretion in the validity and reliability they ascribe to their sources of policy-relevant information.

Third, the discretion that individuals employ in their trust of information sources often is based systematically on fundamental political orientations. Significant amounts of variation in trust in sources of information can be explained by individual demographic and value-based attributes. These attributes themselves may be surrogates for elements of self-interest by which individuals also may guide their policy preferences. Thus, for interest groups to act as effective vehicles for helping individuals to cope with the technical information quandary, citizens must be able to discriminate among information sources in ways that correspond with their policy goals. While the two systems *may* have distinct political cultures, and while Canada and the United States may differ in how they view their natural environment (Atwood 1984), in both cultures citizens and environmental activists evaluate sources of information in ways compatible with the needs of an informed and self-interested type of democratic participation.

Fourth, while significant cross-national similarities exist and tend to dominate findings reported in this chapter, some clear evidence of political cultural differences also is present in these data. The evidence of political culture differences among the older activists in the United States and Canada is noteworthy in this regard. Perhaps the most significant of these political culture differences may be that Canadian group members are more trusting of diverse information sources than are their American counterparts. This clear finding suggests a more corporatist, consensual, accommodating political process. Of importance, though, is the observation that this cross-national difference well may be evaporating as the younger cohorts in the United States and Canada move away from their older fellow nationals and toward each other. While these findings stem from the analysis of citizens and environmental activists in only one Canadian province and one American state, the patterns of belief and attitude reported here seem quite in line with contemporary scholarship on interest group phenomena in Canada generally.

The patterns of trust of interest group information shown here provide significant support to A. Paul Pross's recent observations that the contemporary Canadian interest group system is becoming much more like that of the United States (1986). It seems clear that in both countries strong potential foundations exist for citizens and environmental activists to employ interest groups systematically as sources of policy-relevant information, allowing them to gain some sense of self-reliance in coping with the technical information quandary of postindustrial democracies. Chapter 4 examines the reasons citizens of Canada and the United States offer for joining interest groups, paying close attention to the relative importance accorded information-based reasons for that membership.

NOTES

1. The question used was: "What is your highest level of education?" The following response categories were provided: (1) never attended school; (2) some grade school; (3) completed grade school; (4) some high school; (5) completed high school; (6) some college; (7) completed college; (8) some graduate work; and (9) an advanced degree.

2. To indicate support for the NEP, respondents were asked to indicate agreement or disagreement on these six items: (1) the balance of nature is very delicate and easily upset by human activities; (2) the earth is like a spaceship with only limited room and resources; (3) plants and animals do not exist primarily for human usage; (4) modifying the environment for human use seldom causes serious problems; (5) there are no limits to growth for nations like the United States and Canada; (6) humankind was created to rule over the rest of nature. Five response categories were provided, ranging from "strongly agree" to "strongly disagree." After recoding, the scores on all six items were summed for the additive NEP scale.

3. The question used to ascertain subjective political ideology was: "How would you place yourself on the following ideological scale in your country?" The Likert response format for the United States was (1) very liberal, (2) liberal, (3) moderate, (4) conservative, (5) very conservative; for Canada, the format was (1) very left, (2) left, (3) moderate, (4) right, (5) very right.

4. The question used to construct Inglehart's (1990) postmaterial scale was: "There is a lot of talk these days about what your country's goals should be for the next ten to fifteen years. Listed below are some of the goals that different people say should be given top priority. Would you please mark the one goal you consider the most important in the long run? What would be your second choice? Please mark that second choice as well." The response categories provided were (1) maintaining order in the nation, (2) giving people more say in important governmental decisions, (3) fighting rising prices, (4) protecting freedom of speech. Respondents are considered to profess postmaterialist value orientations (i.e., Maslow's higher-order values) if they selected both the (2) and (4) postmaterialist responses. If the respondent selected items (1) and (3), they are considered to have materialist value orientations (i.e., lower-order values), and any other combination is considered a mixed orientation.

5. The pseudo-R^2 measure has been recommended by Aldrich and Nelson (1984, p. 57) as an acceptable substitute for logit models to replace the conventional R^2 used in regression models.

Chapter Four

The Information Incentive

This study is grounded on the contention that public policy disputes in postindustrial democracies increasingly turn on scientific and technical issues, the presence of which challenges the public's capacity for understanding and influencing the course of government action (Nelkin 1979). Can citizens really be expected to exercise informed influence over public policy when policy issues become complex and difficult (Dahl 1985)? The urgency of this question is underscored particularly in those policy areas, such as the environment, in which there is growing public concern and active political involvement by citizens (Enloe 1975).

In this context of complex policy, we argue that the dynamics of democratic political processes once more bring forward interest groups as one critical mechanism for pressing the public's concerns (Milbrath 1984). By linking citizens to policy processes, interest groups are not only a vehicle for achieving political goals but they also may serve citizens in facilitating the acquisition, processing, and application of policy-relevant information. The analysis of interest groups often focuses on their exercise of political influence. In the context of contemporary policy complexity, however, the present study examines the possible important information transfer role interest groups might play. In this chapter, of particular interest is the role of information as an incentive to interest group membership, how that incentive interacts with purposive political incentives, and how the patterns of interaction among these incentives might differ in two democratic countries with historically distinct political cultures and differing institutional arrangements.

THE INFORMATION INCENTIVE

Consistent with the conventional view of interest groups as primarily a means of influence, A. Paul Pross defines Canadian interest groups as "organizations whose members act together in order to promote their common interest" (1986, p. 3). Jeffrey M. Berry offers a similar definition for the United States; for Berry, an interest group is "an organized body of individuals who share some goals and who try to influence public policy" (1984, p. 5).

Thus, in both Canada and the United States, interest groups exist in major part to influence public policy on behalf of their members. But interest groups can perform other functions as well, both for the individual member and for the political system. Canadian groups are described as performing four "systemic functions": communication, legitimation, regulation, and administration. These functions "meet the needs of members, [and] they facilitate the workings of the political system" (Pross 1986, p. 88). American interest groups are thought to engage in similar activities. Berry lists representing constituents, offering opportunities for people to participate in politics, educating the American public about issues, agenda building, and program monitoring as derivative functions of American interest groups (1984, pp. 7–8).

Whether described as "communication" (Pross 1986) or "educating the public" (Berry 1984), information sharing would seem to be an important attribute of interest group activity in both Canada and the United States. In our view, this information-sharing dimension of group activity may become especially important when policy discussions involve such issues as environmental policy, which tend to be presented in technically and scientifically complex terms and uncommon frames of reference. In such circumstances, the opportunity to acquire information may become an important reason for individual decisions to join an interest group.

To be sure, a number of explanations account for why individuals participate in interest groups, but the information sharing in which groups frequently engage is seldom emphasized as an important inducement for affiliation (for some recent exceptions, see Knoke 1988; Rothenberg 1988; Cook 1984). Indeed, most analyses of group membership consider three types of incentives to individual participation: purposive, material, and solidary (see Clark and Wilson 1961; Wilson 1973). The traditional approach to group politics reflects the presumption that people join interest groups primarily because they support group goals (Truman 1951); group affiliation thereby reflects a purposive incentive.

The work of Mancur Olson has expanded our understanding of motivation for affiliation by suggesting that in large groups individuals sharing group goals participate only when they either are coerced or when organizations offer selective incentives—that is, provide benefits that are not available without group membership (Olson 1965). Terry Moe argues, in turn, that both nonselective group goals and selective benefits can serve as membership incentives, but that even purely purposive incentives must be accompanied by a belief (however true or fanciful) in the achievement of selective benefits. Moe writes: "If an individual is to be attracted purely on the basis of group goals, . . . he must perceive that his contribution makes a difference for the group's political success, resulting in net gains for himself [sic]" (1980, p. 34).

In addition to the purposive goals of environmental groups that may attract members, those groups also may offer a variety of such material incentives as a magazine, newsletter, or cost savings on particular attractive items (maps, trips, etc.). Similarly, group members may be motivated to participate because of solidary social rewards associated with membership in a voluntary organization. Joining an environmental group that sponsors outdoor activities, for example, allows members to interact with others who enjoy nature and share similar environmental values. Helen Ingram and Dean Mann express very well how American environmental interest groups have used these incentives to build their memberships:

The technology for creating mass membership and thus more financial security vastly improved over the past two decades. Direct mailings to individuals on lists of people who are deemed likely to be sympathetic to the environmentalist cause have proven to be a provident source of financial and mass support for environmentalist organizations, as they have to other organizations. Using appeals based on impending environmental crises and offering such benefits as a monthly publication, books, and other benefits, the environmental organizations have been able to tap sources of support which are quite capable of paying the rather modest annual membership fee. (1989, p. 150)

The informational benefits that individuals might obtain from group membership, strictly speaking, may not be purposive, material, or solidary in nature. Knoke, for example, has shown that information incentives comprise a separate dimension of reasons members give for joining organizations (1988, p. 317). Policy-relevant information, selectively available to group members, may represent an independent incentive for group involvement. Some group members may desire such information for its own sake, thereby satisfying some fundamental "need to know" (Lane 1969, p. 31). Others may find environmental policy information "interesting," intellectually stimulating, or entertaining. For such group members, the desire for information may be relatively unrelated to the political purposes of the group.

Nonetheless, it is unlikely that most environmental group members are attracted to affiliation solely by the availability of information. Indeed, it seems probable that many individuals for whom information is an incentive also will be drawn to membership by the group's political goals. For such citizens, the information acquired through group membership well may be viewed as instrumental to the achievement of environmental policy goals. Knowledge may help such individuals understand policy alternatives more fully, persuade others to share policy purposes, or influence decision makers to adopt preferred public policy outcomes.

Why might the information-motivated citizen turn to environmental interest groups for satisfaction? As we have noted, in many ways environmental policy issues frequently take on complex technical and scientific features; as a consequence, those issues place a premium on credible policy-relevant information. It is quite reasonable for citizens who wish to grasp the difficult and complex environmental policy arena to turn to environmental interest groups for information. Such groups and their leaders are close to the policy conflict and they reasonably can be seen as being especially able to identify the "relevant" information members should have about an issue. In addition, interest groups can aggregate the resources necessary to acquire, process, and distribute difficult to assemble information more efficiently than could be accomplished by many individuals acting independently. Moreover, any congruence between the individual's policy preferences and the goals of the organization should provide the citizen with a source of information that can be trusted, one that reflects one's own perspective on environmental affairs.

Unfortunately, except for the several studies noted above, very little is known about the extent to which information actually motivates membership in environmental interest groups. The purpose of this chapter is to assess the salience of this possible role of information as an incentive to environmental group membership. The results, we believe, are critical to understanding the way interest groups may assist citizens in coping with the technical information quandary.

THE CANADIAN AND AMERICAN CONTEXTS

Chapters 1 and 2 examine at some length the political systems and political cultures of Canada and the United States. As a context for this chapter's analysis, we begin by briefly reviewing those discussions.

The Canadian policy-making system has been characterized as being closed rather than open, with channels of influence that tend to be hierarchically organized and based to only a limited extent on a pluralistic, competitive approach to policy formation (Presthus, 1974; Pross, 1975). Consequently, attempts by Canadian elites to generate grassroot public support for policy issues are less apparent than in the American system. In contrast, the American policy-making system reflects a pluralistic, competitive approach to decision making; the emphasis is on conflict-oriented techniques intended to arouse public opinion (Pross 1975, p. 19).

In the Canadian political system, a process of elite accommodation stands in contrast to the competitive American approach (Presthus 1974). The Canadian system favors elite groups and functional, accommodative, consensus-seeking techniques of political communication. These characteristics affect the process of agenda-setting in Canada according to Pross (1975, p. 19). If public authorities are receptive to an issue, they will act with dispatch. Since the system is organized rather hierarchically, information can move quickly and action can be taken with dispatch. However, on issues to which government officials are unreceptive, action may not occur for a long period of time despite considerable public demand.

The structure of the policy process and the character of governmental institutions both affect group access to decision makers in important ways as well. The fragmented structure of American authority allows for access at many points, both at the federal and the state levels of government (Jones 1984). Environmental groups in Canada and the United States consequently operate in quite a different political milieu as they carry out their activities. Pross considers Canadian interest groups to be "political communication mechanisms capable of adapting to the policy system in which they are located" (1975, p. 27). In an analysis of national-level pressure groups in Canada, Dawson concurs with this view and concludes:

Those groups which have operated effectively over a prolonged period have had to tailor both their methods and organization in order to maximize their impact on the political institutions. Established Canadian groups have a tendency to avoid open conflict with associates in the civil service, and . . . to share the points of view of the officials with whom they work. (1975, p. 50)

It is quite possible, then, that the historically distinctive political cultures and the rather different public policy processes and institutional arrangements found in Canada and the United States may affect the extent to which information-seeking incentives motivate environmental group affiliation among Canadians and Americans.

Chapter 1 develops the reasoning underlying an expectation that Canadians would be less likely than Americans to join interest groups for the purpose of obtaining policy-relevant information. This expectation was based in the reduced need for policy-relevant information in a political culture seen as more accommodative and cooperative, and where, historically, citizen-based interest groups have been less active as instruments of shared individual interests than is the case in the United States. It also is important to note that more recently, according to some observers, the Canadian interest group system has become more similar to that found in the United States (Pross 1986). This position of possible similarity in the interest group environment is reinforced somewhat by the findings presented in Chapters 2 and 3. That is, on some very general political values, mixed results have been observed as to differences between the two nations, with the bulk of the evidence leaning in the cultural difference direction. In the evidence about trust of interest groups (Chapter 3), the two countries' citizen and group activist respondents acted in much the same way. We conclude that while cross-national similarities exist and dominate the information presented in the chapter, some remnants of residual political cultural differences are present in the data. In particular, in line with our discussion above, Canadian group members are more trusting of information sources than are their American counterparts. It is this conclusion that may lead to a counterhypothetical finding. This greater trust in information sources may lead to a greater incentive to acquire policy-relevant information from interest groups. It is possible, of course, that information still may be sought for different (i.e., less political) reasons by Canadians than by their American counterparts.

MEMBERSHIP AND INFORMATION

The major concern of this chapter is the degree to which a desire on the part of citizens to acquire policy-relevant information motivates affiliation with environmental interest groups. If information is indeed an important incentive to membership in environmental organizations, members should be distinguishable quite clearly from nonmembers by their desire for more information.

Using the 1985–1986 surveys of the general public and environmental activists, Table 4.1 compares the desire for acquiring additional information about environmental affairs among environmental group members and nonmembers in the general public. Two distinct group member subsamples are employed for analysis. One category of group members is based on the group member sample produced from the membership lists provided by group officials. The second type of group member is the subset of the general public sample with citizens indicating they had joined an organization for the purpose of influencing environmental policy.[1] The nonmember general public subsample is comprised of those respondents to the general public survey who indicate no environmental group affiliation. The measure used for assessing the level of desire for policy-relevant information is based on one item for which respondents indicated on a 7-point scale (1 = not interested to 7 =

Table 4.1
Desire for More Information on Environmental Affairs among Publics and Group Members

Interest in More Environmental Information	NONMEMBER PUBLIC		SELF-IDENTIFIED MEMBERS		GROUP-IDENTIFIED MEMBERS	
	Ontario	Michigan	Ontario	Michigan	Ontario	Michigan
1. *Not Interested*	7%	3%	0%	7%	2%	1%
2.	2%	2%	0%	0%	1%	0%
3.	3%	6%	0%	7%	3%	3%
4.	15%	29%	10%	18%	10%	11%
5.	21%	30%	17%	10%	15%	14%
6.	21%	14%	18%	20%	23%	27%
7. *Very Interested*	32%	17%	54%	38%	47%	44%
TOTAL	101%	101%	99%	100%	101%	100%
N	(504)	(383)	(87)	(84)	(539)	(678)
MEAN	5.3	4.9	6.2	5.4	6.0	5.9

* *Overall anova among means of six groups significant at p ≤ .001*

very interested) their interest in having more information concerning a specific environmental issue (acid rain).

The results in Table 4.1 show that group members (by either definition) indeed are characterized by an uncommon desire for more information on this important aspect of environmental affairs in Michigan and Ontario. In both countries, the nonmember general public is less desirous of additional information than is either the official group membership sample or the self-identified subset of the general public. Moreover, contrary to our earliest expectations, what differences do arise are in the direction of greater Canadian interest in information than is found in the United States' samples. The greatest difference is found in the self-identified group members drawn out of the public sample. In the group-identified members, though, almost no difference exists between Ontario and Michigan respondents. The contrasting magnitudes of difference between the two subsamples may have something to do with the nature of those subsamples. It is possible that the group memberships identified by some portion of the Michigan public sample reflect different kinds of groups than those identified in Ontario. Our sample of interest groups in Michigan tended toward the politically active group, but such activity may not be present in the acid-rain-problem-oriented groups to which many in the Michigan public belong.

In short, in both Ontario and Michigan, group members are more likely to desire greater amounts of information on environmental affairs than are nongroup members of the general public. This is consistent with the required role for interest groups if they are to respond to the public's technical information quandary. Group members do desire more information. But, the cross-national differences in the known group member sample are very small, and in the other subsamples the observed differences are contrary to our simple culture-based expectation (i.e., groups will be less political in Canada) and consistent with our more complex, revised hypothesis. That is, it is possible that interest groups are now just as important in Canadian society as they are in the United States, and that because Canadians are more trustful of interest group information than Americans, their desire for information would exceed that of Americans as a reason for environmental interest group affiliation.

THE ROLE OF ENVIRONMENTAL VALUES

While group members are more likely to desire additional information, it is possible that this relationship could be spurious with respect to the policy positions attendant on group affiliation. That is, the desire for more information simply may be a consequence of distinctive pro-environmental values, adherence to which constitutes a likely purposive

motivation for environmental group membership. To assess this possibility, the strength of desire for more information is examined within
the six subsets of the 1985–1986 study while controlling for low, medium, and high levels of support for the new environmental paradigm
(NEP). The results of this analysis are shown in Table 4.2, which also
reports the outcomes from a two-way analysis of variance.

The results displayed in Table 4.2 indicate that even when controlling

Table 4.2
Sample Mean Differences in Desire for More Information, Controlling for
Support of the New Environmental Paradigm

	NEW ENVIRONMENTAL PARADIGM		
ONTARIO SAMPLES:	*Low*	*Medium*	*High*
Self-Identified Group Members	6.83*	6.17	5.93
Group-Identified Members	5.59	5.83	6.08
Public	4.96	5.37	5.48
MICHIGAN SAMPLES:			
Self-Identified Group Members	5.44	6.15	5.44
Group-Identified Members	5.90	5.74	5.03
Public	4.72	4.81	5.27

ANOVA RESULTS

F Sample 31.41, $p \leq .001$

F NEP 10.95, $p \leq .000$

F Interaction 2.58, $p \leq .004$

* *Desire for more information: 1=low; 7=high.*

for adherence to environmental values, group members desire more information to a greater extent than do nonmembers. At all three levels of NEP support, American and Canadian group members indicate greater desire for additional information about environmental issues than do the respective general public nonmember samples.

Within the overall stable effect of group membership on enhanced desire for policy-relevant information, the respondents' positions on the NEP index have some interesting effects of their own. In both publics, Ontario and Michigan alike, there is a consistent increase in the mean desire for additional information as the support for the NEP increases. Recall that all group members have been removed from the public sample. Thus, these are the members of the public for whom the desire for more information failed to move them to group membership. In each level of NEP support, the public desire for information is greater in Ontario than in Michigan.

The public pattern for the relationship of the NEP index and desire for more information is different from that among the group members. Moreover, the group member patterns differ in the two countries. Among the self-identified group members in Ontario, the desire for more environmental information *decreases* as support for the NEP increases. However, in Michigan the desire for more information among self-identified members is greatest in the middle NEP category, with the two extremes about equal. Again, among the group-identified members, the two countries differ. In Ontario, the desire for more information *increases* with greater support for the NEP; however, in Michigan, among group-identified members, the desire for more information *deceases* with the increase in support for the NEP.

Of these patterns, the most startling contrast is seen in the last, in which the official group members' desire for more information moves in different directions with a change in NEP in the two countries. Why would proenvironmental beliefs enhance the informational desires of known group members in Ontario and depress them in Michigan? In Michigan, it may have to do with the character of the groups to which the members belong, most of which focus on environmental issues. The members expressing the least support for general environmental values may feel that they are the most fully left out of the information network, or that the information that is available is less relevant for their interests than it might be. The same logic may account for the Ontario pattern. Given the nature of environmental interest group activism in Canada, it may be that the members with the strongest proenvironmental values may be the ones who feel less integrated into dominant information systems or feel their values to be more challenging to dominant knowledge sets. Thus, they may feel a greater need to acquire additional information to support that challenge.

Table 4.3 expands this analysis by utilizing logit models to examine the relationship between the desire for more information and membership in an environmental group. Several additional predictor variables plausibly associated with environmental group affiliation also are included in the models as important control variables. They include age (in years), gender (1 = female, 0 = male), formal educational attainment,[2] support for the NEP,[3] subjective political orientation (1 = very left/liberal to 7 = very right/conservative), and postmaterial values. The analytical issue of interest is whether the desire for more information remains a significant predictor of environmental group membership

Table 4.3
Logit Estimates for the Predictors of Group Membership

	MICHIGAN* Coeff. (s.e.)	ONTARIO* Coeff. (s.e.)
AGE	- .07** (.02)	- .09** (.001)
GENDER	.04 (.04)	.03 (.04
INFO-DESIRE	.41** (.11)	.36** (.12)
NEP	.16** (.008)	.18** (.03)
IDEOLOGY	- .09** (.03)	- .12** (.03)
POSTMAT	.21** (.06)	.33** (.07)
Goodness-of-fit Chi-Square =	412.64	532.76
df =	457.	576.
Pseudo-R^2 =	.47	.48

* The dependent variable is coded 1 = self-identified group member and 0 = nongroup member.

when simultaneously taking into account other potential predictors of organizational involvement.

The results in Table 4.3 demonstrate that even when controlling for age, gender, education, environmental, and political values, the desire for more policy-relevant information has a strong independent effect on participation in environmental organizations in both Canada and the United States. The coefficients for desire for additional information are positive and statistically significant for both Canadians and Americans. These findings, in combination with those reported above, indicate that self-identified environmental interest group members do indeed differ from nonmembers in their stronger desire for acquiring policy-relevant information on environmental affairs.

These results are important for this study's fundamental thesis, namely, that environmental interest groups may act as a unique mechanism for assisting democratic publics in dealing with their need for help in evaluating and employing scientific and technical policy-relevant information. Group members are distinguished by their desire for more information. Moreover, this relationship persists in both the Canadian and American settings. Indeed, the two (Michigan and Ontario) sets of coefficients predicting group membership are so similar as to be startling, setting aside any notion that the effect of the desire for more information on group membership is constrained culturally in this particular context.

INCENTIVES TO GROUP MEMBERSHIP

The next question we need to look at is the matter of the relative importance of information as an incentive to group membership for group members as opposed to purposive, solidary (social), and material incentives. For evidence on this question, we turn to the 1987 survey of environmental organization members. Respondents were asked the following question: "As a member of an environmental group, how important were each of the following as reasons for joining this organization?" Five potential reasons were offered: social activities, political goals of the organization, source of information on environmental issues, cost saving on special items, and a particular environmental issue. Respondents were asked to indicate the importance of each reason on a scale from 1 (not important) to 5 (very important). The results are shown in Table 4.4, which reports the mean responses for both Ontario and Michigan environmental group members.

Several important results can be observed in Table 4.4. First, as we had hypothesized, in both the American and Canadian settings information clearly has the highest rating as a self-declared reason for joining environmental organizations. The relative magnitude of information's

Table 4.4
Average Importance Accorded Five Reasons for Joining Environmental Interest Groups

REASONS FOR JOINING:	ONTARIO (N = 375)	MICHIGAN (N = 290)	t-value
Information	4.17[a]	4.33	-2.27*
An Environmental Issue	3.37	3.98	-5.60***
Political Goals	3.24	3.77	-4.55***
Social Activities	2.54	2.43	1.01
Savings on Items	1.52	1.56	-0.47

*$p \leq .05$; ** $p \leq .01$; *** $p \leq .001$

[a] *Mean value on importance of this reason for affiliation as indicated on a 5-point scale: 1 = not important, 5 = very important.*

superiority is considerably greater in Canada than in the United States, but it is nonetheless strongly present in both countries. According to these responses, information is not only an important incentive, but is the most important incentive to membership in environmental organizations in both countries. Second, also as we had expected, there are at the same time significant differences between Canadian and American group members. While the relative importance of information, a specific environmental issue, and group political goals are comparable in Michigan and Ontario, the absolute values are different. In those three cases, the Michigan respondents allocate greater importance to the informational, political, and issue-based reasons for membership than do their Ontario counterparts.

The critical point here is that again these data support some of the fundamental expectations we had laid out as critical to the interest group role in the democratic citizen's response to the technical information quandary. Not only are group members in both countries distinguished by their desire for more policy-relevant information, when asked to rate the importance of information as an incentive to group membership they give it a higher average score than they give to pure purposive, solidary, and material incentives.

In comparing the Canadian and American group members, the Michigan respondents do give greater importance to information and policy reasons, but they do not differ from their Ontario counterparts on the material and solidary reasons. Thus, it appears that the American public turns somewhat more to interest groups for the knowledge-gaining and political goals critical to our thesis. Whether this is actually the case or reflects some cultural baggage about groups and politics is unimportant at this point. What is critical is that groups again appear to be able to respond to the individual's need for information and for political action, although this response is more likely to be perceived among our Michigan sample than among the Ontario group member survey respondents.

The information in Table 4.4 sets forth findings concerning the incentives to participation independent of their interrelationships. It also will be instructive to look at the structure among the separate incentives in the two samples. The question addressed is whether group members in the two countries tend to mix their reasons for joining groups in the same or different ways. We especially are interested in the joining of informational and political reasons for membership. Do group members see informational and political goals as belonging on the same dimension, as interconnected? If so, the evidence will suggest that groups perform much the same role in connecting citizens to the policy process in the two countries.

In order to assess the underlying structure of group membership incentives among the Michigan and Ontario respondents, a factor analysis of the five incentive variables was conducted separately for the Canadian and American group members. The results of that factor analysis, after a principal components varimax rotation, are shown in Table 4.5.

Several significant patterns are in evidence in the factor analysis results. First, at a general level the two factor solutions are very similar in Canada and the United States. Two factors emerge for both samples, the same items load heavily on the two factors, and the overall explanatory power of the solutions is very much the same. Second, for both the Michigan and Ontario group members, those similar item groupings on the factors have important implications for the primary concerns of this book. That is, the political information, environmental issues, and political goals all load heavily on the same factor in both national settings. At the same time, in both the American and Canadian settings the social and material incentive items cluster together on a separate factor.

Table 4.5
Factor Loadings (Principal Component Varimax Rotated) of Reasons for Joining Environmental Groups

	Factor 1	Factor 2
ONTARIO (N=375)		
Information on Environmental Issues	.74137	-.08786
A Particular Environmental Issue	.65038	-.01227
Political Goals	.56688	.17142
Social Activities	-.22717	.84794
Cost Savings on Items	.31889	.72524
Eigenvalue	1.466839	1.26112
Percent of Variance	29.4	25.2 = 54.6*
MICHIGAN (N=290)		
Information on Environmental Issues	.70204	.18397
A Particular Environmental Issue	.58744	.12850
Political Goals	.72911	-.18011
Social Activities	.09454	.73331
Cost Savings on Items	.01903	.83110
Eigenvalue	1.507099	1.18304
Percent of Variance	30.1	23.7 = 53.9*

* Cumulative percent

Thus, it seems clear in the patterns of response registered by Ontario and Michigan environmental group members that the informational incentive indeed is connected empirically to the political/purposive incentives, but not to the solidary and material incentives. This finding reinforces the potential for interest groups to use information as an important means to aid citizens in responding to the technical information quandary. The need for information expressed as a motive for interest group participation is wedded to the desire to promote general political goals and to affect particular environmental issues, both of which are the raison d'être of environmental interest groups.

The only difference between the two national settings is a small one, but it is of sufficient scale to provide a passageway into further analysis. The item on general political goals loads less strongly on the information factor among Ontario subjects than it does among Michigan group members. This suggests that, among Canadians, those who join interest groups for informational purposes may be somewhat less likely than their American counterparts to have a related general political motivation in regard to that activity. This finding raises the possibility that individuals may differ importantly in the conjunction of informational and political reasons for joining groups.

It is likely that for some group members both informational and political goals are important (4 or 5 on the 1-5 scale) reasons for affiliating with the group. We can call such persons *politicos* because they are able to use the information as a means to serve the purposive political goals that also motivate their group membership. At the same time, other individuals may join the group primarily for the purpose of acquiring information. We can label as *purists* those individuals who identify information as a very important (4 or 5 on the 1-5 scale) incentive to their participation while indicating political goals as being a relatively unimportant (1 or 2 on the 1-5 scale) reason for membership.

Table 4.6 shows the relationship between informational and political reasons for group membership in both Michigan and Ontario; these results provide the foundation for the identification of the politico and purist types. After identifying the relative incidence of these two types of group members, it will be possible to determine the extent to which they differ on other predicted attributes.

Clearly, in both countries the predominant type of environmental interest group member is the politico, registering 43% in Ontario and 58% in Michigan. In Ontario, the information purists comprise 24% of the sample as compared with only 14% in Michigan. These two types are the most frequently occurring mixes of the two incentives to group membership. Very few respondents express neither information nor political goals as an incentive, or express strong political goals without an accompanying incentive of information acquisition.

The greater percentage of politicos in Michigan (58%) compared to Ontario (43%) lends marginal support to the political-culture-effects hypothesis. Canadian environmental interest group members are less likely than their American counterparts to connect political goals to their desire for information from interest group membership. The articulated information source role for environmental groups may be less clearly perceived in Canada than in the United States, or interest groups may be perceived in Canada as less fully responsible for providing policy-

Table 4.6
Relationship between Informational and Political Reasons for Joining Environmental Organizations

ONTARIO
Information Incentive

Political Incentive		LOW 1	2	3	4	HIGH 5
LOW	1	2%	2%	1%	9%	7%
						24%
	2	1%	1%	5%	3%	5%
	3	0	0	4%	5%	6%
	4	1%	0	1%	11%	9%
						43%
HIGH	5	0%	1%	2%	7%	16%

MICHIGAN
Information Incentive

Political Incentive		LOW 1	2	3	4	HIGH 5
LOW	1	2%	1%	1%	3%	5%
						14%
	2	0	0	1%	3%	13%
	3	0	0	1%	3%	8%
	4	1%	0	1%	12%	
						58%
HIGH	5	0	0	3%	10%	28%

relevant information to their members (see Chapters 5 and 6 for an analysis of interest group information-oriented activity). Yet again, this difference may reflect some cultural perception that sees interest groups as somewhat less viable as vehicles for effecting public policy outcomes in Canada than in the United States. Indeed, the overall political salience of interest groups may be lower in Ontario than in Michigan. If so, the policy perspectives of group members may differ in the two countries and, consequently, there may be larger differences between purists and politicos in Michigan than in Ontario. It is to this question that we now turn.

The relatively small number of purists in each sample causes some difficulty with the subsequent statistical analysis. The possibility of enlarging the purist category by including individuals who rated the importance of political goals as a 3 in addition to those who rated it 1 or 2 was considered. The rationale would be that they clearly do not rate the political reason very highly (4 or 5). Doing this would increase the number of purists from 24% to 35% in Ontario and from 14% to 30% in Michigan. On the other hand, it is clear from data analysis that such a change decreases the "purity" of the purists without changing the statistical results. That is, the changes move the attributes of the two groups closer together but, because of the increase in the number of cases, there is little or no change in statistical significance. Consequently, the original distinction is maintained at the cost of reducing the number of purists in the analysis.

ATTITUDINAL DIFFERENCES BETWEEN PURISTS AND POLITICOS

If the information-incentive-based purist–politico distinction is substantively important, one would expect certain other kinds of differences to exist between the two types. In particular, the two types may be distinctive in their political attitudes. Purist versus politico differences in three types of environmental attitudes are shown in Table 4.7. The results generally confirm our expectations, but with an important cross-national twist. Among the Michigan group members (but not among Ontario activists), politicos and purists differ on each of the three attitudinal measures. In Michigan, politicos are more likely to view acid rain as a serious problem, to see acid rain as a serious threat to the environment, and to be more preservationist-oriented than purists. As for the Canadians, individuals who add political goals to information as an incentive to group membership fail to differ significantly in their political environmental attitudes from those who are motivated by information alone.

The political differences between purists and politicos in Michigan are

Table 4.7
Attitudinal and Informational Differences between Purists and Politicos

Attitudinal Variables	ONTARIO		MICHIGAN	
	Purists	Politicos	Purists	Politicos
Relative Seriousness of Acid Rain Issues[a]	6.3	6.3 $p=ns$	4.8	5.8 $p \leq .01$
Acid Rain Threat to Environment[b]	5.5	5.2 $p=ns$	4.4	5.5 $p \leq .01$
Preservationist Sentiment[c]	4.3	4.6 $p=ns$	3.4	4.4 $p \leq .01$

[a] Single item in which respondents are asked how serious the acid rain problem is relative to other problems in society such as crime, unemployment, and inflation. Responses were recoded on a seven-point scale, 1=not serious and 7=very serious.

[b] Single item in which respondents are asked to indicate how threatening acid rain is to humans and nature. Responses were recoded on a seven-point scale, 1=not a threat and 7=significant threat.

[c] Single item in which respondents are asked to locate themselves on a preservationist-developmentalist continuum containing the following categories: (1) Strong Developmentalist; (2) Developmentalist; (3) Moderate; (4) Preservationist; and (5) Strong Preservationist.

consistent with what one would expect to be the purposive incentives to environmental group membership. This helps to validate the separation of members into the analytical categories of purists and politicos. Group members who share an interest in information but differ in their articulated political motivation do in fact also differ in their political attitudes. Group members who are more likely to say that political goals are important to their organizational affiliation are more likely to have political attitudes consistent with their organization's putative political purposes.

Ontario, obviously, remains another case. These political differences between politicos and purists do not appear among Ontario group members. This observation leads to two comments. First, it again underscores the importance of cross-national analyses in identifying patterns of political communication. The particular political/cultural context clearly may structure the dynamics of the links between individual motivation and the role played by interest groups in political communication in complex issue areas. Second, this finding raises the question of just what accounts for the Ontario–Michigan difference. There may be two parts to the answer, one focusing on the role of interest groups in Canadian politics and the other reflecting the special status of Canadians vis-à-vis the acid rain issue.

The less influential role of interest groups in the Canadian political system historically may serve to dampen their functioning as a source of purposive benefits to members, even for those who join for that reason. It seems more likely, though, that the pervasiveness and high salience of the acid rain issue among Canadians has raised the consciousness of all group members, regardless of their espoused reasons for membership. That is, the importance of the environment and the acid rain issue may be so much a part of the political communication system that it is not important as a discriminator among group members. Indeed, even the Canadian purists perceive acid rain as more serious an issue than do the American politicos.

At this point, it is appropriate to tie in the role of information as an incentive to interest group membership to our earlier analysis of the trust given to various information sources (see Chapter 3). Our expectation is that the combination of information and political goals will lead to more favorable views of like-minded sources of information and more critical perspectives of potential political opponents. Moreover, given the patterns to this point, we would expect this distinction to have a greater impact in the Michigan setting than in the Ontario environment. Table 4.8 shows the mean trust score given to each potential information source by the purists and politicos in Michigan and Ontario. It also shows the average individual differentiation among the information sources in each of the four subgroups. Individual differentiation as mea-

Table 4.8

Average Information Source Trust Levels among Purists and Politicos

Group Information Source	ONTARIO ACTIVISTS Purists	Politicos	P
Business	2.2[a]	2.3	ns
Environmental	3.7	4.0	$\leq.01$
Citizen groups	3.2	3.6	$\leq.05$
Hunter groups	2.8	2.9	ns
Energy Companies	2.1	2.0	ns
Experts	3.8	3.7	ns
Legislators	2.2	2.5	$\leq.05$
Labor Unions	1.9	2.4	$\leq.001$
Developers	1.6	1.5	ns
Timber Companies	1.8	1.7	ns
News Reporters	2.6	2.8	ns
Educators	3.9	3.7	ns
Federal Agency	3.0	2.8	ns
State Agency	3.0	2.9	ns
Local Agency	2.7	2.7	ns
Individual $\bar{x}$[b]	2.68	2.79	ns
Individual Differentiation[c]	.97	1.00	ns
	MICHIGAN ACTIVISTS		
Business	2.7[a]	2.1	$\leq.01$
Environmental	3.1	4.1	$\leq.001$
Citizen groups	2.9	3.9	$\leq.001$
Hunter groups	3.2	3.2	ns
Energy Companies	2.6	2.0	$\leq.05$
Experts	3.9	4.0	ns
Legislators	2.1	2.5	$\leq.05$
Labor Unions	2.0	2.5	$\leq.05$
Developers	1.7	1.6	ns
Timber Companies	2.1	1.7	$\leq.05$
News Reporters	2.5	3.0	$\leq.05$
Educators	3.3	3.9	$\leq.01$
Federal Agency	2.9	2.9	ns
State Agency	3.0	2.9	ns
Local Agency	2.5	2.7	ns
Individual $\bar{x}$[b]	2.69	2.87	ns
Individual Differentiation[c]	.91	1.11	$\leq.01$

[a] The entry in each cell is the average trust level given to the particular information source by the purists or the politicos in Ontario or Michigan. The trust score ranges from low of 1 to a high of 5.

[b] This figure refers to the overall average trust score across all information sources given by the purists or politicos in Ontario or Michigan.

[c] This figure is the average standard deviation of trust scores given by individuals who are politicos or purists in Ontario or Michigan.

sured by a standard deviation (SD) calculation represents the degree to which each individual respondent varies in the extent to which he or she attributes trust to differing information sources (that is, according some interests high trust and others low trust as opposed to giving all sources very similar trust ratings). These individual respondent SDs of the respondent's set of trust ratings then are averaged for purists and politicos among Ontario and Michigan group members.

Several significant patterns appear in Table 4.8. First, it is clear that the purist–politico distinction has a greater effect on trust of information sources in the Michigan setting than in the Ontario context. Among Ontario group members, the purists and the politicos differ in their trust on only 4 of the 15 information sources. In contrast, among Michigan environmental activists, the two groups differ in their trust levels with regard to information coming from 9 of the 15 potential sources. Thus, the confluence of the informational and the political goals pulls out some feelings about information sources that are not visible when only information acts as the motivation to group membership.

Second, in the Canadian setting in each case where there are significant purist–politico differences in trust, the politicos are more trustful than are the information purists. In Ontario, politicos are more likely than purists to trust environmentalists, citizen groups, legislators, and labor unions, all of which have obvious political implications. In Michigan, the politicos also are more likely than the purists to trust those same groups, as well as several others (news reporters and educators). However, unlike their Canadian activist counterparts, there are several information sources that politicos are *less* likely to trust than are purists. These differences in trust seem consistent with the political goals of the organizations to which the politicos belong. Thus, the American environmental interest group members who are politicos are less likely than purists to trust information from business, from energy companies, and from timber companies. Again, then, the American context seems to produce a more "political" pattern in the effects of political incentives to environmental interest group membership than does the Canadian setting.

Third, in both countries the politicos overall are more likely than the purists to trust information sources. While the differences in the average trust scores are not significant statistically, they are the same in both countries. Perhaps the person who joins an organization to acquire information but not necessarily to achieve a political goal is more suspicious of all information regardless of its political content. If all information sources are to be treated as being of relatively equal value, the possible result might be considerable skepticism as to the validity of information from any specific source.

Fourth, as the individual differentiation mean scores show, politicos in Michigan differ from purists in the variability of their trust levels, but such is not the case in Ontario. The political motivation to group membership clearly alters the perspectives with which group members view information sources. It also suggests that information seeking, when it occurs in conjunction with political goal seeking, leads group members to evaluate interest-relevant information sources (either positive or negative) in a way that argues for groups to serve as an important resource for the citizen seeking help in dealing with the technical information quandary. The groups are seen as a source of policy-relevant information for group members and they also appear to assist in acting as a guide to the discriminating search for and evaluation of the information being sought.

Finally, the degree of discrimination existing among information sources can be compared cross-nationally by purist or politico type. The Michigan politicos are more discriminating in regard to information sources than are their Ontario counterparts. On the other hand, the Michigan purists are less discriminating in regard to information sources than are their Ontario counterparts. The combination of informational and political goals or, put another way, the presence or absence of political goals really is much more important in the American setting. If political goals combine with the pursuit of information motive, then a greater source discrimination does surface in the Michigan setting as hypothesized in Chapter 1. That important merger of incentives is required, though, to produce the hypothesized outcome.

CONCLUSION

The thesis of this chapter is that in such complex policy areas as those dealing with the environment and natural resources, interest groups can provide a significant means by which citizens can acquire information and employ that information for political ends. If this is indeed the case, environmental interest groups may be viewed as social mechanisms linking microlevel individual activity to macrolevel political processes. The findings reported here would seem to provide direct empirical evidence to support this thesis.

In both American and Canadian settings, environmental group members are more likely than nonmembers to desire more policy-relevant information, even when controlling for various background factors and environmental and political values. In both national contexts, information has the highest rating among group members as a reason for joining groups when compared to purposive (general policy), solidary, and material reasons. Members who join for both informational and purposive reasons (politicos) are more prevalent in both locations than are members who join primarily for informational reasons (purists). In Ontario, purists and politicos are very similar in their policy preferences, but in Michigan politicos are more preservationist than their fellow group members who joined primarily for informational reasons. Moreover, politicos and purists are more distinct in their level of trust of other groups' information in the American than in the Canadian setting. Indeed, Michigan politicos discriminate more broadly among information sources than do the Michigan purists or either purists or politicos in Ontario. The findings of this chapter again support the potential role interest groups can play in assisting citizens to overcome the technical information quandary of postindustrial democracy. This potential micro–macro political linkage role has implications for individual citizens and for interest groups alike.

Individual citizens seem to have developed a reasonable strategy for responding to the difficulty posed by complex policy questions: if more information about the policy area is desired, the citizen is rather likely to make affiliation with an interest group that is active in that policy area. That strategy is reasonable because the resources of the group provide it with much greater capacity than that of the individual for assembling, sifting, and interpreting the policy implications of available information. The organization can condense and restructure the information around the central policy issues. Because of the clarity of the group's position in the policy arena, the individual is given a shortcut to the political end of assessing and applying policy-relevant information.

These results also have a message for interest groups, at least in the environmental arena. First, the investment that groups make in the generation and dispersion of policy-relevant information does play a significant role in linking the organization to its members. That provision of information is a way to attract members, a way to retain them, and a way to enhance group political influence. It is true that most members who value group-provided information do so apparently because of its instrumental connection to their desire for policy influence. At the same time, it also is true that a smaller set of members come to the group primarily for the information the group can provide to inform members of how their interests and values are being affected by developments in public policy. Even these information purists become potentially mobilizable for political and issue-grounded goals. Groups that seem to offer more benefits to membership in the way of information (newsletters, updates, legislative hotlines, speakers' bureaus, etc.) may be more likely to recruit individuals who join groups for both informational and political reasons. Thus, the information activities of groups can be related directly to their ability to attract members who can provide them with the membership base needed to exercise political influence.

In summary, these several patterns of relationship from the Ontario and Michigan environmental interest group member surveys and the surveys of the general public indicate how, in complex policy arenas, a mass public environment exists within which interest groups can position themselves as important links between the public and the policy process as a consequence of their policy-relevant information activities. The dynamics are present that would enhance the capacity of the interest groups to respond to the technical information quandary confronting contemporary postindustrial democracies.

It is this dual economy of information for both individuals and organizations that provides at least one potential means for citizens to deal with the micro–macro difficulties posed by complex policy questions. Turning to interest groups for the means to understand complex policy information allows the individual to economize on information costs by reliance on information from trusted sources; providing information to members allows the group to employ an effective means of recruiting individuals to the organization who share its goals and who become dependent on it for the distribution of selective incentives. Both the individuals and the groups are operating in their particular self-interests—the former reducing costs of information relevant to policy goals and the latter effectively attracting members.

Importantly, the democratic political process also is a beneficiary of this exchange of private benefits. Democratic polities thus have developed a means by which contemporary citizen involvement in complex policy issues can be enhanced. To be sure, the information to which individuals will be exposed via their group membership will be shaded by the group's political purposes. But, the color to that information is consistent with the reasons people join environmental organizations—for information and for politics.

What can be said about the cross-national differences encountered in the analysis of incentives for group affiliation? Are there important differences between Canada and the United States in these patterns? The answers clearly are ambivalent.

1. Among the general publics, Ontario citizens express a somewhat greater desire for information about environmental affairs than do their Michigan counterparts. But, among the formal environmental interest group members, no differences exist between the two countries in the desire for more information.

2. In both the Canadian and the American settings, at each level of support for the NEP, group members desire additional information to a greater extent than do nonmembers. However, among known, formal group members, in the Ontario setting it was found that as support for the NEP increases so does the desire for more information; in contrast, in the Michigan context among known group members, the desire for more information actually decreases as the NEP support increases.

3. In both countries, the strongest incentives to group membership are policy-relevant information, direct interest in a particular environmental issue, and general political goals. However, viewed cross-nationally, each of those three incentives is more important to the American group members than to the Canadian counterparts.

4. In both countries, information, interest in specific issues, and political goals load on the same primary incentive factor, while social activities and specialized goals and services load on a separate factor. However, viewed cross-nationally, on that factor primary political goals are more important in the Michigan setting than in the Ontario context.

5. In both countries, information and political goals represent the most predominate *combination* of active incentives to environmental organization membership. But, information is more likely to stand alone as an incentive among Ontario group members than among their Michigan equivalents, while it is more likely to be accompanied by political goals in Michigan than in Ontario.

6. As noted above, politicos and purists are more likely to differ on environmental issue positions in Michigan than in Ontario. In Ontario, the purists appear just as political as the politicos.

7. Politicos and purists differ in their trust of certain information sources in both Canada and the United States. But, those differences are more frequent in Michigan than in Ontario. In addition, Michigan group members are more likely to discriminate among potential information sources than are Ontario group members.

Chapters 5 and 6 move from the individual level of analysis of publics and group members to the level of the groups themselves. We have seen that the rudiments of group linkage around information are present, but that those linkages differ to some extent in Michigan and Ontario. At this point, we shall begin to find out if environmental organizations in these American and Canadian settings respond differently to the demands posed by the technical information quandary.

NOTES

1. Respondents in the general public sample were asked if they had "joined a group or organization" concerned about environmental and natural resource issues. These respondents were considered "self-identified" members in the following analyses.

2. Respondents were asked to indicate their level of formal education by locating themselves on an 8-point continuum: (1) never attended school, (2) some grade school, (3) completed grade school, (4) some high school, (5) completed high school, (6) some college, (7) completed college, (8) some graduate work or an advanced degree.

3. To indicate support for the NEP, respondents were asked to indicate agreement or disagreement on these six items: (1) the balance of nature is very

delicate and easily upset by human activities, (2) the earth is like a spaceship with only limited room and resources, (3) plants and animals do not exist primarily for human usage, (4) modifying the environment for human use seldom causes serious problems, (5) there are no limits to growth for nations like the United States and Canada, (6) humankind was created to rule over the rest of nature. Five response categories were provided, ranging from "strongly agree" to "strongly disagree." After recoding for consistency of direction, responses on all six indicators were summed to constitute the NEP scale.

A pro-NEP position consists of agreement on the first three items and disagreement on the last three items. The distribution on the additive NEP index was trichotomized into high, medium, and low levels.

Chapter Five

Organizational Resources and Informational Capacity

Environmental interest groups, in their lobbying efforts, clearly serve as important mechanisms for pressing the public's concerns in the scientifically and technically complex environmental policy area (Milbrath 1984). Moreover, environmental groups clearly contribute importantly to citizen participation through their efforts to inform and mobilize their members on current policy issues (Heyrman 1989).

The advocacy role taken by interest groups frequently is framed in the context of the information-sharing function they can perform in modern, postindustrial democracies—activities that A. Paul Pross characterizes as "communication" (1986, p. 88) and Jeffrey M. Berry refers to as "educating the public" (1984, p. 5). In their role as information sharers, environmental interest groups constitute a potentially critical link between their respective members and policy-making elites. Presthus argues that in both Canada and the United States information is the most valuable benefit government decision makers receive from interest groups (1974, p. 215).

The earlier chapters examine the importance of information for interest group members. This chapter focuses on the factors that might facilitate the communication of information both to members and to government officials by environmental interest groups in the two research sites of the province of Ontario and the state of Michigan. To this end, the information provided by leaders of 61 Canadian and American environmental organizations is analyzed to explore relationships among four factors: traditional organizational resources (e.g., staffing level, funding support, size of membership, extent of networking capability), group capacity to generate policy-relevant information, range of group communication efforts, and extent of group contacts with government officials. The goal of this chapter is to assess the impact of traditional organizational resources, informational capacity, and the scope of group communication efforts on the strategies used to influence government policy-making and on the self-perceived effectiveness of group attempts to communicate information.

In looking at the communications activities of environmental organizations, the following assumptions are made: (1) groups use information both to educate their members and to attempt to mobilize this attentive public around issues of environmental policy and (2) groups use information to define policy issues and to structure the public debate in an effort to influence public policy at all levels of government decision making. These assumptions emphasize similarities in the information-sharing roles of environmental interest groups active on the acid rain issue in Ontario and Michigan. Although the specific means by which groups of individuals organize around environmental concerns in an attempt to mobilize their attentive publics and influence actors in the public policy process are expected to differ somewhat cross-nationally, the concern in this chapter is primarily on the resources, capabilities, and communication efforts that are important for environmental groups in any national setting.

The impact of political system differences on communication activities must not be ignored, of course; however, few distinctions will be made between the 38 Ontario groups and the 23 Michigan groups. Chapter 6, in due course, focuses specifically on cross-national differences between the Canadian and American groups. The emphasis in that analysis is on variations in the way environmental organizations actually carry out their information-sharing role in the settings of Michigan and Ontario.

In exploring factors that affect the ability of environmental groups to communicate with their own members and with government officials, the following expectations guide the analysis. First, it is anticipated that groups with high levels of traditional organizational resources will be able to generate high levels of informational capacity, and that the possession of both conventional organizational resources and informational capacity allows environmental interest groups to broaden the scope of their communication efforts substantially. Second, a broad and intense communication effort is expected to increase both the scope and frequency of all types of government contacts.

Finally, traditional resources, informational capacity, and communication effort are expected to affect the perceptions group leaders entertain concerning their own effectiveness in communicating information to members, to contributors, and to government officials. Is effective communication associated exclusively with high levels of conventional organizational resources? If so, it could be said that contemporary interest groups remain trapped in playing the old pluralist game of direct lobbying and indirect electorate mobilization by means of the strategic employment of tangible resources. If, however, environmental interest group leaders systematically associate communication success with the possession of informational capacity and the mounting of communications efforts as well as group resources and government contacts, then evidence would be at hand to suggest that interest group politics in this Canadian province and the American state are taking a different form. Such findings would be consistent with the picture of the agenda-setting and context-shaping dynamics of the "information age" politics widely commented upon in contemporary critiques of postmodern social concept formulation (Foucault 1980; Goodman 1983; Bruner 1985; Edelman 1988). Some writers go so far as to label our period the "postjournalism" era in reflection of this hypermediated political environment (Altheide and Snow 1991, pp. 51–80).

THE SAMPLE OF GROUPS

An organizational profile survey was conducted by mail (with telephone follow-up) in the summer and fall of 1987 as a supplement to the surveys sent to directors and members of environmental organizations in Ontario and Michigan. All of Michigan's 71 known state and local environmental groups, including affiliates of national organizations, were contacted. Of the several hundred environmental organizations identified in Ontario, a representative cross-section of 98 groups was chosen. The larger number of groups in Ontario reflects a plethora of newly formed, locally based associations. From this initial contact, 63 Ontario groups and 43 Michigan organizations agreed to distribute survey questionnaires to their respective members and staffs, and to members of their respective boards of directors. In Michigan, 23 of the 43 participating groups (53%) completed detailed organizational profiles; in Ontario, 38 of the 63 participating groups (60%) returned their completed profiles.

ENVIRONMENTAL GROUPS AS ORGANIZATIONS

Environmental groups can be categorized as public interest groups (McFarland 1976), citizen groups (King and Walker 1989), or as amateur, theme-oriented, or issue groups (Canadian Study of Parliament Group 1989). These several terms are used to distinguish among environmental groups, which generally differ considerably from interest groups representing established business or professional interests (Wenner 1990). Although interest groups of all types differ widely in their respective human, financial, and organizational resources (Pross 1986), environmental groups are generally relatively poorly financed and understaffed vis-à-vis other organized interest groups.

Many environmental groups are operated by a paid staff and claim very few official members (Heyrman 1989; Berry 1984); others develop large memberships and/or long lists of generous financial contributors. Whatever their structure or resource base, there has been a noticeable growth in the number and size of environmental groups in recent decades (Ingram and Mann 1986). Among environmental groups that focus on recruiting group members, Milbrath speculates that two primary motives account for the growth in group affiliation: the widespread perception of threats to the environment (*purposive motive*), and a desire on the part of many to be out in nature with others sharing similar interests (*solidary motive*) (1984, p. 73). Interest groups, moreover, can have two fundamentally different types of memberships, one composed of individual citizens, and another that consists of "representatives of large institutions, business firms or state and local governments" (King and Walker 1989).

Volunteer workers can be an extremely valuable resource for those environmental groups that do not have the funding to hire a paid staff. In a study of 57 neighborhood organizations' reactions to fiscal stress, community groups that managed fiscal strain most effectively were those that had volunteer help, the assistance of specialists and experts, extensive grassroots fundraising efforts, large memberships, and had formed affiliations with other organizations (Hawkins et al. 1986). The affiliations with other groups characteristic is a problematic resource, however, since one could argue that a coalition or network of groups is only as strong as its weakest link (Canadian Study of Parliament Group 1989). The opposite argument is quite plausible, of course, to the effect that affiliations with other likeminded organizations—especially at the state or provincial or national level—are very important for local community groups (Pross 1986). The logic of this argument is that such interest groups can maximize their local influence by building mutual assistance agreements with more distant groups espousing similar positions on related issues (Ingram and Mann 1989).

A. Paul Pross used information on the organizational features of interest groups to develop a typology of pressure groups (1986, pp. 120–121). (Pross prefers the term "pressure group" over "interest group" because the former clearly designates the political activities of groups, while the latter includes nonpolitical activities as well.) Those pressure groups with extensive human and financial resources are on the high resource end of the continuum and are labeled *institutionalized*. Second, *mature* pressure groups are those that form alliances with other groups and have a staff that includes professionals. *Fledgling* pressure groups are membership groups with a small staff. Finally, on the lowest end of the continuum are *issue-oriented* groups—those with a small membership and no paid staff. Since Pross links the possession of such resources to the ability to maintain regular interaction with government officials and to exercise political influence, his categorization highlights the importance of extensive human and financial resources and a professional staff for environmental organizations.

In the organizational profiles, leaders of the 61 groups were asked to provide information on a number of traditional organizational characteristics, and the following measures were created: the presence or absence of a paid staff,[1] the size of the group's annual budget,[2] the number of volunteer workers upon which the organization can call,[3] whether or not the group has individual memberships (a dichotomous variable where 1 = yes and 2 = no), whether or not the group has organizational members (1 yes; 2 = no), the extent to which funds are raised from member dues,[4] the extent to which funds are raised from external sources,[5] whether or not the group is organized into local chapters (1 = yes; 2 = no), whether there is a national or provincial/state affiliation,[6] and whether or not the group enjoys tax-exempt status (1 = yes; 2 = no).

As a first step in the analysis of the organizational features of the 61 environmental groups in Ontario and Michigan, the 11 characteristics were analyzed by means of a principal components (varimax rotated) factor analysis; these results are reported in Table 5.1. This analysis verified the expectation that group characteristics are multidimensional and 3 quite distinct dimensions—financial, human, and networking—appear for the set of 11 traditional organizational characteristics investigated. The first dimension is defined by four features of the groups' financial resources: size of the annual budget, extent of external funding, presence of a paid staff, and tax-exempt status. The second dimension relates to human resources: whether there are local-level chapters (which have their own members), the number of volunteer workers, number of individual memberships, and the proportion of funding raised from members' dues. The third dimension contains provisions for organizational memberships and the presence of affiliations at the provincial or state or national levels; this dimension represents the coalition-building or networking resources of groups. Summary measures were created as indicators of these three dimensions of organizational characteristics.[7]

A summary profile of the 11 individual measures of traditional organizational characteristics is reported in Table 5.2. The table lists the mean, standard deviation, and the range of each of the 11 characteristics; in addition, for the dichotomous variables, the number of groups in each of the categories is included. The environmental organizations could represent all the points along the resource continuum presented by

Table 5.1

A Principal Component (Varimax Rotated) Factor Matrix of Measures of Group Resources

Group Resources (N=61)	Factor 1	Factor 2	Factor 3
Size of Annual Budget	.83524	.01798	-.10365
Extent of External Funding	.81708	-.02482	.05581
Paid Staff (1=yes; 0=no)	.73049	-.15692	-.22121
Tax Exempt Status (1=yes; 0=no)	.66264	.19025	.12727
Organized in Chapters (1=yes; 0=no)	.18209	.68397	-.25315
Number of Volunteers	.19227	.67746	.21098
Individual Members (1=yes; 0=no)	-.40016	.64235	.21596
Percent Raised from Dues	-.39511	.53442	-.16593
Groups as Members (1=yes; 0=no)	.08243	-.12960	.7950
Provincial/State Affiliation (1=yes; 0=no)	-.33674	.07655	.65347
National Affiliation (1=yes; 0=no)	.34579	.32187	.42643
Eigenvalue	2.99836	1.85163	1.42997
Percent of Variance	27.3	16.8	13.0

Cumulative Percent = 57.1

Table 5.2
Summary Profile of the Measures of Traditional Organizational Characteristics

	Mean	S.D.	Range
Monetary Resources			
Annual Budget (in 1000's)	$252	$827	$200 to $6 million
Percent Funding from External Staff	14%	24%	0% to 100%
Paid Staff	0.53	0.26	0=no (29)*;1=yes (32)
Tax-Exempt Status	1.31	0.47	1=yes (40); 2=no (18)
Member Resources			
Organized into Chapters	1.64	0.48	1=yes (22); 2=no (39)
Volunteer Workers	139	246	0 to 1,000 volunteers
Individual Memberships	1.11	0.32	1=yes (53); 2=no (7)
Percent Funding from Dues	53%	39%	0 to 100%
Networking Resources			
Organizational Members	1.51	0.50	1=yes (30); 2=no (31)
Affiliated with State/ Provincial Organization	1.46	0.50	1=yes (30); 2=no (31)
Affiliated with a National Organization	1.75	0.44	1=yes (15); 2=no (45)

* Figures in parentheses are number of groups in category.

A. Paul Pross (1986). The standard deviations for measures that are continuous rather than dichotomous clearly indicate that there is considerable variability within the sample of groups on many of the organizational characteristics. In the category of monetary resources, there are groups with very sizable annual budgets (in the millions of dollars) and up to 40 full-time paid staff. On the other hand, there are groups in the sample that have minuscule budgets ($200 was the lowest amount), and 29 groups did not have any paid staff. In addition, the environmental organizations receive, on average, 14% of their funding from external sources (the standard deviation is 24%), and many groups (40) have tax-exempt status.

When considering the category of member resources, almost two-thirds of the groups (39) are not organized into chapters; nearly all (53) have individual members; they can call on an average of 139 volunteers; and the groups raise, on average, 53% of their funding from dues. In the category of networking resources, approximately half of the environmental groups have organizational members; this includes groups in the sample that are either one of these two basic types or a combination of the two, that is, (1) coalitions of groups or clubs or (2) groups with civic, business, labor, research, and/or government organizations as members. Finally, more environmental groups are affiliated with a state or provincial organization (30) than are affiliated with an organization that is national in scope (15). As was the case with monetary resources, the groups in this sample are not uniform in the extent to which they are able to rely upon human labor resources or in their ability to network with other organizations.

Although not reported here in a table, it should be noted that Ontario–Michigan differences in the 11 organization characteristics were explored using difference of means tests and chi-square values produced through cross-tabulations. In both types of analyses only the percentage of funding that the environmental groups raised through membership dues showed a significant cross-national difference, with Ontario organizations relying more heavily on dues as a funding source than did their counterpart groups in Michigan. This set of results suggests that although the 61 groups included in the study show considerable variability on many of the organizational characteristics, this variation exists primarily irrespective of national boundaries as opposed to within the confines of a national setting.

ENVIRONMENTAL GROUPS AS
TRANSMITTERS OF POLICY INFORMATION

While much has been written about pressure groups, both as voluntary organizations and as significant political actors with diverse policy agendas and employing a wide range of strategies for implementing these agendas, relatively little work has been done to document the growing ability of groups to generate and disseminate a wide variety of types of information. Rather than operating exclusively in the realm of conventional lobbying and membership electoral mobilization, environmental groups increasingly are concerned with the gathering and distribution of complex scientific and technical information (DiMento 1986, pp. 147–154). This combination of political activity and information-creation roles is evident in Weisskopf's (1990) observation:

No match for huge industries such as steel, oil and automobiles 20 years ago, the groups have borrowed the techniques of their rivals, fielding a team of skilled lobbyists to press their demands on Congress, issuing original scientific reports and relying on contacts within the bureaucracy for intelligence on shifts in administration policy. (p. 10)

Some environmental organizations concentrate primarily on science and the creation of scientific information. Ingram and Mann argue that "two of the basic distinctions among the environmental groups is their orientation toward science versus activism and their willingness to engage in negotiations with those whom they consider to be the adversary" (1989, p. 143). On the other hand, many conservationist and preservationist groups, which at one time did not try to influence legislators and administrative officials, are now active in "influencing specific legislative and administrative actions" (1989, p. 144). Ingram and Mann note that such "groups had to know how the political system worked, how to identify decision makers and how their minds worked" (1989, p. 144).

For example, the Natural Resources Defense Council (NRDC) is described as a "team of crack scientists and lawyers that functions as an *ad hoc* EPA" (Gifford 1990, p. 75). The NRDC litigates and lobbies quite effectively in Washington D.C., but it also formed an alliance with the Soviet Academy of Sciences, which led to the "first superpower test-ban monitoring arrangement" (p. 75). It is quite clear that this powerful and widely respected environmental organization has both considerable organizational resources (a staff of 140, a budget of $16 million, and 168,000 members) and the capacity to create scientific, technical, economic, and legal information that can be used effectively to advance the NRDC's political agenda.

In the organizational behavior literature, communication is understood to be the process of creating and exchanging of messages between transmitting and receiving parties, and the primary purpose of the communication process is to convey information (Vasu et al. 1990). Just as environmental organizations differ in their capacity to generate information, they are likely to vary in the degree of effort expended in communicating this information and in the scope or range of types of information communicated. In addition, efforts by groups to communicate a broad range of types of policy-relevant information to government officials is an area in which cross-national political system differences may become a significant factor. The following observation is pertinent to the communications efforts of the environmental groups under study since interaction between group representatives and government officials goes both ways—and quite possibly is affected by cross-national differences in the political systems of Ontario and Michigan:

Messages are communicated through an interaction process. There is constant mutual feedback between sender and receiver so that both parties are communicators, or givers and receivers, at the same time. The environment within which communication occurs is a significant part of the communication picture because of its role in shaping both the process and contents of communication. (Vasu et al. 1990, p. 147)

Providing information to group members is typically not viewed as a primary type of group-to-group member interaction by serious students of interest groups. Following the reasoning of Mancur Olson, specialized information (publishing newsletters, magazines, or journals; providing information or data services; sponsoring research activities; organizing and staging seminars, conferences, or workshops) is considered a private good and a separate incentive to group membership (Ingram and Mann 1989; Knoke 1988). However, other scholars turn Olson's reasoning on its head by arguing that "provision of private goods is a by-product of the lobbying function . . . magazines and outings serve to reinforce or increase members' utility for environmental goods the group seeks to obtain and to impress members with the groups' accomplishments" (Mitchell 1979, p. 109).

When group communications with government are considered, the interactional nature of information sharing becomes more evident. For example, communications between interest groups and Canadian Members of Parliament (MPs) is broadly considered a two-way street. "The information interest groups provide is helpful to MPs, but MPs can also use the groups as a channel for conveying messages back to the group's membership" (Canadian Study of Parliament Group 1989, p. 10). In addition, there is interaction in another sense; interest group representatives use the specialized information they have to insure their access to government officials. Information provided by environmental organizations that pertains to highly complex economic, technical, or scientific problems is especially important to legislative staff and both high-ranking and middle-level civil servants (Schlozman and Tierney 1986).

Measures for both concepts—informational capacity and communication effort—were created from several of the responses registered on the organizational profiles. Indicators of *informational capacity*, which is defined as the ability of the environmental group to gather and create a variety of types of research information, were constructed from items found in the organizational profile questionnaire: (1) the number of external sources of information used by organizations to compile information on environmental problems,[8] (2) the range of types of research findings and specialized information (scientific/technical, legal, political, or economic) used by the organization,[9] and (3) the extent to which the environmental group generates its own research.[10]

As a complement to informational capacity, the scope of *communication effort* was conceptualized as the extent to which environmental group personnel worked to disseminate a broad range of types of information to group members and government officials. The items used to construct indicators of communication effort were (1) the percentage of total staff time devoted to communication,[11] (2) the number of ways used by the organization to inform members or contributors about environmental issues and group activities,[12] and (3) the range of types of information (scientific, technical, legal, political, or economic) communicated both to elected government officials and career service government officials at the state or provincial level of government.[13]

Table 5.3 reports the mean, standard deviation, and the range of possible scores for each measure of informational capacity and commu-

Table 5.3
Summary Profile of the Measures of Informational Capacity and Scope of Communication Efforts

	Mean	Standard Deviation	Range
Informational Capacity			
Number of External Sources of Information	4.39	1.95	0 to 7 sources
Range of Types of Information Used	3.25	1.23	0 to 4 types
Group Generation of Its Own Information	2.00	1.41	0 to 4 times
Scope of Communication Efforts			
Percent Staff Time Spent on Communication	47%	39%	0% to 100%
Number of Means Used to Inform Members	4.92	1.89	0 to 9 means
Information Types Communicated to Elected Officials	2.16	1.71	0 to 5 types
Information Types Communicated to Bureaucrats	2.12	1.68	0 to 5 types

nication effort. In the section, "Informational Capacity," the sample groups use an average of four sources external to the group (out of a possible seven, including affiliates or central offices of the organization, other environmental organizations, scientists or experts in universities or research institutes, lawyers or legal experts, elected government officials or their staff, nonelected government personnel, or some other external source). The range of types of information used includes scientific/technical, legal, political, and economic. The groups use, on average, three of the four types. On the last measure of informational capacity shown in Table 5.3, the groups manage to generate some or all of their own research in an average of two of the four research areas.

Four measures of communication effort are included in Table 5.3. The first is the percentage of total staff time that is devoted to communication activities; these activities include educational, political, and scientific or technical research activities. Staff in these environmental organizations spend an average of 47% of their time on this combination of activities related in one form or another to communication. The second measure is a count of the number of ways the group uses to communicate with members or contributors. Nearly all of the groups have some type of written communication with their members, and of the nine total means of informing members that were listed on the organizational profile (see Note 12) the groups use an average of five. Group communication efforts are the same on the last two indicators; an average of two out of five types of information are communicated both to elected and bureaucratic officials. Cross-national differences between the Ontario and Michigan environmental groups on the informational capacity and scope of communication efforts measures are explored in the next chapter.

ENVIRONMENTAL GROUPS AND THEIR
CONTACTS WITH GOVERNMENT

In the literature on political communication, the position is taken that "the field is constituted by research that makes claims about relationships between communication processes and political processes" (Nimmo and Swanson 1990, p. 7). There are significant differences in the political processes of the Canadian province and the American state, and these differences are likely to affect types of access routes frequently used by environmental groups in their communication efforts. Effective communication of information to government officials is dependent on access, and the "strategies of environmental groups can best be understood as attempts to gain access to government decision making" (Ingram and Mann 1989, p. 143).

It has been argued that lobbyists seek access at the sources of power in a political system (Presthus 1974). This means the cabinet and the bureaucracy in the parliamentary system and the legislature, legislative committees, and the bureaucracy in the presidential system. However, a recent study of the Ontario Legislative Assembly concludes that "Interest group leaders often make public presentations to legislative committees not so much because they believe that they can affect policy, but because they wish to justify themselves to their membership. Nevertheless, lobbyists do take the legislature and its members seriously as contributors to the policy process" (White 1989, p. 255). Lobbying efforts by environmental interest groups in Canada and the United States are likely to differ somewhat, but the differences may be a matter of degree only (Presthus 1974). There are, however, rather significant differences in the use of litigation strategies between the two nations. A Canadian government official made this observation: "In Canada, we tend to work a little more through discussion and consensus. As Canadians, we are often amazed by the litigation processes that go on in the United States" (Cronin-Cossette 1988, p. 110).

In the Canadian Study of Parliament Group's report on Canadian interest groups, the observation was made that there would be a gap between the communication and influence capabilities of well-financed, highly skilled, and effectively organized groups and those with fewer resources. This resource difference was viewed as the source of some serious problems because "confrontational politics and playing to the media may be the only options left to the latter" (Canadian Study of Parliament Group, 1989, p. 12). Thus, organizational characteristics as well as political system differences may affect the kinds of strategies pursued by interest groups as they attempt to influence the public policy process.

Several dimensions of government contacting were included in the study: (1) the frequency of interaction with a range of government officials within each level of government (national, provincial/state, and local),[14] (2) the frequency of interaction with four types of government officials (elected officials, top-level bureaucrats, mid-level bureaucrats, and legal or scientific experts across all three levels of government),[15] (3) the range of services typically provided for members of the provincial parliament or state legislators,[16] (4) the range of services typically provided for provincial or state civil servants,[17] and (5) the variety of methods used to influence government actions or policies affecting the interests of members.[18] It should be noted that cross-national differences on many indicators of these dimensions of government contacts are apparent readily in the organizational profile data. These differences are explored in Chapter 6; the focus here is on the relationships among organizational characteristics and how those characteristics affect the behavior of environmental interest groups.

Table 5.4 reports the mean, standard deviation, and the range of possible values for each of the measures of the various dimensions of government contacting. For the first measure listed, group representatives interact most frequently with a range of officials on the provincial or state level of government; interactions with local officials represent a secondary practice, and the extent of interaction is the most limited with national officials. The indicator for interactions at the provincial/state level is a count of only the "very frequent" (the high value on a 5-point

Table 5.4
Summary Profile of the Measures of Government Contacts

Interaction with Officials WITHIN Levels	Mean	Standard Deviation	Range
National Level	0.87	1.31	0 to 5 frequent interactions
Provincial/State Level	1.03	1.44	0 to 5 very frequent interactions
Local Level	1.28	1.50	0 to 5 frequent interactions
Interaction with Officials ACROSS Levels			
Elected Officials	8.97	2.90	0 = low to 15 = high
Top-Level Bureaucrats	8.95	3.26	0 = low to 15 = high
Mid-Level Bureaucrats	9.08	3.01	0 = low to 15 = high
Legal and Scientific Experts	13.10	5.43	0 = low to 30 = high
Services Provided to:			
Provincial/State Legislators	1.87	1.32	0 to 4 services
Provincial/State Civil Servants	2.23	1.49	0 to 4 services
Group Strategies			
Methods Used to Influence Policy Making	4.46	3.10	0 to 10 methods

scale) interactions group leaders have with elected officials, top- or mid-level bureaucrats, and legal or scientific experts. For interactions with the same officials at national and local levels, the top two values were counted, and the measures represent somewhat frequent and very frequent rather than exclusively very frequent interactions.

When the measures of the intensity of interaction with these same officials is examined across (rather than within) the three levels of government, the averages for interactions with elected officials and top- and mid-level bureaucrats are very similar—mean values of 8.97, 8.95, and 9.08, respectively, on additive indexes that range from 0 to a possible high of 15. The interactions with scientific and legal experts are represented by a scale that ranges from 0 to 30, and the mean value of 13.10 is below the midpoint of this index. The standard deviations are all relatively high, suggesting that significant differences among the groups do exist.

The environmental groups were given the opportunity to indicate whether they provided four specific services for their legislators and officials within the provincial or state bureaucracy. The legislative services include testifying at hearings, providing information on pending legislation, building public support for legislative proposals, and campaign support. The services to bureaucratic agencies included participation in public advisory bodies, providing information on public attitudes, mobilizing support for agency policies, and making recommendations on appointments to high-level posts. The mean (2.23) for the number of services provided to provincial or state civil servants was higher than the mean value (1.87) for the number of services provided to legislators. The standard deviations, however, for these two composite measures indicate considerable variability around the mean values. Finally, when a count is made of the methods or strategies the sample groups are using to attempt to influence policymakers in the area of the environment, the groups use an average of 4 methods out of a possible 10. It should be noted, however, that the sizable standard deviation (3.10) again indicates substantial variation across groups in this regard.

THE EFFECTS OF RESOURCES AND COMMUNICATION CAPABILITY

A number of expectations were set forth regarding how the several aspects of group resources and capacities might be related to what environmental pressure groups do to influence government decision making and how successful the groups see themselves being in that endeavor. Table 5.5 presents the results of cross-tabulations among measures of group resources and capacities (conventional organizational resources,

Table 5.5
Bivariate Relationships among Group Aspects, Government Contacting, and Self-Perception of Group Effectiveness (Measured as Gamma Coefficients)

		GOVERNMENT CONTACTING			
		Contacts With State/Provincial Officials	Legislative Services Provided	Bureaucratic Services Provided	Range Of Methods Employed
Conventional Resources	*Funds*	.47	.49	.37	.38
	# of Members	-.14	.27	.19	.14
	Coalitions/ Affiliations	.12	.09	.38	-.12
Informational Capacity	*External Sources*	.46	.71	.58	.73
	Range of Types	.67	.67	.52	.76
	Generates Own Research	.48	.50	.44	.59
Scope of Group Communication Efforts	*Time Devoted*	.37	.20	.09	.36
	Range of Information to Members	.28	.25	.34	.26
	Range of Information to Government	.79	.73	.57	.84

PERCEPTIONS OF GROUP SUCCESS

		Informing State or Provincial Officials	Informing Group Members
Conventional Resources	*Funds*	.42	-.03
	# of Members	.45	.63
	Coalitions/ Affiliations	-.01	.13
Informational Capacity	*External Sources*	.34	.58
	Range of Types	.49	.53
	Generates Own Research	.43	.54
Scope of Group Communication Efforts	*Time Devoted*	.43	.26
	Range of Information to Members	.15	-.21
	Range of Information to Government	.77	.67

informational capacity, communication effort) (independent variables), government contacts, and group leaders' estimations of the effectiveness of their group's communication efforts[19] (dependent variables). Gamma coefficients are used to report the strength of the bivariate associations.

When the three measures of organizational resources (monetary, membership, and networking capacity) are considered, there are more noteworthy relationships (gamma of 0.40 or better) between the monetary resource indicator and the dependent variables than there are for the indicators of member and networking capacity resources. The combination of a large annual budget, sizable amounts of external funding, a paid staff, and tax-exempt status has a moderate and positive impact on both the number of types of government-contacting behavior undertaken and the degree of success group leaders attribute to their attempts to inform state/provincial government officials. Having monetary resources, however, is not associated by group leaders with more positive estimates of their group's success in communicating with members (gamma = −0.03).

Networking capacity as a group resource, consisting of group memberships and affiliations with provincial/state or national organizations, is correlated weakly with the measures of government contacting and communication success. The member resource indicator—which includes separate measures of group chapter structure, the number of volunteers available, availability of membership by individuals, and the percentage of group funds raised from member dues—has a positive relationship only with the two measures of communication success—success in informing government officials (gamma = 0.45) and success in informing group members (gamma = 0.63).

Having informational capacity, which is measured as the ability to rely on a large number of external sources of information, to use a wide range of types of research information, and to be in a position to generate some or all of the research information used by the organization, is related strongly to all the measures of government contacts (gammas range from a low of 0.44 to a high of 0.76). In addition, informational capacity is associated moderately and positively with the two indicators of communication success (gammas of 0.34 and 0.58 for informing state/ provincial officials and organization members, respectively). The ability to create and compile a wide range of scientific, technical, economic, legal, and political information appears to be a particularly important aspect of the influence potential of these environmental organizations, perhaps even more important than conventional organizational resources.

The scope of communication efforts is measured as the time group personnel spend on information-sharing activities, the number of means used to communicate with members, and the range of types of information communicated to government officials. The results of the several cross-tabulations indicate that only the range of information types communicated to government officials is associated positively with all the measures of government-contacting behavior and communication success. Environmental groups that share with government officials a wide variety of types of specialized (scientific, technical, legal, political, and economic) information are likely to have frequent interactions with provincial/state officials, provide lots of services to legislators and bureaucrats, and engage in a wide variety of strategies to influence policy process (gammas of 0.57 to 0.84).

In addition, increasing the scope of the group's communication efforts is associated positively with perceptions of communication success (gammas of 0.77 and 0.67 for state/provincial officials and organization members, respectively). Although the other two indicators of communication effort, for the most part, are associated positively with indicators of government contacts and self-perceptions of success, the correlations are rather weak. Only the staff time spent on communications shows a noteworthy, positive relationship to one of the self-assessed success measures (success in informing state or provincial officials) (gamma = 0.43).

In the analyses of the bivariate relationships above, for the most part the traditional organizational resources did not perform as well as might be expected given the emphasis placed on monetary, human, and networking capacity characteristics in the literature on interest groups. Although 11 organizational characteristics were included in the factor analysis that produced these 3 dimensions, more information was collected on the organizational profiles than was used in constructing the 11 measures. For example, after group leaders were asked if their organization provides for types of members other than individuals, they were asked to indicate all the types of memberships they have from a list of environmental organizations, clubs, civic or community organizations, units of government or government agencies, research organizations, businesses or corporations, labor organizations, and any other types of group members not listed. To test whether type of organizational membership provided by a group affects either the nature or the extent of group attempts to influence environmental policy-making, the seven organizational membership types were cross-tabulated with the indicators of contacts with government officials. The results of this cross-tabulation are listed in Table 5.6.

Two types of memberships—other environmental groups and civic or community organizations—are associated with each of the government contacts in a relatively strong, positive manner. Having these types of members increases group attempts to influence public policy and to

Table 5.6
Relationships between Types of Organizational Members and Measures of Government Contacts

TYPES OF ORGANIZATIONAL MEMBERS

GOVERNMENT CONTACTS:	Environ- mental	Clubs	Civics	Govern- ments	Research	Business	Labor
Interaction-- National Level	.57	-.01	.48	.06	.40	.35	.88
Interaction-- Provincial or State Level	.50	.16	.71	.55	.49	.45	.40
Interaction-- Local Level	.40	.10	.71	.68	.58	.39	-.06
Legislative Services	.53	.25	.65	.26	.36	.50	.29
Bureaucratic Services	.66	.28	.73	.50	.70	.71	.31
Methods of Governmental Influence	.43	.01	.52	-.06	.26	.15	.16

Note: *Each of the member types is a dichotomous variable, where 1=group has this type of member; 0=group does not have this type of member.*

communicate information. In contrast, those groups with clubs as members are not very active in approaching any of the government officials. What is interesting is the association between having research organizations as members and the measures of government contacts. Environmental groups with research organization memberships tend to increase their interactions with officials at the national, provincial/state, and local levels of government; they are also likely to provide a wide range of services to bureaucratic officials. This finding is consistent with our evolving view of contemporary environmental organizations very likely being quite important providers of scientific and technical information to citizens, potential group members, their own members, and to officials of government.

COMBINED EFFECTS

The second part of the analysis is an assessment of the combined effects of the measures of monetary resources, informational capacity, and communication effort on several measures of government contacts and the two indicators of communication success. Only the measure of monetary resources is included from the original set of three indicators of conventional organizational resources; this indicator is included because it had a few noteworthy relationships with government contacts and communication success in the bivariate analysis above. Only two of three capacity indicators are included (number of types of information used by environmental groups and the extent to which groups generate their own research) because the former is correlated strongly with the number of external sources used ($r = 0.82$). An additional dichotomous variable indicating whether the environmental group is in Ontario or Michigan is included in the multivariate analysis to provide a control for the possible effects of Canadian/American cross-national differences.

The previous analysis focused on the frequency with which group representatives interacted with provincial or state-level officials. These provincial/state-level government officials included elected officials or their staff; heads of departments, divisions, agencies, or commissions; mid-level personnel in departments, divisions, or agencies; legal experts in government; and scientific experts in government. In this analysis, measures are used that were created to represent interactions with the five types of government officials across (rather than within) the levels of government—national, provincial/state, and local.

Table 5.7 reports the cumulative and relative effects of the measures of monetary resources, information capacity, communication effort, and country on contacts with types of government officials across all levels of government. These independent variables explain similar percentages of the variance for each type of government contact; the adjusted R^2 values ranged from a low of 0.34 in the equation in which interaction with experts was the dependent variable, to a high of 0.40 in the equation in which interaction with top-level bureaucrats was the dependent variable.

Two of the communication effort measures—the number of means used to inform members and the range of information types communicated to government officials—have statistically significant independent impacts in either two or three of the four multiple regression equations. Using a variety of means to inform members and communicating a wide range of types of information to government officials tends to increase

Table 5.7
Combined Effects of Measures of Resources, Capacity, Communication Efforts, and Country on Measures of Contacts with Government Officials (Multiple Regression Analysis Results)

	CONTACTS WITH NATIONAL, PROVINCIAL/STATE, AND LOCAL OFFICIALS			
STANDARDIZED BETA COEFFICIENTS:	Elected Officials	Top-Level Bureaucrats	Mid-Level Bureaucrats	Government Experts
Group Monetary Resources	.05	.07	.19	.01
Number of Types of Information Used	.08	.04	.30*	.20
Extent to Which Group Generates Its Own Research	.17	.15	-.01	.09
Staff Time Spent on Communication	.10	.15	.21	.21
Number of Means Used to Inform Members	.28**	.33**	.01	.22*
Range of Information Types Communicated to Government Officials	.24*	.27*	.09	.18
Country (Ontario=0; Michigan=1)	.11	.07	.24*	.12
Adjusted R²	0.36	0.40	0.35	0.34
F Statistic	5.81***	6.66***	5.65***	5.35***

* $p \leq .05$; ** $p \leq .01$; *** $p \leq .001$

the frequency with which environmental groups interact with elected officials, top-level bureaucratic officials, and government experts, but these indicators do not increase the interactions with mid-level career civil servants. Informational capacity (the indicator of the number of types of research information used by the groups) and country effects are the two factors that have independent effects on interactions with mid-level bureaucrats.

Table 5.8 reports the cumulative and relative effects on measures of

Table 5.8
Combined Effects of Measures of Resources, Capacity, Communication Efforts, and Country on Measures of Group Success in Informing Government Officials and Group Members (Multiple Regression Analysis Results)

	SELF-PERCEIVED SUCCESS IN INFORMATION TRANSMISSION	
	To Provincial/ State Officials	**To Group Members**
Adjusted R^2	0.24	0.17
F Statistic	2.90**	2.21*
STANDARDIZED BETA COEFFICIENTS:		
Group Monetary Resources	.02	-.17
Number of Types of Information Used	.19	.10
Extent to which Group Generates Its Own Research	-.08	-.11
Staff Time Spent on Communication	.08	.13
Number of Means Used to Inform Members	-.20	-.24
Range of Information Types Communicated to Government Officials	.40*	.23
Number of Legislative Services Provided	.13	.14
Number of Bureaucratic Services Provided	.28	.24
Number of Methods Used to Influence Policy Making	-.13	.06
Country (Ontario = 0; Michigan = 1)	-.03	-.00

$**p \leq .01; *p \leq .05$

self-perceived communication success of these same independent variables and three additional related factors: number of legislative services provided, number of bureaucratic services provided, and the number of methods used to influence policy-making. When the group leaders' perceptions of success in informing provincial/state officials and in informing group members are the dependent variables, the cumulative impact of these independent variables is quite weak (adjusted R^2 values of 0.24 and 0.17, respectively), although both equations produce statistically significant F statistics. The sole variable that has a statistically significant independent impact on perceptions of success in informing provincial or state-level officials is the range of information types communicated to government officials.

DISCUSSION AND CONCLUSIONS

The empirical findings reported here would appear to provide considerable support to those who urge close attention to the centrality of "information" phenomena in postindustrial society. By tradition and earlier training, students of politics and political economy are inclined to focus upon the more tangible aspects of political struggle. Those subjects of study are most likely things that can be observed and counted, such as votes, number of people a group can move into action, and the size of an interest group's bank account.

Increasingly, however, students of contemporary society are inclined to call attention to the salience of "language games" in the highly mediated environment of postindustrial society. For example, Murray Edelmon aptly notes that the "linguistic turn in philosophy, social psychology, and literary theory has called attention to language games that construct alternative realities, grammars that transform the perceptible into nonobvious meanings" (1988, p. 103). Perhaps what has been exposed in these findings is evidence that interest group politics is beginning to focus as much on the transformations of the perceptible into nonobvious meanings as upon the conventional activities of direct lobbying and indirect social mobilization.

While these traditional activities always will be an important aspect of interest group work, it is quite possible that the "real" battles lie in capturing the definition of problems and structuring the context for the discussion of alternative public policies. From the evidence gathered in these recent surveys of environmental group leaders, it would appear that these environmental interest groups are inclined to attach high importance to their information-gathering and information-dissemination roles, and to assess their own potential for influence primarily in terms of their command of agenda-setting and discussion-molding information. The fact that findings along these lines are very similar in the Canadian and American settings—political environ-ments that share a clear postindustrial character but differ in their insti-tutional design and political cultures—adds further to the importance of the language game aspects of interest group politics in contemporary society.

In a period of declining conventional political participation and parti-san affiliation, falling newspaper readerships, and widespread televi-sion dependency on the acquisition of understanding of social reality, the major struggle to capture influence likely lies in the language games of contemporary politics (Kellner 1990, pp. 161–174). The raiding of animal labs, the announcement of having spiked old-growth trees, the futile occupation of fragile sections of land—what sense do these actions of "eco-warriors" make in terms of votes, contributions, or influence in a state legislative process? Unlike the groups studied here, some environmental activists have forsaken the conventional routes to influ-ence completely and devoted their entire attention to the symbolic level of politics (Scarce 1990). While the environmental groups that partici-pated in this study maintain a faith in the propriety of remaining within the boundaries of conventional political struggle, they quite clearly are sensitive to the centrality of information phenomena and understand well the language game aspects of their work.

NOTES

1. Both full-time and part-time staff were considered in the creation of the measure representing the availability of a paid staff; groups having no paid staff were coded 0 and those with a paid staff were coded 1. In Ontario, 20 groups (53%) have paid staff; 12 Michigan groups (52%) have paid staff.

2. The size of the groups' annual budgets ranged from a low of $200 to a high of $6 million (mean = $252,006; S.D. = $827,663). Because of this varia-tion, budget amounts were placed into categories of low (up to $2000), medium ($2,200 through $100,000), and high ($118,000 through $6 million), and these categories were coded 1, 2, and 3, respectively.

3. The number of volunteers associated with these groups ranged from 0 to 1000 (mean = 139; S.D. = 246). These values were placed into three catego-ries—few (0–20), average (25–60), and many (100–1000)—and coded 1, 2, and 3, respectively.

4. The percentage of group funding raised from dues ranged from 0 to 100 (mean = 53; S.D. = 39). In the cross-tabulation analyses, these values were placed into three categories coded 1 (0% through 25%), 2 (30% through 75%), and 3 (80% through 100%).

5. Three items were combined to create the percentage of funds raised from sources external to the group: the percentages raised from foundations, govern-ment sources, and private corporations. No money from any of these external sources was raised by 33 groups; consequently, these groups were coded 0 and groups with some funding from external sources were coded 1.

6. Group leaders were asked if their groups were affiliated with a national organization (1 = yes; 0 = no), and leaders also were asked if their groups were affiliated with a provincial or state organization (1 = yes; 0 = no).

7. After recording the variables included in the three dimensions of organizational resources to dichotomous variables where 1 = high amounts/presence of the resource and 0 = low amounts/absence of the resource, indicators of the three dimensions were created by adding the variables found in each. These additive indexes then were recorded as dichotomous variables for the cross-tabulation analysis.

8. Group leaders were asked to indicate whether their organizations used any of the following external sources to compile information on environmental problems: (1) affiliates or offices of the organization, (2) other environmental organizations, (3) scientists or experts in universities or research institutions, (4) lawyers or legal experts, (5) elected government officials or their staffs, (6) nonelected government personnel, and (7) others (which could be named). The number of external sources used was counted across these seven types (mean = 4.39; S.D. = 1.95). For this study, number of external sources was categorized as 0 through 4 = 1 (26 groups) and 5 through 7 = 2 (35 groups).

9. Four types of research information were listed: scientific or technical, legal, political, and economic. Leaders indicated whether their groups used these types of specialized information in their research. Number of types of research information used was counted across the four types (mean = 3.25; S.D. = 1.23). All four types of information were used by 41 groups (coded 2); the remaining 20 groups used no sources or up to 3 (coded 1).

10. When respondents were asked about the types of information, they also were asked to check whether any types of information used by the group were self-generated, provided by others, or a combination of the two. The number of times research was self-generated or produced by a combination of efforts was counted across the four types of research information. These results then were recorded to indicate that the group either generated none or very little of its research information (coded 1) or generated substantial amounts of its research information (coded 2).

11. The percentages of total staff time devoted to three activities (educational programs, political activities, and scientific or technical research) were combined to create the measure of staff time spent on informational activities (mean = 46.98; S.D. = 38.57). These percentages were placed into three categories coded 0 (no staff time), 1 (5% through 75% of time), and 2 (80% to 100% of time).

12. Many ways of communicating with members were listed—a newsletter, magazine, periodic membership meetings, special reports or pamphlets, workshops or short courses, videotapes or films, community or regional newspapers, radio, television, and other forms (which could be named). Number of means of communication was counted across these 9 forms (mean = 4.92; S.D. = 1.89). Thirty-eight groups used from 1 to 4 forms (coded 1); the remaining 23 groups used 5 to 9 forms (coded 2).

13. The measure of the range of information types communicated to state/provincial government officials came from two items on the organizational profile. Respondents were asked to indicate the types of information—scientific, technical, legal, political, and economic—that were communicated to elected

and career service government officials in their state or province. These separate measures (number of types of information communicated to each category of officials) are reported in Table 5.3. The overall composite measure was developed by counting the types of information checked across the two items and categorizing the results into two categories: a smaller range of information types (2 through 6) coded 1 and a wider range of information types (7 through 10) coded 2.

14. Group leaders were asked how frequently representatives from their organizations interacted with different types of government officials: elected officials; heads of departments, divisions, agencies, or commissions; mid-level bureaucratic personnel; legal experts; and scientific experts at the national, provincial/state, and local levels of government. Five response categories were listed with endpoints of "never" (coded 1) and "often" (coded 5) and a midpoint of "occasionally" (coded 3). For the measure of frequency of interaction with national officials, the two categories (coded 4 and 5) at the "often" end of the scale were counted across the five types of officials (mean = 0.87; S.D. = 1.31). Thirty-eight groups had no frequent interactions with national-level officials (coded 1); the remaining 23 groups had frequent interactions with from 1 to 5 of these officials (coded 2). The measure of frequency of interaction with local officials was constructed in exactly the same manner as the measure for contacts with national officials (mean = 1.28; S.D. = 1.50). Twenty-nine groups had no frequent interactions with local officials (coded 1); the remaining 32 groups had frequent contacts with from 1 to 5 of these officials (coded 2). The 61 groups had most of their contacts with officials at the provincial or state level; consequently, for this measure only the "often" category (coded 5) was counted across the 5 types of officials (mean = 1.03; S.D. = 1.44). Thirty-four groups did not interact "often" with any provincial or state officials; 27 did have frequency of contacts with these 5 types of officials that were considered "often."

15. For the indicator of contacts with elected officials, the items on frequency of interactions with elected officials on the national, provincial/state, and local levels of government were added (mean = 8.97; S.D. = 2.90). Similar procedures were followed for the remaining three items: (1) interactions with top-level bureaucrats across all three levels of government (mean = 8.95; S.D. = 3.26), (2) mid-level bureaucrats across all three levels of government (mean = 9.08; S.D. = 3.01), and (3) legal and scientific experts across the three levels of government.

16. Four types of services were listed that groups could provide to members of the provincial parliament or state legislature: testifying at hearings, providing information on pending legislation, building public support for legislative proposals, and providing campaign support. Leaders were asked to indicate which of these services were provided by their organizations, and the number of services provided was counted across the categories (mean = 1.87; S.D. = 1.32).

17. Similarly, four types of services were listed that groups could provide to provincial or state civil servants: participation in public advisory bodies, providing information on public attitudes, mobilizing support for agency policies, and making recommendations on appointees to high-level posts. The number of services provided was counted across the categories (mean = 2.23; S.D. =

1.49). Both measures (legislative services and bureaucratic services) were re-corded as follows: 0 services = 1, 1 or 2 services = 2, and 3 or 4 services = 3.

18. Ten methods used to influence government actions or policies were listed: (1) briefs to parliamentary committees or testifying before legislative commit-tees, (2) briefs to cabinet ministers or submitting reports to the governor's office, (3) appeals to executive assistants of cabinet ministers or appeals to agency personnel, (4) briefs or appeals by outside experts, (5) contact with government regulatory bodies, (6) filing law suits, (7) instigating a letter-writing campaign, (8) building coalitions with other groups, (9) releasing information through the mass media, and (10) organizing political protests. The number of methods used was counted across these 10 categories (mean = 4.46; SD = 3.10). These values were recoded as follows: 0–3 methods = 1; 4–10 methods = 2.

19. The following question was asked: "On matters affecting the environ-ment, how successful is your organization in its attempts to inform provincial or state government officials and members of the organization?" Five response categories were listed with endpoints of "not successful" (coded 1) and "very successful" (coded 5) and a midpoint of "not certain" (coded 3). Both measures were recoded for the cross-tabulation analysis so that the two successful re-sponses (4 and 5) were coded 1, and the remaining responses were coded 0.

Chapter Six

Environmental Groups as Communicators

The comparisons of underlying conceptions of societal arrangements and the polity in the Canadian and American settings presented in previous chapters suggest that environmental groups in Canada and the United States operate in quite different cultural and institutional milieux as they seek to influence public policy processes (Gibbins and Nevitte 1985; Horowitz 1966; Presthus 1974; Lipset 1985, 1990). Nevertheless, it is likely that A. Paul Pross is quite correct in noting that interest groups are "political communication mechanisms capable of adapting to the policy system in which they are located" (1975, p. 27). In this chapter, the focus is on cross-national differences (adaptations) in the activities of the Canadian and American environmental interest groups taking part in this study. Also of interest, of course, is any evidence that such differences as might have typified a comparison of Canadian and American interest groups in the past are diminishing under the common weight of postindustrial conditions in Canada and the United States (Yang 1988).

The assumption is made that environmental interest group members and their leaders in both national settings are attempting to influence the public policy process, but the expectation is that precisely how environmental activists actually do this is quite likely affected by the structure and values of their respective political systems (Milbrath 1983). The structure of both governmental systems—the parliamentary format of Canada and the presidential system in the United States—will have a significant impact on the access environmental groups have to government officials (Lowe and Goyder 1983, pp. 163-175). In addition, cross-national variation in the political cultures of Ontario and Michigan are expected to produce different viewpoints concerning the proper role of interest groups in the two political settings, and concerning the acceptable tactics and most effective strategies that group leaders might put into use (Fry 1985, pp. 1–8).

In writing about the political culture of Ontario, A. Paul Pross makes the following observations:

Analysts of Ontario's political culture tend to emphasize the importance of features such as continuity, social order, stability, elitism, and ascription . . . this conservatism tends to be leavened with a persistent concern with progress and reform, so that the province is more aptly characterized as "progressive conservative" or "red tory." (1985, p. 16)

Pross quotes Gad Horowitz as saying that "Canadian socialism and conservatism share an organic collective notion of society, which finds expression in a positive if paternalistic state," and he concludes that these characteristics are nowhere more prominent than in the Province of Ontario (Pross 1985, p. 16).

Peter Kobrak also emphasizes progressivism in his summary account of Michigan's political culture, although he emphasizes a different dimension of that value orientation:

The commitment to progressivism was an easy one to make. Expanding resources eliminated the need to make painful choices between heavy taxation and extensive services . . . Michiganions could also continue to manifest a belief in individualism even while big business, the automobile companies, the United Automobile Workers (UAW), and big government itself were creating an increasingly interdependent, and to some extent vulnerable, state economy. (1984, p. 101)

Kobrak views Michigan politics as a "vehicle through which virtually every major group at one time or another attempts to gain the resources necessary to cope with the state's rapidly changing economic and social environment" (p. 99).

Both of these brief descriptions of the prevailing values underlying the Michigan and Ontario political systems conform to the general outlines of the Canadian and American national political cultures. The value systems of Ontario and Michigan should not be thought of as residing on opposite ends of a libertarian versus communitarian continuum. The basic classical liberal values of individualism, love of personal liberty, and a constitutionally restricted role for government are important in the province of Ontario (Pross 1985) as well as in the state of Michigan, but there are important cross-national differences in how such conventional classical liberal values are expressed and institutionalized in the two national settings. Moreover, in Ontario the "great issues of state tend to be national rather than provincial'' (White 1989, p. 258), and the province is considered the political and economic center of Canada. Michigan certainly does not play the same pivotal role in American political and economic life. These several considerations led to the conclusion that it is likely that state and provincial political cultures do produce a distinctive impact upon interest group politics in Ontario and Michigan.

What was unknown, of course, was the extent to which political culture and political system differences might affect the way environmental interest groups communicate information to government officials and to their own members. Consequently, cross-national differences in the way environmental groups perform their information-sharing role are explored in this chapter (Groth et al. 1984). In addition, an analysis of differences and similarities in perceptions of group roles and in beliefs concerning the most effective ways to influence the public policy process are presented.

It is the intention here, first, to assess the extent to which the more centralized Canadian political system, which has been described as a policy process of elite accommodation, and the more fragmented and competitive American political system produce differences in activities undertaken by groups to influence public policy. To explore the possible effects these several differences in national settings might have on interest group behavior, both qualitative and quantitative information collected in Ontario and Michigan are presented. Qualitative material from personal interviews held with 24 public policy process elites is combined with quantitative data collected from organizational profiles completed by the leaders of the 61 environmental groups taking part in the Ontario–Michigan study of the acid rain issue.

The second major intention of the analysis presented here concerns cross-national communication patterns. Differences and similarities are explored in the character and focus of the information that comes into play in interest group communication efforts. Given the scientific and technological complexity inherent in many environmental issues, do interest groups in both national settings devote special attention to the task of providing understandable scientific and technical information (or possibly specialized economic and legal policy-relevant information) in their frequent interactions with government officials, or are group communications primarily political in nature? In addition, cross-national differences and similarities are investigated in the bivariate relationships existing between government contacts and separate measures of organizational capacity, communication effort, and the types of information interest groups transmit to government officials. Does the ability to obtain, generate, and disseminate a wide range of types of information affect either the frequency or focus of government contacts in the two political systems? Are the effects of these organizational characteristics the same or different in Ontario and Michigan? These are the types of communication pattern questions investigated here.

ELITE OPINIONS ON GROUP ACCESS AND TACTICS

To explore how cross-national differences in perceptions of the proper role as regards group access and tactics of environmental interest groups in the policy process might play out in elite circles, a series of lengthy interviews focusing on acid rain issues was held with numerous prominent government officials and the directors of the most influential environmental organizations in Ontario and Michigan.[1] All interviewees were promised absolute anonymity, hence none of the comments reported in the following pages are attributed to their original source.

Governmental policy elites in Ontario tend to concur that the provincial government—meaning the premier and his or her cabinet—is very important in the environmental policy process in the province. The provincial government creates important public policy largely independent of Ottawa, establishes important regulations, and is viewed by the public and industry as having broad administrative discretion in carrying out its governmental duties (Segsworth 1990). The Ontario elites interviewed believe that the environmental minister's office is very well connected to the environmental community, and that environmental interest groups are in regular contact with the ministry. Most environmental organizations lobby various ministers (as well as other government officials) by letter, and a small number of the larger groups have representatives that meet personally with cabinet ministers and their deputy ministers.

Many environmental interest groups also have quite regular contacts with members of the legislative assembly, most usually through letters, newsletters, conferences, and informal meetings. As one might expect from a system featuring a strong element of elite accommodation, the Ontario interviewees believe that groups taking a conciliatory rather than a confrontational approach are most effective in their contacts with government officials. In the Canadian case, environmental interest groups rarely enjoy access to either upper- or mid-level civil service officials in the ministries, and it was reported that some ministry staff even carry some resentment against environmental organizations precisely because they are seen as having the ear of the current minister.

There is little coordination and centralization of policy-making power evident in the Michigan elite's picture of the state's environmental policy system. The state legislature is considered to be one of the most prominent actors, but it seldom speaks with one voice on environmental issues. Policy proposals that manage to obtain bipartisan support in both houses are subject to rules made by the legislature's Joint Committee on Administrative Rules (JCAR). Both agency and environmentalist elites in Michigan view the committee as the key obstructionist element on environmental issues because of its pro-industry viewpoint. Its exercise of a "legislative veto" on agency implementation efforts gives it both direct and indirect influence over policy in all areas of state government. Several interviewees accused JCAR of letting its pro–automobile industry bias influence its decisions on environmental administrative rules. Given the power of this committee, agency personnel are said to shelve needed rules and regulations from time to time that they know will not clear the obstacle of JCAR review.

The interviewees in Michigan agree unanimously that no one policy actor has enough power and authority to centralize decision making on environmental issues. Environmental interest group leaders, consequently, feel they must maintain contacts with as many actors in the policy process as possible. Most statewide groups have developed relationships with officials in the governor's office, top-level and mid-level people in the Department of Natural Resources, and members and staffers of the relevant legislative committees. In addition, interviewees among both the group leaders and agency officials report that some environmental groups are asked to make recommendations to the governor's office on appointees to the state's important Air Quality Control Commission.

It is not surprising that cross-national political system differences would affect how strategically located policymakers and major interest group leaders see the proper role and most effective activities of organized environmental groups. The Ontario interviewees concur in the view that, in Canada, environmental interest groups serve an important watchdog function, and that their role is to be the primary educator of the public and the primary bearer of petitions to the government on issues of major import. Environmental groups in Michigan also are viewed as providers of information to the public and government, but they are considered to be only one legitimate voice among many competing voices; utility companies, local governments, industry, chambers of commerce, and labor organizations also are participating in the choir in question. Interviewees in Michigan are inclined to express the view that environmental interest groups must develop a broad political power base to be effective. This might be accomplished in several ways, including having staff in the state capital who have regular contacts with state officials, proving to state legislators and agency officials that the group's position is backed by a large membership and a large number of sympathetic citizens, and getting involved either directly or indirectly in campaign financing and partisan electoral politics.

As expected, the elites interviewed in Michigan and Canada confirm that environmental interest group tactics are likely to be quite different in the two political systems. In Ontario, as in Michigan, environmental groups engage in a variety of tactics, but the Ontario groups are seen as pursuing active, albeit quiet, involvement in the public policy process. In contrast, environmental interest groups in Michigan express the view that they must remain visible and appear to the public as exercising power in order to compete effectively in Michigan's highly fragmented power structure. One elite informant expressed the belief that the parliamentary practice of the public "questions period" held regularly in the legislative assembly presents the most effective opportunity for influence for environmental groups in Ontario. Needless to say, there is no direct analogue for the questions' period in the American presidential system.

A tactic that is considered important in both countries is the use of the media, especially the press. An important caveat concerning media use in Ontario was offered by one informant, who observed that the media play a less important role when environmental organizations are granted access to government and believe that their viewpoints are heard. If the provincial government did not allow this access, the use of the media presumably would become more important. A major difference in tactics between Ontario and Michigan environmental interest groups involves the use of lawsuits. Canadian groups are not permitted to sue the Crown, in keeping with English common law traditions of Canadian jurisprudence, and this restriction promotes a considerably less adversarial relationship between interest groups and government in Canada than in the United States. In Michigan (as in the United States generally), of course, suits filed by environmental interest group are a very common phenomenon (Rummands 1970).

The comments of the 24 elite government officials and directors of well-known environmental organizations affirm some expected differences in the interest group dynamics of the two political systems. The power structure in Ontario is described as centralized, and environmental group leaders—either through personal meetings or letters—contact the top-level government officials in the ministries frequently. However, no contact with mid-level career civil servants is reported in the Ontario setting. In contrast, many actors play important roles in the power structure of Michigan; the picture presented is one of broadly diffused rather than centralized power. Consequently, leaders of environmental organizations, in their attempts to penetrate this fragmented structure, make contacts with decision makers in both the legislative and executive branches, and seek to maintain contacts with all levels of the state bureaucracy as well.

Although environmental interest groups in both national settings play important information-sharing roles, the way this particular role is performed differs in the two countries. In Ontario, the emphasis, according to the interviewees, is on groups as educators. The common view is that environmental groups seek to represent the public interest honestly and therefore are accorded respect as watchdogs in the area of environmental issues. Group involvement in the public policy process is expected to be quiet, respectful of authority, and cooperative as opposed to openly confrontational.

In stark contrast, environmental interest groups in the Michigan setting tend to be regarded as just another special interest; as such, group leaders must strive to be highly visible and to endeavor to create a broad political power base so they will enjoy an adequate degree of credibility with Michigan's environmental policy decision makers. As a consequence of these differences, the strategies most frequently adopted and the tactics used most frequently and effectively by environmental groups in Michigan are often different from those adopted by their counterparts in Ontario.

CROSS-NATIONAL DIFFERENCES IN GOVERNMENT CONTACTS

The information on organizational characteristics collected through the organizational profile instruments completed by leaders of the 61 groups tends to validate the elite perceptions offered in personal interviews. Table 6.1 reports mean values among Ontario and Michigan groups on several measures of governmental contacts: (1) interactions with provincial/state officials, including elected officials or their staffs; heads of departments, divisions, agencies, or commissions; mid-level personnel in departments, divisions, or agencies; legal experts in government; and scientific experts in government; (2) such types of legislative services provided as testifying at hearings, providing information on pending legislation, building public support for legislative proposals, and providing campaign support; and (3) such types of bureaucratic services provided as participating in public advisory bodies, providing information on public attitudes, supporting agency policies, and recommending appointees to high-level posts.

In all cases in which statistically significant mean values are in evidence, the higher mean is associated with the Michigan environmental interest groups. The Michigan groups contact state-level officials more frequently than groups in Ontario contact provincial officials, and this pattern is consistent for the measures of interactions with elected officials, top- and mid-level agency personnel, and legal and scientific experts. Reporting frequent contacts with all types of government officials is consistent with the demands imposed upon interest groups by fragmentation of power in the American political system. Such a govern-

Table 6.1
Cross-National Differences (Differences of Means Tests) on Measures of Interaction with Provincial/State Officials and Legislative and Bureaucratic Services

	ONTARIO GROUPS (N=38)	MICHIGAN GROUPS (N=23)	t-value
FREQUENCY OF INTERACTIONS WITH PROVINCIAL/STATE OFFICIALS (The range of values is from 1=never to 5=often.)			
-Elected Officials	3.19	3.91	-2.60**
-Top-Level Bureaucrats	3.17	4.22	-3.65***
-Mid-Level Bureaucrats	3.19	4.52	-5.21***
-Legal Experts	2.03	2.78	-2.62**
-Scientific Experts	2.67	3.74	-3.68***
LEGISLATIVE SERVICES PROVIDED (The values were 1=service is provided; 0=service not provided.)			
-Testify at hearings	0.42	0.70	-2.16*
-Provide legislative information	0.61	0.65	-0.36
-Build public support	0.61	0.70	-0.71
-Campaign support	0.08	0.09	-0.11
BUREAUCRATIC SERVICES PROVIDED (The values were 1=service is provided; 0=service not provided.)			
-Serve on advisory bodies	0.63	0.82	-1.72
-Provide information on attitudes	0.58	0.74	-1.29
-Support agency policies	0.42	0.74	-2.57**
-Recommendations on appointees	0.18	0.61	-3.48***

*$p \leq .05$; ** $p \leq .01$; *** $p \leq .001$

mental system of fragmented power creates burdens for the would-be interest group representative to be sure, but it also provides a variety of executive and legislative access routes for a plethora of interest group representatives.

There are no significant mean differences for three of the legislative services listed in Table 6.1. Environmental organizations in both national settings provide information to their respective legislative bodies, and both Canadian and American environmental groups build public support for proposals at relatively high levels (mean levels ranged from

0.61 to 0.70, where 1 = service provided and 0 = service not provided). Similarly, both Canadian and American environmental interest groups tend to exhibit low levels of campaign activity (mean values were 0.08 and 0.09, respectively). Differences, however, are evident when testifying at hearings is considered, with the Michigan groups being considerably more likely to engage in this type of activity than are comparable groups in Ontario.

The environmental groups in the American state provide two bureaucratic services—voicing support for agency policies and making recommendations on high-level appointees—at higher mean levels than do their Canadian counterparts. Both activities involve a more political, policy-relevant interaction with state agency personnel than the bureaucratic services in which Michigan and Ontario groups are similarly active (serving on advisory bodies and providing information concerning public attitudes on environmental issues). This active policy involvement on the part of the Michigan groups suggests that they are adapting to the expectation in the state that interest groups must be visible and must compete actively to have their particular concerns and viewpoints heard by policymakers.

Table 6.2 reports the percentage of Ontario and Michigan environmental interest groups using the various methods of advocacy investigated in their attempts to influence governmental policy-making. Once more, the environmental groups in this American state are more aggressive in pursuing both traditional interest group tactics and protest activities than are the Canadian groups. Presthus reported similar findings two decades ago, and he drew the conclusion that "the historic benefices for the private sector, has made lobbying less of a functional requisite in Canadian politics, i.e., governmental elites have less frequently had to be convinced of the propriety of accommodating group claims, compared with the United States" (1974, p. 218). The Canadian and American environmental interest groups studied are relatively similar on only 2 of the 10 strategies. Of the environmental organizations in Ontario, 50% report contacting cabinet ministers, and the same proportion (52%) of the Michigan groups submit reports to the governor's office. Approximately one in five of the Ontario groups (21 percent) pursue the organization of political protests, and about one in four of the comparable environmental organizations in Michigan do the same (26 percent).

Cross-national differences were expected on two other lobbying methods. Ontario groups were believed to be engaged in quiet techniques—like letter writing—to a greater degree than those in Michigan; the reverse pattern was expected concerning the use of lawsuits. The greater American propensity for litigation is evident among the Michigan groups; 30% of these groups have filed lawsuits, compared to only

Table 6.2
Cross-National Differences in Methods Used to Influence Policy-Making at the Provincial or State Level of Government

METHODS USED TO INFLUENCE GOVERNMENT POLICY MAKING	ONTARIO GROUPS	MICHIGAN GROUPS	Chi-Square (p)
Briefs to parliamentary committees (ONT) OR testifying before legislative committees (MI)	47%	61%	1.05 (.31)
Briefs to cabinet ministers (ONT) OR submitting reports to the governor's office (MI)	50%	52%	0.03 (.87)
Appeals to executive assistants of cabinet ministers (ONT) OR appeals to agency personnel (MI)	42%	74%	5.84 (.02)
Briefs or appeals by outside experts-- lawyers, former officials, scientists	21%	44%	3.46 (.06)
Contacts with government regulatory bodies	55%	74%	2.12 (.15)
Filing court suits	11%	30%	3.84 (.05)
Instigating a letter writing campaign	58%	70%	0.83 (.36)
Building coalitions with other groups	55%	70%	1.23 (.27)
Releasing information through the mass media	63%	70%	0.26 (.61)
Organizing political protests	21%	26%	0.21 (.65)

11% of the Ontario groups. However, the Michigan groups also engage in higher levels of letter writing (70% percent) when compared to their Canadian counterparts (58%).

While 61% of the Michigan groups indicated that they testify regularly before legislative committees, fewer than half (47%) of the Ontario groups do so. From the impressions gained in the interviews with group leaders, moreover, it would seem that even those Canadian environmental groups that do engage in this form of government contacting do not do so as frequently as comparable groups in the United States.

An explanation for this finding might be found in Graham White's recent analysis of the Ontario Legislative Assembly (1989). He reports that while this legislative body has displayed only limited independence from control by the premier and cabinet governmental authorities historically, it has gathered increased capacity to act as a policy-making body in recent years by means of a series of institutional reforms. White concludes that "interest groups in Ontario, particularly those of greater size and influence, are increasingly seeking to legitimize their positions . . . by appearing before legislative committees" (p. 259). It would seem that the historical differences separating Ontario and Michigan are diminishing; this is an observation we have made earlier with respect to other comparisons, and it is a theme to which we return in the concluding chapter of this book.

Lobbying agency personnel is another method used extensively by environmental interest groups in Michigan (74%), but this activity is used much less frequently among the Ontario groups (42%). In the interviews held with government officials and group leaders, it was clear that access to civil service employees is much more restricted in the Canadian province than is the case in the American state's setting. These survey results serve to confirm the view that contact with ministry personnel continues to be far less frequent in Ontario than in Michigan.

CROSS-NATIONAL COMPARISON OF COMMUNICATION PATTERNS

The second part of the analysis explores cross-national differences in the way the Michigan and Ontario environmental interest groups perform their information-sharing role in their respective political settings. The exploration of this area of activity begins with a look at the types of information most likely to figure in group communication efforts. Canadian–American differences and similarities are assessed in terms of the types of information—scientific, technical, legal, political, and economic—communicated and the frequency of interactions reported with respect to several categories of provincial and state government officials.

The next step in the investigation of cross-national differences in this area relates to two dimensions of group communicative activities, namely, informational capacity and communication effort. The first dimension reflects the group's ability to gather and create a variety of types of research information, and the second concept pertains to the extent to which environmental group personnel work to disseminate a broad range of types of information to both group members and government officials. The empirical analysis of data gathered concerning these activities in the profile surveys concludes with an exploration of cross-national differences in bivariate relationships between informational capacity and communication effort, and the comparison of the relative foci of organizational efforts and frequency of group contacts with specific government actors.

Table 6.3 sets forth results on bivariate relationships between information types communicated and the focus of interactions with government officials. In this table, gamma coefficients are listed separately for Ontario and Michigan for relationships between each of five types of information—scientific, technical, legal, political, and economic—and indicators of the frequency of interaction with elected officials, top-level bureaucrats, mid-level bureaucrats, public agency legal experts, and public agency scientific experts. In answer to the question posed earlier regarding what types of information would be transmitted to government officials most often, the answer is all types except political information. Among the Ontario groups, there is a relatively strong relationship (gamma = 0.72) between political information and frequency of interactions with elected officials in the province, but it is the only noteworthy coefficient associated with the measure of political information.

The types of information that figure in frequent contacts with provincial officials among Ontario group personnel are primarily legal and economic, and these are followed in importance by the transmission of technical and scientific information. The Michigan organizations also concentrate on communicating scientific, legal, and economic information in their frequent interactions with a variety of government officials, but there are fewer noteworthy relationships between type of information and frequency of interactions with government officials in Michigan than there are in Ontario.

Table 6.4 lists results for the analysis of cross-national differences on measures of informational capacity and scope of communication efforts. Percentages are reported for the highest value of each indicator of informational capacity and scope of communication effort, which was cross-tabulated with the variable representing Ontario or Michigan; chi-square values also are listed.

The indicators of informational capacity reported are (1) number of external sources utilized to compile advocative information on environmental problems, (2) number of types of research information (scientific/technical, legal, political, economic) used by groups, and (3) the extent to which groups generated some or all of their own information across the four types of information listed above. Four indicators are reported for the concept of scope of communication effort: (1) the percentage of total staff time devoted to educational activities, political activities, or

Table 6.3
Relationships between Type of Information Communicated to Provincial/State Government Officials and the Frequency of Group Interaction with These Officials by Country

Frequent Interaction with Government Officials		TYPE OF INFORMATION COMMUNICATED				
		Scientific	Technical	Legal	Political	Economic
Elected Officials	ONT	.46[a]	.55	.79	.72	.72
	MI	.53	.38	.76	.28	-.02
Top-Level Bureaucrats	ONT	.27	.43	.58	.14	.58
	MI	.55	.26	.46	.17	.27
Mid-Level Bureaucrats	ONT	.37	.69	.51	.33	.59
	MI	.45	.04	.09	.16	.39
Legal Experts	ONT	.17	.27	.66	.19	.74
	MI	.49	.42	.56	.27	.54
Scientific Experts	ONT	.56	.20	.49	-.07	.48
	MI	.13	.10	.33	.15	.48

[a] Gamma coefficients

Note: Each of the information types is a dichotomous variable, where 1 = type of information *is* communicated; 0 = type of information is *not* communicated.

Table 6.4
Cross-National Differences on Measures of Informational Capacity and Scope of Communication Efforts

	ONTARIO GROUPS (N=38)	MICHIGAN GROUPS (N=23)	Chi-Square (p)
Informational Capacity:			
Use of 5 to 7 External Sources of Research Information	50%	70%	2.24 (.13)
Use of All Four Types of Research Information	58%	83%	3.97 (.05)
Groups That Generate Much of Their Own Research	18%	26%	11.34 (.02)
Scope of Communication Efforts:			
Staff Spends from 80% to 100% of Time on Communication	34%	30%	3.06 (.22)
Group Uses 5 to 9 Means to Communicate with Members	58%	61%	0.05 (.82)
Many Types of Information Are Communicated to Elected Officials	32%	57%	5.46 (.02)
Many Types of Information Are Communicated to Career Civil Servants	32%	57%	8.56 (.07)

scientific research, (2) the number of means groups employ to communicate with their members from among a list of nine possible methods, (3) the number of types of information communicated to state or provincial elected officials, and (4) the number of types of information communicated to state or provincial career civil servants.

The Michigan groups have higher values on the three measures of informational capacity than do their Canadian counterparts. While 70% of the Michigan groups use from 5 to 7 external sources to compile information on environmental problems, only 50% of the Ontario groups use as many external sources. Similarly, 83% of the Michigan groups rely on all types of information; the comparable percentage for the Ontario groups is 58%. Finally, while 26% of the Michigan groups generate a considerable amount of their own research information, only 18% of Ontario groups do so.

When the measures of communication effort are compared, however, the results are not nearly as one-sided. The environmental groups in both national settings are relatively similar in the amount of time staff members devote to the communication of information; 34% of the Ontario environmental interest groups and 30% of those in Michigan report staff spending from 80% to 100% of their time on educational activities. There is also little difference in the number of means used to inform group members, which could include the distribution of a newsletter, the publication of a magazine, the holding of periodic membership meetings, the issuance of special reports or pamphlets, the organization of workshops or short courses, the making of videotapes or films, and the preparation of articles or new releases for community or regional newspapers, radio, and television. Well over half of the groups (58% in Ontario and 61% in Michigan) report using from 5 to 9 of these methods to communicate information to their members, contributors, and potential members.

The Ontario and Michigan environmental groups, however, differ rather considerably in the number of types of information communicated, both to elected officials and to career civil servants. Of the 5 types of information considered (scientific, technical, legal, political, and economic), 57% of the Michigan groups report communicating from 3 to 5 of these types of information, and this percentage is the same for activities directed toward elected officials and toward career civil servants. Only 32% of the Ontario environmental groups report the same range of types of information being communicated to Ontario's elected officials and career bureaucrats.

These results demonstrate that the Michigan environmental interest groups surveyed have a greater capability to gather and create policy-relevant information and to communicate a wider range of types of information to government officials than do their Canadian counterparts. The next step is to explore the profile survey findings for cross-national differences and similarities with respect to bivariate relationships between communication resources (informational capacity and communication effort) and the nature and frequency of these groups' governmental contacts. Gamma coefficients are reported in Table 6.5 for the relationships among each of the measures of government contacts and two indicators of informational capacity (number of external sources used and the range of information types gathered) and two measures of communication effort (number of means of communication

Table 6.5
Relationships between Measures of Informational Capacity and Scope of Communication Efforts and Measures of Contacts with Government Officials

		Range of External Sources Used	Range of Information Types Gathered	Range of Means Used to Inform Members	Percentage of Time Spent by Staff on Information
Contacts with Government Officials:					
Frequent Interaction with National Officials	ONT	.61*	.63	.21	.43
	MI	.32	.37	.56	.18
Frequent Interaction with Provincial/State Officials	ONT	.59	.85	.42	.35
	MI	-.06	-.16	.11	.49
Frequent Interaction with Local Officials	ONT	.50	.77	.63	.20
	MI	-.20	-.27	-.45	.24
Number of Services Provided to Legislators	ONT	.61	.69	.15	.22
	MI	.86	.48	.45	.18
Number of Services Provided to Career Civil Servants	ONT	.45	.53	.21	.15
	MI	.65	-.08	.56	-.06
Number of Methods Used to Influence Government Policy-Making	ONT	.83	.81	.33	.30
	MI	.38	.47	.11	.49

*Table entries are gammas.

with members and the time spent by staff on transmitting information). The results are reported separately for the Ontario and Michigan environmental interest groups.

The patterns of bivariate interrelationships for the Ontario and Michigan environmental interest groups differ considerably. For the Ontario groups, both number of external sources and breadth of types of information communicated are associated with all of the following: frequency of interactions with government officials at the national, provincial, and local levels; the number of services provided to legislators and civil servants; and the number of types of interest group strategies employed. Environmental organizations in the Canadian province may have fewer informational capacity resources than their counterparts in Michigan, but these results suggest that Ontario groups with high levels of informational capacity in fact are engaging in quite frequent interactions with government officials. Although the Michigan environmental interest groups, in comparison, use a wider range of outside sources than do their counterparts to the north to generate policy-relevant information, the range of external sources used by groups in Michigan has a noteworthy correlation with only two types of contacts—services provided to state legislators and to Michigan state career civil servants.

Michigan environmental groups also are more likely than Ontario groups to use all types of information (scientific, technical, legal, political, economic); however, the range of information types is correlated moderately with only two of the six types of government contacts listed in Table 6.5. These two types of contacts are breadth of services provided to legislators in the state and number of interest group strategies employed.

Environmental groups using a wide variety of means to communicate with their memberships in Michigan tend to have frequent contacts with national-level officials, and they are inclined to provide a wide range of services to legislators and career civil servants. For Ontario groups, in contrast, the number of means used to communicate with members is related to frequent contacts with government officials on both the provincial and local levels but not on the national level. Finally, those groups in Ontario reporting considerable amounts of staff time being spent on informational activities tend to have more frequent interactions with national officials. Their environmental activist counterparts in Michigan, in comparison, report more frequent contacts with state officials and use a wider variety of lobbying techniques if considerable amounts of their association's staff time is being devoted to informational activities.

This bivariate analysis of the organizational profile survey results suggests that relationships between communication resources and both the nature and the frequency of government contacts are rather different in the two national settings. Although in the aggregate the Ontario environmental interest groups do not give evidence of the same levels of informational capacity and the same scope of communication effort as do their counterparts to the south, the ability to gather a broad range of information types from a large number of sources is more important in distinguishing among Canadian groups than it is among their American opposites. In Ontario, the transmission of policy-relevant information—including that which is scientific, technical, legal, economic, and political—from sources other than the group itself consistently is associated with more frequent group interactions with government officials at all levels of Canadian government. It also is associated with a larger number of services being provided to legislators and career civil servants, and with a more extensive range of lobbying techniques being employed by the groups in question.

The patterns of statistical interrelationships between separate measures of informational capacity and government contacts in Ontario supports the prescription offered by elites in this Canadian province that environmental interest groups should contribute to the policy process primarily by performing an educational role, one that is regarded as a quiet, dignified, and nonconfrontational type of political involvement. In contrast, the relationships between the measures of communication effort and government contacts, which may be interpreted as a more action-oriented way of assessing the information-sharing role of interest groups than is the assessment of informational capacity, suggest that government contacts increase with communication effort for the Michigan groups to a greater degree than for their Ontario counterparts. This pattern, however, is not consistent across all of the indicators.

One interesting finding to be noted in the Michigan profile survey is that group efforts to communicate with their members and contributors tend to be associated with a reduction in the level of interaction occurring with local officials; at the same time, interactions with national-level officials, state legislators, and Michigan state career civil servants are correlated positively with communication effort. This finding likely reflects the realistic assessment that effective control of environmental problems very often requires a regional, state, national, or even global perspective, even though the effects of such problems might seem localized to those most directly affected by them (Gorz 1980; Nash 1989, pp. 55–86). For example, while the protection of the northern spotted owl in the ancient forests of the states of Oregon and Washington might be seen as a salient problem for timber and logging towns in those states, the real issue is one of great consequence not only to those two states and to the timber and housing industries nationally, but also to the movement of forest products trade around the Pacific Rim global region (Wenk 1986, pp. 187–228). Of course, the same line of reasoning applies to the issue of acid rain, the particular common focus of the Canada and American environmental interest groups studied here (Fiorino 1990).

CONCLUSION

Political system differences do affect the communication patterns of environmental interest groups in Ontario and Michigan primarily because access to government officials differs importantly cross-nationally. Environmental interest groups in Michigan actively and visibly interact with a broad range of government officials to a significantly greater degree than do comparable groups in Ontario. The focus of efforts to secure access in a political system "is determined by where power lies in the system" (Presthus 1974, p. 220). The environmental interest group leaders in Michigan apparently recognize well the fragmented nature of power in their system of government, and they clearly make great effort to interact with many of the various actors involved in the environmental policy-making process.

Access to many types of policymakers in the American state, however, should not be interpreted as being equivalent to exercising effective political influence. Environmental group leaders in Michigan tend to act on the belief that, in order to be effective in their advocacy of pro-environmental positions, environmental organizations have to be as visible and active as the many private sector interests that are competing for the attention of state decision makers and the media reporting on their activities and decisions. Their voice is only one among many voices deemed to be legitimate participants in the democratic political process of the United States. Depending upon the financial condition of the automobile industry and Michigan's general economic outlook, the voices of those representing the utilities and major industries sometimes exercise disproportionate influence on policy-making in this arena notwithstanding a public citizenry that generally is quite sympathetic to the environmental lobby.

The greater centralization of power present in the parliamentary system of Ontario has a noticeable effect on contacts with mid-level bureaucratic officials. Contact with career civil servants in the provincial ministries is far less common in Ontario than in Michigan. In the American state, civil servants are quite clearly among several of the most important targets of environmental interest group lobbying efforts. This finding is consistent with Leman's (1980) conclusion that bureaucrats in the United States are more independent and freer to pursue policy goals than are their counterparts in the Canadian parliamentary system. What was true of the welfare policy arena in his research also would appear to be true of the environmental area as well.

Although information has been referred to as the "most valuable benefit legislators receive from interest groups" (Presthus 1974, p. 215), there are clear cross-national differences in legislative contacts. Members of the Ontario Legislative Assembly currently play a more prominent role in policy formulation than they did in the past, but interacting with legislators is not yet as vital to groups in Ontario as it is to interest group representatives in Michigan. White draws the following conclusions about group interactions with the Ontario Legislative Assembly: "Interest group leaders often make public presentations to legislative committees not so much because they believe that they can affect policy, but because they wish to justify themselves to their membership. Nevertheless, lobbyists do take the legislature and its members seriously as contributors to the policy process" (1989, p. 255). Ontario group leaders who were a part of this study do not ignore legislative contacts, but they accord them less significance than do environmental group leaders in Michigan. There is some evidence to suggest that this is an area in which convergence in political practices likely is coming about in Canada and the United States. It is possible that the "green lobbies" of Canada and the United States will come to display more similar behaviors in the 1990s than they have hitherto (Mitchell 1990).

Political system differences affect both the role environmental interest groups play in the two policy systems and the tactics those groups employ to transmit policy-relevant information. Here, the consensual nature of the Canadian setting stands in sharp contrast to the competitive flavor of the American political system. Although groups in both governmental systems provide information on environmental issues to the authorities and to their members and contributors, the Ontario environmental interest groups are not as actively engaged in the range of strategies environmental groups in Michigan use to influence the policy process. Ontario group leaders, more so than their Michigan counterparts, use policy-relevant information as the basis for their interactions with government officials. Many groups in Ontario do pursue a less obvious, quiet involvement in politics, and this involvement relies rather extensively on the communication of policy-relevant information.

NOTE

1. Personal interviews were conducted with 24 government officials and directors of prominent environmental organizations in Michigan and Ontario in the summer of 1987. The 13 individuals interviewed in the American state included appropriate representatives from all significant state governmental bodies and statewide environmental groups actively involved in the issue of acid rain deposition. The 11 individuals interviewed in the Canadian province also included the relevant government officials, but only leaders from a representative cross-section of the types of groups involved in this policy arena could be included because of the large number of environmental organizations active in the province. Efforts were made to match all group and governmental interviewers in one country with their equivalents in the other national setting.

Chapter Seven

Interest Groups, Individuals, and the Technical Information Quandary

This study addresses the question of how citizens in contemporary democratic countries might cope with the "technical information quandary." That quandary stems from diverse effects attributable to the advent of postindustrial society. The postindustrial condition is one of long-lasting economic and physical security, relative affluence in standard of living for a broad spectrum of citizens, and a high degree of development of communications channels and the widespread dissemination of knowledge via high levels of literacy and easy access to mass media. These societal conditions are associated with rapid technological, social, and economic change, followed in time by predictable changes in societal values, particularly with respect to cross-generational differences in outlook and beliefs.

Under these conditions, democratic publics are inclined to express increasingly greater desire for influence over issues of public policy, while at the same time many of these public policy controversies in question are becoming significantly more scientifically complex and difficult for the average citizen to understand. How is the conscientious, involved, committed citizen to cope with such scientifically and technologically complex issues as acid rain deposition, endangered species protection, in vitro fertilization, and the like in a way that will produce informed and reasoned behavior in the pursuit of either individual interests or their own view of the public interest? Are the knowledge barriers to informed participation so great that it is necessary to give up the hope of the public effectively acquiring, processing, and applying policy-relevant information to their decisions about the appropriate directions government should take on such questions? Has the postindustrial democratic polity progressed to a point where its own successes in conquering the mysteries of science and technology have created the conditions for failure in accommodating the higher-order needs of civic involvement and sense of personal connection to public life (Kaplan 1976, pp. 115-130)?

Various apparent solutions to the technical information quandary are available, many of which seem rather inconsistent with Western traditions of liberal democratic thought. As we noted in Chapter 1, most efficiency-oriented solutions advocate that the public be restricted from having direct access to the arenas of decision making, leaving the most critical public policy choices to elites of one kind or another—technocratic, political, or social/economic (Abrahamson 1977; Brooks 1975, 1984). Some optimists argue, of course, that mass education efforts could be invoked in attempts to bring all participating citizens to some essential minimal knowledge level, thereby providing the foundation for genuine mass participation in any area of public policy seriously affecting the public welfare (Habermas 1971; House 1981; Miles and Gershung 1986; Yankelovich 1991). The option is available, of course, for us to throw up our hands in despair and let the existing processes of collective choice continue to muddle along, counting on the vagaries of good luck and fortune and the public spiritedness of a few exemplary citizens to carry us through to the future (Kelman 1988).

This study has investigated the role interest groups might play as one important means for the public to cope with the extraordinary demands of democratic participation in the postindustrial era. In some ways, the investigation of this topic represents a leap backward into the past to glimpse a view of what the future might hold. Interest group democracy has been a staple of political science theory and practice since the early part of this century, with particular prominence being given group theories of politics in the 1950s and 1960s. There followed this period of virtual paradigmatic disciplinary dominance a time of rapid and severe decline in the putative legitimacy and analytical efficacy of the concept of interest group democracy. Not only were interest groups seen as being unlikely to represent the total array of legitimate interests in modern society, but they also were seen as too often being irrelevant to the kinds of citizen concerns and policy preferences characterizing the contemporary political environment of postindustrial democracies. The new politics issues that produced the single issue interest group and the public interest group did not fit well with the traditional economic-based organizations that had dominated the political playing field in the days of the early group theorists (White 1988, pp. 23-36).

Our study has examined the possibility that interest groups may be newly relevant to the kinds of public policy issues that produce the technical information quandary. We have tried to identify some of the conditions that would lead one to conclude that there exists the potential for interest groups to act as a link between democratic publics and the effective resolution of public policy issues entailing significant scientific and technological content. These conditions are of three quite distinct kinds: effects of political culture, interests and motivations, and group characteristics.

The first condition pertains to the effects of political culture upon both the individuals and the interest group organizations operating in differing national settings. In order to investigate this aspect of interest group phenomena, we designed a study that allowed us to compare individuals and organizations operating on the same issue (acid rain) in two different political cultures, with the differences in culture having direct potential implications for the resolution of the technical information quandary. The second condition has to do with the interests and motivations of citizens among the general public and those citizens who choose to affiliate with environmental interest groups. In this regard, we looked at whether individuals are driven, at least in part, to participate in interest groups on the basis of a desire for information about salient public policy issues, and whether their evaluations of the sources of policy-relevant information are tied to their own public policy orientations in any systematic way. The third condition we investigated entailed focusing on the characteristics of the interest group organizations themselves. Here we were interested in the degree to which the interest groups devoted efforts to respond to the public's need for policy-relevant information and used such information themselves in attempting to influence the course of public policy on the acid rain issue.

On the matter of cultural effects, just as the role of interest groups in a political system may change over time as the conditions and expectations for group activities and objectives also change, so may the nature of interest group activity differ among political systems at any single point in time to the degree that the respective political cultures differ in conditions and expectations for interest groups in their society. To isolate the impact of differing political cultures on the role of interest groups, it is important to find cases in which the prevailing relevant conditions are relatively similar. In this case, we needed to compare the American case with that of another country that has had evidence of important historical interest group activity, a lengthy tradition of democratic institutions and practices, and postindustrial attributes that would produce public policy issues exacerbating the technical information quandary.

These several analytical requirements led us to examine simultaneously the potential information-disseminating role of environmental interest groups in the Canadian province of Ontario and the American state of Michigan. The two countries indeed do share a common historical heritage of British rule and English common law, but their respective political cultures and governmental institutions have been regarded widely to have developed along distinct though parallel tracks (Lipset 1990a). Both Canada and the United States clearly are situated among the set of distinctly postindustrial democratic nations. Finally, very important for the analysis undertaken here, these two countries share a common concern with environmental politics generally, and with the issue of acid rain deposition in lakes and forests in particular (Cooper 1987).

The shared salience of environmental policy in Canada and the United States and politics generally, and the mutual salience of acid rain deposition issues specifically, is particularly critical to the study presented here. The environmental policy arena is one that taps directly into the core of postindustrial politics, with connections to distinctive value structures that arise among mass publics in such societies and that contribute directly to the advent of the technical information quandary. Such value structure changes as are in evidence, moreover, would appear to be concentrated among younger age cohorts, suggesting that environmental concerns and the desire for citizen involvement in policy formation are likely to persist or even intensify as generational replacement occurs (Dunlap 1989).

Environmental policy choices involve clear trade-offs between the traditional materialist values of economic growth and national security and the postmaterial values of empathy for the disadvantaged, aesthetics, nature preservation, and the integration of the needs and interests of humans with all other species sharing the world's ecology. The environmental policy arena has a direct connection to the distinctive postmaterial values of younger postindustrial age cohorts, the members of which manifest a strong attachment to public involvement in the political and administrative processes that produce policy outcomes for contemporary society. And, importantly, environmental policy questions frequently are of such extreme technical and scientific complexity that making informed choices among rival policy options is problematic at best, even for the specially trained experts. Acid rain clearly falls into this category of scientifically complex content (National Academy of Sciences 1983).

As a case of environmental policy generally, acid rain seems particularly appropriate for this analysis. Acid rain deposition is environmentally degrading, it is relatively diffuse and unrestricted to national borders, its sources can be identified with some specificity, its control will exact significant economic costs, there has been significant political activity within both Canada and the United States (and between the two countries) in attempts to influence acid rain policy, and many of the arguments about the sources, consequences, and proper ameliorative policies for minimizing acid rain are heavily laden with both scientific and technical content (Cowling 1982). Moreover, acid rain relates directly to the value trade-offs between the materialist and postmaterialist values that are central to postindustrial politics. Consequently, one finds a rich context within which to compare Canadian and American interest group responses to the technical information quandary as they are played out in the acid rain issue setting.

Chapter 2 presented findings that show how some of the most widely discussed hypotheses accounting for differences existing between the American and Canadian political cultures—differences that might structure the political communication role of interest groups—hold some empirical weight. However, as is generally the case in complex social phenomena, the empirical results are considerably more complicated than the several literature-based hypotheses would suggest. That is, as expected, Ontario residents are more likely to be postmaterialists than are their Michigan counterparts, but cross-national convergence in these values in the Canadian and American settings is greater among environmental interest group activists than among the general public.

There is also some empirical evidence of Canadian–American convergence in libertarian values among the young people who share adherence to postmaterial values. Canadians also perceive greater cooperation in politics and are more accepting of government regulations than are Americans. Consequently, it would appear that the value convergence occurring among activists is taking place in the face of continuing partial cultural separation in the larger society; these conditions serve to exert some important cross-pressures on the interest group system. The result is a pattern of similarity at the groups' activity levels that may or may not permeate into the relationships of those groups to the remainder of their respective political communities.

In order to delve more deeply into the connections existing between Canadian and American citizens and their respective interest groups active in the environmental arena, Chapter 3 investigated the extent to which Michigan and Ontario citizens and environmental interest group activists differ in their trust of various sources of policy-relevant information and in the foundations of variations of that trust. The findings reported in that chapter suggested only marginal evidence of a political culture effect on the informational trust beliefs of Americans and Canadians. In both Canada and the United States, activists and lay citizens accord some information sources more trust than they do other sources. In both locations, the same types of sources of information are given more trust than others. In both Michigan and Ontario, variations in the trust of certain information sources are associated systematically with variations in individual attitudinal and demographic attributes that may be surrogates for self-interest. Within these overarching similarities, though, Canadian citizens remain somewhat more trusting generally than do their American counterparts, although the differences in general trust level are less extreme within the younger cohorts than within the older age groups.

Chapters 2 and 3 thus indicated some divergence in the traditional political cultures of Canada and the United States, but also mounting evidence of growing similarity among activists and younger cohorts. Indeed, as the focus of analytical attention narrows more precisely on interest group-relevant concerns, some of the cross-national similarities uniting Canada and the United States emerge even more clearly. These similarities suggest a common potential for having interest groups play an important political communication role in linking contemporary citizens to the public policy process in highly complex policy areas in both countries.

In Chapter 4, the analysis shifted to a consideration of whether individuals are motivated to any noteworthy degree by the desire for additional information in coming to their individual decisions to affiliate with environmental interest groups. Our survey results indicate rather clearly that environmental interest group members are more likely than nonmembers to desire additional policy-relevant information, even when holding constant the respondent's environmental policy values. Moreover, group members in both countries identify information as a more important factor in their group membership than political, material, or solidary incentives. In both the Ontario and Michigan settings, information gathering as an incentive to group membership tends to be joined by political goals for many individuals; this inclination to join informational and political incentives is somewhat stronger in the American location than in the Canadian setting. Group members in Ontario are more likely to report information as an incentive without associated political goals than is the case in Michigan. In addition, joining political goals with information goals makes a greater difference among Michigan group members than among their Ontario counterparts in terms of the kinds of environmental policy preferences they express. Thus, from Chapter 1 through Chapter 4, the study documents the presence of evidence from two postindustrial democratic countries that conditions clearly exist for policy-relevant information seeking to be a salient source of interest group membership. In addition, the results reported in the first four chapters indicate that, while common conditions exist within the two political cultures generally, there is greater cross-national similarity at the activist level than at the level of the general public.

Chapters 5 and 6 shifted the analytical focus from individual group members to an examination of the interest groups themselves. Do environmental interest groups endeavor to develop and disseminate policy-relevant information as an important aspect of their work? What kinds of environmental information capacity and scope of communication efforts do they exhibit? Do the information-relevant resources available to an organization serve to structure its contacts with government officials, its own members, and potential members? How do information-relevant resources available to a group relate to the perception of group successes entertained by group leaders?

Some common patterns of group activity do indeed appear in the Michigan and Ontario settings, but more cross-national differences are evident in organizational behavior than in the analysis of individual members of the public or individual members of environmental organizations. For example, Michigan environmental organizations interact with a much broader range of officials than do their Ontario counterparts. Moreover, the Ontario environmental interest groups studied are not as actively engaged in the full range of interest group strategies as are the Michigan groups included in our study. It should be noted, of course, that both Michigan and Ontario environmental interest groups rely extensively in carrying out their activities on the communication of policy-relevant information to their members and lay citizens.

THE INTERSECTION OF INDIVIDUAL
AND GROUP ATTRIBUTES

This final chapter takes the analysis of interest group potential for overcoming the technical information quandary one more brief step in trying to fit together the puzzle of interest group political communication phenomena. To this point, we have looked separately at individuals as members of groups and at the groups themselves. However, it remains to be seen whether there is an empirical coupling of individual behavior and group behavior in such a way as to demonstrate that citizens who seek policy-relevant information systematically turn to the most relevant interest groups as important sources of aid in overcoming the technical information quandary.

Individual Incentives and Group Characteristics

In this aspect of our analysis, it is useful to recall that information gathering surfaced as a primary incentive for individual citizens making the choice to join environmental interest groups in both Michigan and Ontario. It is also important to recall as well that the environmental interest groups studied in both Ontario and Michigan varied considerably in their uses of information. The question then surfaces, of course, as to whether citizens affiliate with groups possessing characteristics that match their own motivation vis-à-vis information seeking. The findings reported in Table 7.1 serve as a first step in answering that question.

Table 7.1 presents the relationship between organizational attributes and the reasons given by members of their organization for joining the group. In the context of our study, our primary interest is in whether interest groups that give greater emphasis to information in their interactions with members and with government officials than other groups are more likely to have members for whom information is a major motive for joining the group. The causal connection between the two, of course, may be reciprocal. That is, individuals may join a group in order to maximize their information returns and thus choose the organization that offers the most information to them. Conversely, the environmen-

Table 7.1
Relationship of Organizational Attributes and Member Reasons for Joining Groups*

	ORGANIZATIONAL ATTRIBUTES					
	Number Of Ways To Inform Members		Number Of Types Of Research		Number Of Sources Used For Information	
Reasons for Joining	U.S.	Can	U.S.	Can	U.S.	Can
Social	-.06	.18[b]	.11	-.11[a]	.10	-.11
Political	-.02	.17[b]	.47[c]	.24[c]	.40[c]	.22[c]
Informational	-.19[b]	-.08	.14[a]	-.09	.06	-.01
Economic	-.20[b]	.13[a]	.12	-.26[c]	.05	-.21[b]
Issue	-.11	.14[a]	.23[b]	-.07	.16[a]	.04

[a] $p \leq .05$

[b] $p \leq .01$

[c] $p \leq .001$

* *Entry in each cell is the correlation (r) between individuals' reasons for joining a particular group and the information attributes of the organizations they joined.*

tal organization and its leaders may be responding to the information needs and demands of group members.

The organizational attributes of the environmental interest groups studied here were introduced in Chapters 5 and 6. The first attribute is the number of different ways—from the following listing—the organization tries to inform its members: publishing a newsletter or magazine; holding regular meetings; issuing special reports; conducting short courses; producing videotapes or films; preparing stories for newspaper, radio, and television journalists; and "other" forms. The second organizational attribute is the number of types of research employed by the organization: scientific or technical, legal, political, and economic were the types provided. The third indicator is the number of sources used by the organization to compile its information: organizational affiliates, other environmental organizations, scientists or experts in universities, lawyers, elected officials and their staffs, nonelected government personnel, and "others" were the options of choices. The measure of member reasons for joining is drawn from Chapter 4; each respondent was asked to indicate on a scale that ranged from one to four the importance of each of five possible reasons for joining their particular interest group. Those reasons include social, political, informational, and economic motivations, or the presence of a concern for a specific environmental issue.

It is clear from Table 7.1 that certain of the organizational information attributes are related to the reasons given by their members for joining the particular organizations they have chosen. It is important to note, however, that those relationships vary by the reason for joining, the organizational attribute in question, and the particular national setting in which the members and their organizations operate.

The "political" incentive to interest group membership is the most sensitive to variation in the organizational attributes. Significant relationships exist in five of the six possible cases. Moreover, the largest relationships in the entire table also appear in the row for political incentives. Generally speaking, then, the more important the political incentive is to an interest group member, the more likely it is that the member belongs to a group with greater numbers of ways to inform members (Canada only), greater numbers of types of research, and a greater number of sources used for compiling policy-relevant information. Thus, independent of the importance of information to the individual, the information activity of the group is critical to attracting politically motivated individuals to group membership. It is important to note as well that the magnitude of this relationship is much greater in Michigan than it is in Ontario. Thus, for American activists, the correlations between the importance of political incentives and number of types of research and number of information sources are $r = .47$ ($p \leq .001$) and $r =$

.40 ($p \leq .001$), compared to $r = .24$ ($p \leq .001$) and $r = .22$ ($p \leq .001$) among the Canadian activists. This pattern may reflect the hypothesized cultural and political system differences in which Canadian interest groups are thought to be less political than are American interest groups. Recall, as well, from Chapter 4, that the political and the informational incentives to group membership are less likely to be joined in the same individuals in the Canadian province than they are in the American state.

Ironically, the information incentive has only two significant relationships to the organizational information attributes, and both of those are present in the Michigan sample. In fact, the information incentive has a negative relationship ($r = -.19$; $p \leq .01$) to the number of ways groups inform their members in Michigan, but a positive relationship with the number of types of research the groups utilize ($r = .14$; $p \leq .05$). Thus, it appears that the information motivation connects with group affiliation through the quality and substantive scope of the information types used by the group rather than through the number of channels used to disseminate that information to group members. Environmental interest group members in the United States who are driven by the information incentive may need fewer mechanisms for obtaining that information from their group if they are convinced that the group has done its job well in acquiring that information.

The economic incentive is related significantly to organizational attributes in four of the six possible cases, with three of the four significant correlations occurring in the Ontario columns. In the Canadian setting, greater internal group investment in the generation of information is related *negatively* to having members with economic motives for joining, but positively associated with the number of channels employed for disseminating information to members. The members who give priority to the specific environmental issue-based incentive are linked to increased group investment in information gathering in Michigan in a way similar to the pattern found for the political incentive for affiliation.

Overall, then, the most prominent finding with respect to which incentive is the most directly connected to group characteristics is the preeminence of the linkage between group information activities and the recruitment of members who join in order to pursue political goals. This strong connection stands in contrast to a weak relationship between the information-gathering incentive to membership and the level of the organization's commitment to information gathering and dissemination to its members.

An important second perspective on the relationships evident in the findings displayed in Table 7.1 is found when focusing on the relative impact of the three types of organizational attributes. Generally speaking, little difference emerges among those attributes with respect to the absolute number of statistically significant relationships with group member motives for affiliation. However, there is some interaction between attribute and national setting in the direction of those relationships. Often, the significant relationships found are in opposite directions when they appear simultaneously in the Ontario and Michigan findings. For example, the measure of the number of channels the group uses to inform its members is related negatively to all of the incentives for affiliation in Michigan, but positively related to all of them in Ontario. Similarly, the number of types of research used in developing organizational information generally is correlated in a positive direction with the incentives for affiliation among Michigan group members, but in a negative direction among their Ontario counterparts (with the exception of the political incentive). A similar, though less dramatic, pattern of cross-national difference exists for the number of sources used to compile policy-relevant information. It is important to note that one of the incentives for affiliation does not follow this general pattern of opposite effects in Michigan and Ontario. The political incentive for membership is related positively to the three characteristics in five of the six correlations listed in Table 7.1. The primary role of this member motivation for affiliation once again is apparent from this review of the effects attributable to organizational characteristics.

An additional cross-national difference should be noted. Canadian and American citizens differ in how their individual incentives for affiliation relate to the information activities of the groups to which they belong. Generally, among Michigan environmental interest group members, the internal *information-generating* activities tend to induce membership from individuals with high values on most of the incentives for affiliation, while among their Ontario counterparts, the inverse relationship exists. Similarly, among Michigan group members, the number of information-dissemination activities to members has a negative relationship with the importance of all five affiliation incentives, but a positive relationship with all five among Ontario environmental interest group members. As noted repeatedly in previous chapters, the way in which the dynamics of interest group operations play themselves out in the Canadian and American settings has been quite different in the past. More recently, some scholars have noted changes in the Canadian political system that have given Canadian interest groups a great deal more room to operate, and have argued that Canadian interest groups are becoming more like American interest groups in their activities and in the role they might play in linking citizens to public policy processes. These findings from Ontario and Michigan would suggest, of course, that Canadian–American differences remain quite strong in how interest groups connect to their members. If there is some degree of convergence occurring in the operation of interest groups in Canada and the United

States, it is safe to say that full equivalence of form and role function are quite far off yet, at least as judged from environmental interest groups in Ontario and Michigan.

The exception that stands out in these analyses is the political incentive for affiliation. A political goal as a highly valued incentive is linked strongly to all of the organizational attributes among both Canadian and American group members. Moreover, the absolute magnitudes of these correlations are the greatest given in the table, reinforcing the conclusion that the relationship between the information activities of the groups and their members' desire to influence public policy direction is an important aspect of interest group life in both the Canadian and the American settings investigated here.

Group Effort and Member Perceptions

Another important question is the degree to which group information effort is perceived by members to be useful to them. Table 7.2 reports findings concerning the relationship among group members' perceptions of the usefulness of group-provided information and the same three group information activities attributes used in the previous discussion. Three of the six bivariate relationships are statistically significant, albeit not particularly strong in their magnitude. In the Ontario setting, environmental interest group member perceptions of the usefulness of group information have a positive association with the number of ways the group informs its members ($r = .20$; $p \leq .001$) and the number of types of research in which the group engages ($r = .14$; $p \leq .01$). The latter relationship also is significant in the Michigan setting ($r = .16$; $p \leq .05$). In a somewhat sketchy form, then, these data suggest that interest group behavior with regard to information development and dissemination does make a difference in member perceptions of the utility of that information.

The first two parts of this analysis show evidence of a link between group information activity and the attitudes of group members, first with respect to incentives to group membership and second with respect to perceptions of information utility. We now move to the question of whether the incentive composition of a group's membership is linked to the group's own pattern of political communication activity. The question addressed here, of course, is whether group members pick and choose among groups in such a way that they affiliate with those groups offering the kind of informational feedback and action inventory consistent with their own preferences. Table 7.3 shows the methods of political influence used by groups in conjunction with the proportion of purists and politicos who are members of groups reporting that type of activity.

Table 7.2
Relationship of Organizational Attributes and Member Perceptions of Group Information Utility*

Organizational Information Attributes	United States	Canada
Number of Ways to Inform Members	-.08	.20[c]
Number of Types of Research by Group	.16[a]	.14[b]
Number of Sources used by Group for Information	.11	.11

[a] $p \leq .05$

[b] $p \leq .01$

[c] $p \leq .001$

* *Entry in each cell is the correlation (r) between perceptions of organizational information usefulness and three measures of organizational information activity.*

Group Characteristics, Purists, and Politicos

It is clear that purists and politicos (see Chapter 4 for definitions) belong to different kinds of interest groups in terms of the methods of political influence employed by these groups. It is also clear, moreover, that the difference between these two key types of group members is much greater in the Michigan setting than in Ontario. In both locations, the groups to which information politicos belong employ more methods of political influence than do the groups to which information purists belong. On only one such method is the difference the same in both countries. In both Michigan and Ontario, interest groups with numerous politicos are more likely to form coalitions with other interest groups than are the groups in which purists are more numerous. In the Canadian setting, the environmental interest groups in which politicos predominate are more likely than the groups in which purists are found in large percentages to appeal to executive assistants, to contact regulatory bodies, and to engage in political protest activities. In the American

Table 7.3
Methods of Political Influence Used by Groups of which Purists and Politicos are Members[a]

Method	Ontario		Michigan	
	Purists (55)	Politicos (97)	Purists (21)	Politicos (84)
Briefs/Legislator	.36	.45	.24	.82***
Briefs/Executives	.49	.55	.29	.68***
Appeals to Executive Assistants	.25	.52**	.76	.83
Briefs by Experts	.11	.20	.29	.51
Contact Regular Bodies	.45	.63*	.67	.82
Court Suits	.05	.10	.19	.45*
Letter Writing	.44	.60	.67	.77
Group Coalitions	.31	.52*	.52	.89***
Information by Media	.55	.67	.52	.89***
Political Protest	.05	.18*	.24	.80***
Number of Methods	3.07	4.40**	4.38	7.08***

* Difference is significant $p \leq .05$
** Difference is significant $p \leq .01$
***Difference is significant $p \leq .001$

[a] *The entry in each cell is the proportion of the purists or politicos in either Ontario or Michigan who belong to a group that uses the political influence methods listed along the left of the table.*

setting, the groups to which politicos belong are more likely to submit briefs to legislators and state executives (ministerial equivalents), to engage in court suits, to distribute information via the media and to engage in political protest activities. The predominant pattern to be noted in Table 7.3 is the substantial difference between results observed in the Canadian and American settings. The differences between politicos' and purists' groups are much greater among the Michigan groups than among their Ontario counterparts, and the level of political activity in general is much higher among the American environmental interest groups than among their Canadian counterparts. These differences are large enough that the purists' groups in Michigan are as engaged in political influence methods as are the Canadian politicos' groups. Similarly, the politicos' groups in Michigan used many more influence methods than the politicos' groups in Ontario.

Table 7.4 displays results indicating the frequency of external interaction with various types of policy-relevant informational sources located at both national and provincial/state levels by the citizen interest groups in which politicos and purists are members. The two types of groups differ in a number of cases, both at the national level and at the provincial/state level of political contact. Perhaps among the most interesting results concern cross-national differences in group interactions with sci-

Table 7.4
Average Frequency of Interaction with Others on National and State/Provincial Level for Groups of which Purists and Politicos are Members[a]

Object of Interaction	Ontario		Michigan	
	Purists	Politicos	Purists	Politicos
NATIONAL				
Elected Officials	2.37	2.87**	2.52	3.42***
Department Heads	2.35	3.05**	2.00	3.36***
Mid-level Bureaucrats	2.28	2.78**	2.05	3.54***
Legal Experts	1.58	1.88**	1.29	2.36***
Scientific Experts	2.37	2.56	1.81	3.25***
PROVINCIAL/STATE				
Elected Officials	2.93	3.74***	3.86	4.37*
Department Heads	2.70	3.45**	4.48	4.51
Mid-level Bureaucrats	2.74	3.35*	4.57	4.65
Legal Experts	1.78	2.18*	2.14	3.31***
Scientific Experts	2.52	2.86	3.43	4.07**
X̄	2.36	2.87	2.82	3.68

* Difference is significant $p \leq .05$
** Difference is significant $p \leq .01$
***Difference is significant $p \leq .001$

[a] *The entry in each cell is the average frequency of interaction by groups with others at the national and provincial/state level for groups of which purists and politicos are members. A higher average indicates a greater frequency of interaction.*

entific experts. Among the Michigan groups, but not so among their Ontario counterparts, politicos' groups are much more likely to interact with scientific experts than are the purists' groups. It is also noteworthy that the American groups of which politicos are members are more likely to interact with scientific experts than either Canadian purists' or politicos' groups. Again, from these findings, it is evident that policy-relevant information appears to be substantially more politicized in the American setting than in the Canadian context, and thus perhaps more amenable to group-based responses to the technical information quandary.

CONCLUSION

This book has examined a number of stages in a necessarily complicated process—namely, how citizens in contemporary postindustrial democracies may exercise influence over policy questions of highly scientific and technical content. We have suggested the possibility that today's interest groups may assist in that process in a way that is at once distinct from the role of interest groups depicted by the traditional model of interest group pluralism and from the mass mobilization role of single issue groups that arose in the 1970s and 1980s. That assistance to the citizen comes in the form of cue-giving, resource-pooling, and influence-exerting activities that share a special focus on policy-relevant information. The underlying context for the analysis developed here has been the comparison of observations simultaneously collected among environmental interest groups in comparable Canadian and American settings.

Two primary answers can be given to the central questions posed throughout the book. First, it is indeed the case that interest groups in both the United States and Canada have the capacity to assist citizens in coping with the problem of the technical information quandary. Second, it does make a difference in which national political culture those interest groups operate. In particular, it was observed that Canadian–American cultural differences with respect to the role of groups in society emerged gradually and subtly throughout the analysis. The remainder of this chapter ties together some of these culturally connected strands of empirical evidence gathered in the course of our work reported here.

Understanding the cross-national patterns emerging in this analysis requires a brief retreat to the book's beginning. Chapter 1 presented several related views of the role accorded to groups in Canadian life and in the American society. In this regard, it is useful to recall anew the observations of Lipset, Presthus, and Merelman. Lipset has noted that "Canada has been and is a more class-aware, elitist, law-abiding, statist, collectively oriented and particular (group oriented) society than the United States" (1990, p. 8). Presthus, almost two decades earlier, wrote that "Canada's political culture includes a generally affirmative perspective of interest groups . . . (but) neither government nor interest groups have enjoyed a similar legitimacy in the United States" (1973, p. 4). Merelman similarly argues that "In Canada, the culture of political participation is dominatingly group oriented. . . . In the United States the culture of political participation is fluid, egalitarian and individualistic" (1991, p. 11). The results of our research on environmental interest groups in Ontario and Michigan lead us to the conclusion that, while Canadians may well have a more positive view of interest groups than Americans do generally, the American institutional setting produces a higher level of policy process participation by interest groups. It seems fair at this time to speculate that the American system thus exhibits greater potential for assisting citizens in dealing with the political communication consequences of the technical information quandary than the Canadian social system does. What specific observations led us to this essential conclusion?

Several examples stated in rather summary form illustrate the greater political content to American interest groups and to their patterns of political communication. Chapter 3 reported that Canadian group members show somewhat higher overall levels of trust in information sources than their American counterparts, regardless of the political orientation of those sources. On the other hand, American group members are inclined to differentiate more systematically among groups viewed as potential sources of political information. Chapter 4 reported that information is more likely to be combined with political goals as incentives to group membership in Michigan than in Ontario. Chapter 6 concluded on the basis of findings drawn on interest group characteristics that Michigan environmental interest groups have developed greater policy-relevant communication capacity than have their Ontario counterparts. This final chapter has presented results indicating that political incentives are more strongly linked to membership in groups placing emphasis on research activities and the use of diverse information sources in the American setting than in the Canadian context.

We conclude that even though groups may be seen as more legitimate in a particular political culture, it does not follow that they will be oriented politically in their policy-relevant information gathering and communication activities. What factor is it, then, that deflects the more group-oriented political culture of Canada into a less active role for environmental interest groups in the political communication system of environmental policy formation? The answer most likely rests among other relevant aspects of the Canadian and American political cultures. The Canadian political culture, which is broadly taken to be the more collectivistic, communal, organic, and corporatist when compared to the American culture, actually may serve to suppress a recognition of the need and legitimacy of that sort of distinct political communication activity on the part of interest groups. Policy-relevant information may be thought to be shared more broadly, or at least more likely to reflect a consensus among Canadian interests than is the case in the American setting. In the United States, in contrast, there is an individualistic foundation to attitudes and interest groups and to citizen behavior generally that likely leads to more frequent group involvement as an instrument to satisfy individual needs for influence, information, and belongingness (Knoke 1990). Sensing these variegated needs among their members, then, American groups likely have gone further in developing their policy-relevant information-gathering and dissemination activities than have their Canadian counterparts.

What does all of this mean for political communication and the technical information quandary? Our study of environmental interest groups in Ontario and Michigan suggests that the conditions definitely exist at three different levels for interest groups to engage in bridging the political knowledge and communication gaps in scientific and technical policy areas. The salience of these three levels clearly was demonstrated in the case of interest groups active on the commonly experienced problem of acid rain deposition in Ontario and Michigan (Johnson 1985). These three levels are the individual, the organizational, and the cultural. At the individual level, it is clear that many people have the desire for acquiring a larger store of policy-relevant information, that they tend to exhibit systematic discretion in their trust of sources of that information and that they participate in organizations in good measure due to a felt need to acquire policy-relevant information and join it with their political goals and policy preferences. At the organizational level, many environmental groups engage in a number of information-producing efforts and conduct political communication activities that serve their members who demonstrate the need for such information as they can provide reliably (Stanfield 1985). Moreover, we have seen in this final chapter that there is some evidence of systematic selection occurring between group members with pronounced political needs and organizations with relatively greater information and communication products. At the cultural level, finally, it is clear that the organizational response to the technical information quandary plays out in ways somewhat consistent with the traditions and values of the political culture within which interest groups operate. This study has shown somewhat divergent patterns in the Ontario and Michigan settings, but this divergence has been consistent with what is broadly thought to be known about the differences separating the American and Canadian political cultures.

In making these observations, we do not mean to suggest that one culture or the other provides a more appropriate crucible in which to concoct an effective response to postindustrial society's technical information quandary. Rather, our findings suggest strongly that as interest group organizations respond to the demands made of them in postindustrial democracies, their reactions to those demands likely will be channeled within the constraining boundaries imposed by tradition, history, and existing institutions. In different ways, perhaps, each modern democratic polity must face the dilemma of the technical information quandary and provide for a creative interplay of information, individual citizens' needs, and interest group activities. Gary Mucciaroni may be correct in arguing that the interest groups of a newer, information-based orientation are "unclogging the arteries" of the American interest group system (1991). Hopeful, though somewhat weaker, indications of such change are afoot in Canada. In many areas, younger interest group members in Ontario and Michigan share more common sentiments on issues and on some basic political values than do their more senior compatriots. The future may belong to these younger activists, and the likelihood is that they will develop more fully the potential of their groups to assist citizens in coping with the technical information quandary.

Appendix
Survey Questionnaires

ONTARIO-MICHIGAN SURVEY OF ENVIRONMENTAL ORGANIZATIONS

Board of Directors/Staff Member Survey

In recent years there has been a lot of discussion about acid rain and general environmental quality in Cananda and the United States. We are interested in finding out what you <u>think</u> about some important issues in this and related areas of concern. This survey has been sent to you with the cooperation of the environmental organization in which you hold a leadership position. Your participation in this survey is completely VOLUNTARY; however, in order to gather a fair impression of how leaders of environmental organizations feel about these issues, it is important that as many people as possible respond to the survey. Your answers will be kept completely CONFIDENTIAL.

Thank you for your time and effort.

Sincerely,

Brent S. Steel, Ph.D.
Department of Political Science
Oakland University
Rochester, Michigan 48063
(313)370-2365/2352

Mary Ann E. Steger, Ph.D.
Department of Political Science
Washington State University
Pullman, Washington 99164

BOARD OF DIRECTORS/STAFF MEMBER SURVEY

DIRECTIONS AND OVERVIEW

This survey has been sent to you with the cooperation of the environmental organization in which you hold a leadership position (serve on the board of directors or serve in a staff capacity). Please comment on any question in the survey which you feel deserves additional attention.

YOUR ANSWERS AND COMMENTS ARE CONFIDENTIAL THROUGHOUT THIS SURVEY

SECTION I

1. As a board or staff member to what extent do you think each of the following is an effective way for your organization to influence environmental policy? Please circle the appropriate responses.

	Not a good idea-------- Uncertain--------			A very good idea
Election campaign contributions	1	2	3	4	5
Media campaigns	1	2	3	4	5
Letter writing	1	2	3	4	5
Coalitions with other groups	1	2	3	4	5
Publications	1	2	3	4	5
Legislative lobbying	1	2	3	4	5
Administrative lobbying	1	2	3	4	5
Taking public opinion polls	1	2	3	4	5
Testimony at hearings/consultations	1	2	3	4	5

2. How much do you think your group's dissemination of scientific and technical information on the environment contributes to the political success of your organization? Please circle the appropriate number on the following scale:

Does not ----------- 1 ---------------- 2 ---------------- 3 ---------------- 4 ---------------- 5 ------ Contributes a
contribute to | great deal to
group's success   Contributes a   group's success
                                   little to group's success

3. When the sharing and dissemination of information on the environment is involved, organizations tend to focus their resources on either communicating this information to members and contributors OR communicating this information to government officials. Which focus does your organization have?

Sharing of ---------- 1 ---------------- 2 ---------------- 3 ---------------- 4 ---------------- 5 -------- Sharing of
information | information
with governmental   Equal focus on   with members
officials exclusively   sharing information   and contributors
                                            with members/contributors   exclusively
                                            AND government officials

SECTION 2

The problem of ACID RAIN DEPOSITION in Canada and the United States has led to a great deal of commentary in both countries. There are differing opinions as to the degree of seriousness of the problem, the sources of this form of pollution, the appropriate means to address the problem, etc. We would like to ask your opinion on these several matters.

4. Compared to other problems in Ontario and Michigan (for example, unemployment, inflation, crime, and the like) how would you rate the seriousness of acid rain? Please circle the appropriate response.

Not serious ---------- 1 ---------- 2 ---------- 3 ---------- 4 ---------- 5 ---------- 6 ---------- 7 ---------- One of the
                                              | more serious
                                         A somewhat   problems facing
                                         serious problem   North America

5. Many possible negative effects of acid rain have been discussed in recent years. We would like to know your assessment of these possible effects using the following risk scale. Write the number that most accurately describes your position in each blank.

Low degree ---------- 1 ---------- 2 ---------- 3 ---------- 4 ---------- 5 ---------- 6 ---------- 7 -------- High degree
of risk | of risk
                                         Uncertain

____ respiratory ailments/lung disease

____ corrosion of buildings or monuments

____ deforestation

____ destruction of wildlife

____ contaminated drinking water

____ lower agricultural productivity

____ decimation of freshwater fish stocks

____ soil depletion

6. Based upon all you have heard about the issue of acid rain, where would you locate yourself on the following scale? Circle your response.

A public health/environ- 1 ----------- 2------------- 3 ----------- 4 ----------- 5----------- 6 ----------- 7 -------- Continue current
mental emergency should   practices involving
be declared in both the U.S.   Undecided   the occasional use of
& Canada, and a MORATORIUM   high sulphur coal,
declared on all acid rain-causing   smokestacks without
activities until appropriate   scrubbers, etc., until
technologies are installed   more research has
to curtail pollutants.   been conducted.

7. Below we have listed terms that are found in reports on acid rain and in discussions about what to do about it. We are asking if you know each term, have heard of the term but perhaps don't know its meaning, or have not heard of the term at all. Please circle the number of the most appropriate answer.

	Know meaning	Heard of but don't know meaning	Have not heard of term
Sulphur dioxide	1	2	3
Acidification	1	2	3
Scrubbers	1	2	3
Ecosystem	1	2	3
Alkaline	1	2	3
Phrenologesis	1	2	3
Nitrogen oxide/dioxide	1	2	3
pH	1	2	3
Oligotrophication	1	2	3
Toxic metals	1	2	3
Desulphurization	1	2	3
Hydrocarbons	1	2	3

8. A variety of TECHNOLOGIES for clean air have been discussed recently. Which of the following do you think have been suggested as possibilities? Place the number of your response in front of each technology.

    1 = a possibility   2 = not a possibility   3 = don't know

    ____ coal/oil desulphurization

    ____ scrubbers in smokestacks

    ____ using low sulphur coal instead of high sulphur coal

    ____ redesigning furnaces to have a higher combustion temperature

    ____ taller smokestacks

    ____ the use of nuclear energy in place of fossil fuels

    ____ catalytic converters on cars

    ____ the use of oil instead of coal

    ____ the burning of clay/sand with coal in the combustion process

9. Many SOURCES of air pollutants, which lead to acid rain, have been discussed recently. Which of the following would you say are definite sources, probable sources, or not likely to be sources of these pollutants? Circle the number of appropriate answers.

	Definitely a source	Probable source	Not a source	Don't know
Car exhaust	1	2	3	4
Ammonia in the air	1	2	3	4
Lime in the air	1	2	3	4
Natural causes	1	2	3	4
Coal combustion	1	2	3	4
Oil combustion	1	2	3	4
Wood burning	1	2	3	4
Aerosol sprays	1	2	3	4
Pesticide sprays	1	2	3	4

10. The term POLLUTION is used to label things whose presence in the environment constitutes a danger to the public health. Below we have listed things that some people say are harmful and other people say are not harmful. Please circle the number that best reflects your position on the degree of harm associated with the following things.

	Definitely not harmful		Not sure		Definitely harmful
Fireplace smoke	1	2	3	4	5
Auto exhaust	1	2	3	4	5
Nuclear waste	1	2	3	4	5
Herbicides	1	2	3	4	5
Residential sewage	1	2	3	4	5
Agricultural runoff	1	2	3	4	5
Neon signs	1	2	3	4	5
Airport noise	1	2	3	4	5
Vulgar language	1	2	3	4	5
Pornography	1	2	3	4	5
Acid rain	1	2	3	4	5
Food additives	1	2	3	4	5

11. The five questions listed below are relevant to the study of ecology. Please circle the number of the most appropriate answer to each question.

a. Soil pollution is generally due to: 1. sparse rains; 2. improper farming methods; 3. poisonous metals; 4. large trucks; 5. refuse disposal.

b. Most smog in our big cities comes from: 1. automobiles; 2. supersonic jets; 3. industrial plants; 4. large trucks; 5. refuse disposal.

c. Which of the following does not appreciably reduce pollution by automobiles? 1. properly tuned engines; 2. high octane gas; 3. low lead gas; 4. smog control devices; 5. propane engines.

d. The most common pollutants of water are: 1. arsenic, silver nitrates; 2. hydrocarbons; 3. carbon monoxide; 4. sulphur, calcium; 5. nitrates, phosphates.

e. Practically all of the lead in our atmosphere is caused by: 1. cars; 2. industrial plants; 3. airplanes; 4. burning refuse; 5. cigarettes.

SECTION 3

People concerned about the environment have a variety of opinions about the way environmental policy is made, the appropriate focus of this policy, the role of science and technology in solving environmental problems, etc. We are interested in your opinions on these various topics.

12. If you were to describe the way natural resource and environmental politics usually operate, which of the following do you think is the most accurate? Please circle the number of the best description.

    1. A clash of big ideas, philosophies or ideologies (differing views of the proper role of man and nature).

    2. A clash of groups or interests (groups of people trying to achieve goals that benefit the interests of their followers).

    3. A clash that depends on the issue (concerns change over time, depending on how things are going in the country, such as the economy or national defense).

    4. A clash based on personal goals (the interests and ambitions of individuals who are interested primarily in benefiting themselves).

13. Some people concerned about the environment advocate the conservation of natural resources while others concerned about the environment advocate the preservation of natural resources. To which of these views do you subscribe? Please locate yourself on the following conservationist-preservationist scale.

Strong conservationist--- 1 ----------- 2 ------------ 3 ----------- 4 ----------- 5 ----------- 6 ----------- 7 ---- Strong preservationist
(Public lands should | (Public lands
always be managed to   Moderate   should always be
allow for multiple uses   (Both positions should   managed to keep
and access points)   be considered when making   them in a pristine
                                                decisions concerning   and undeveloped
                                                public lands).   condition.)

14. Please circle the number indicating whether you agree or disagree with each of the following statements.

	Strongly Disagree		No Opinion		Strongly Agree
Technology will find a way of solving the problem of shortages of natural resources	1	2	3	4	5
People would be better off if they lived without so much technology	1	2	3	4	5
Future scientific research is more likely to cause problems than to find solution to problems	1	2	3	4	5

14. Continued:

	Strongly Disagree		No Opinion		Strongly Agree
Technical and scientific experts are usually biased	1	2	3	4	5
Environmental issues are hard to understand	1	2	3	4	5
The balance of nature is very delicate and easily upset by human activities	1	2	3	4	5
The earth is like a spaceship with only limited room and resources	1	2	3	4	5
Plants and animals do not exist primarily for human use	1	2	3	4	5
Modifying the environment for human use seldom causes serious problems	1	2	3	4	5
There are no limits to growth for nations like the United States or Canada	1	2	3	4	5
Mankind was created to rule over the rest of nature	1	2	3	4	5

15. Many individuals and groups supply information about the environment. We are interested in how much trust you have in the information provided by each of the information sources listed below Please circle the appropriate number.

	None		Some		A great deal
Business or industry representatives	1	2	3	4	5
Environmentalists	1	2	3	4	5
Citizen groups	1	2	3	4	5
Hunting or fishing groups	1	2	3	4	5
Energy companies	1	2	3	4	5
Technical and scientific experts	1	2	3	4	5
Legislators	1	2	3	4	5
Labor unions	1	2	3	4	5

15. Continued:

	None		Some		A great deal
Developers/construction companies	1	2	3	4	5
Timber companies	1	2	3	4	5
News reporters	1	2	3	4	5
College/university educators	1	2	3	4	5
Federal agency representatives	1	2	3	4	5
State/provincial agency representatives	1	2	3	4	5
Local government representatives	1	2	3	4	5

16. All things considered, what would you say was the relative impact of each of the following individuals or groups on environmental policy in your country?

	None		Some		A great deal
Business or industry representatives	1	2	3	4	5
Environmentalists	1	2	3	4	5
Citizen groups	1	2	3	4	5
Hunting or fishing groups	1	2	3	4	5
Energy companies	1	2	3	4	5
Technical and scientific experts	1	2	3	4	5
Legislators	1	2	3	4	5
Labor unions	1	2	3	4	5
Developers/construction companies	1	2	3	4	5
Timber companies	1	2	3	4	5
News reporters	1	2	3	4	5
College/university educators	1	2	3	4	5
Federal agency representatives	1	2	3	4	5
State/provincial agency representatives	1	2	3	4	5
Local government representatives	1	2	3	4	5

17. The next two questions deal with WHAT groups ought to communicate to their members (or contributors) and policy makers in government.

    A. What emphasis do you think leaders of environmental organization should give to each of the following types of information when they are communicating to or sharing information with governmental policy makers?

	No emphasis		Some emphasis		A lot of emphasis
Political information (evidence of support or opposition to specific policies)	1	2	3	4	5
Scientific/technical information (results of research, news on technol-- ogical breakthroughs, etc.)	1	2	3	4	5
Economic information (cost-benefit information on policy options)	1	2	3	4	5
Legal information (analysis of cases at law, trends in judgments, new admin- istrative regulations, etc.)	1	2	3	4	5

    B. What emphasis do you think leaders of environmental organizations SHOULD give to each of the following types of information when they are communicating to or sharing information with their members or contributors?

	No emphasis		Some emphasis		A lot of emphasis
Political information	1	2	3	4	5
Scientific/technical information	1	2	3	4	5
Economic information	1	2	3	4	5
Legal information	1	2	3	4	5

SECTION 4

The answers you profiled above must be interpreted with appropriate attention to differing personal backgrounds and interests. The following section pertains to your personal values and background.

18. How would you place yourself on the following ideological scale in your country? Circle your response.

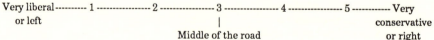

Very liberal ---------- 1 ----------------- 2 ----------------- 3 ----------------- 4 ----------------- 5 ------------ Very
    or left | conservative
                                        Middle of the road   or right
                                          or moderate

19. There is a lot of talk these days about what your country's goals should be for the next ten or fifteen years. Listed below are some of the goals that different people say should be given top priority. Would you please mark the one you yourself consider the most important in the long run? What would be your second choice? Please mark that second choice as well.

	1st Choice	2nd Choice
Maintaining order in the nation	_____	_____
Giving the people more say in important decisions	_____	_____
Fighting rising prices	_____	_____
Protecting freedom of speech	_____	_____

20. We are interested in knowing the frequency of your outdoor recreational activity. Please use the following scale and designate the number that most accurately describes your frequency of use.

Seldom --------------- 1 ----------- 2 ------------ 3 ----------- 4 ----------- 5 ----------- 6 ----------- 7 ---------------- Very
if ever | frequently
                                              Sometimes

____ fishing	____ swimming
____ camping	____ gardening
____ hunting	____ boating
____ hiking/backpacking	____ wildlife watching/photography
____ snowmobiling	____ skiing

SECTION 5

These final questions pertain to YOU personally. We would like to know something about the background you bring to your work with your organization.

21. Year of birth ____ .   22. Gender: 1. Female   2. Male

23. How many years have you lived in Ontario or Michigan? _____ .

24. Your highest level of education:

1. Never attended school   6. Some college
2. Some grade school   7. Completed college
3. Completed grade school   8. Some graduate work
4. Some high school   9. An advanced degree
5. Completed high school

25. Your approximate annual family income before taxes?

       1. Less than $4,000   6. $20,000 - $24,999
       2. $4,000 - $6,999   7. $25,000 - $29,999
       3. $7,000 - $9,999   8. $30,000 - $49,999
       4. $10,000 - $14,999   9. $50,000 and above
       5. $15,000 - $19,999

26. A. How many organizations concerned with environmental issues do you support with regular dues or contributions?

Number: _____

   B. Please list these organizations in the space provided below. For each organization you list, please indicate whether you are a general member, serve on the organization's board of directors, or serve as a staff member (either paid or voluntary) in the organization.

	Serve on board of directors	Serve as paid or voluntary staff	General member only
1. _____	_____	_____	_____
2. _____	_____	_____	_____
3. _____	_____	_____	_____
4. _____	_____	_____	_____
5. _____	_____	_____	_____

PLEASE WRITE ANY ADDITIONAL COMMENTS YOU WOULD LIKE TO MAKE ABOUT ANY OF THE QUESTIONS OR ISSUES RAISED IN THE QUESTIONNAIRE IN THE REMAINING SPACE. THANK YOU VERY MUCH FOR YOUR COOPERATION. A COPY OF THE RESULTS OF THIS STUDY WILL BE SENT TO THE ENVIRONMENTAL ORGANIZATION THAT DISTRIBUTED THIS QUESTIONNAIRE TO YOU.

ORGANIZATIONAL PROFILE: This form should be filled out by a staff member (paid or voluntary).

Part 1

This initial section of the survey deals with general information concerning your organization. Please feel free to add youR comments in the margins next to any of the questions or enclose any information brochures that describe the organization in greater detail.

1-1   Year the organization was created: _____

1-2   In your own words, please state the major purposes of this organization.

_____

_____

_____

1-3   What is the total number of paid staff currently working for the organization?

        Full time _____ Part time _____

1-4   Approximately how many volunteer workers can your organization call upon?

        Number of volunteers _____

        How many of these volunteers do staff work on a regular basis? _____

1-5   Does your organization provide for individual membership? Yes ____ No ____

        If yes, approximately how many members do you have at present? _____

1-6   A. Does your organization provide for other types of membership--such as institutional, governmental, club, or group members?

        Yes ____ No ____ If yes, how many such memberships do you have? ____

     B. In the list below, please check off the types of members you have. (Please check all that apply):

        ____ environmental organizations

        ____ clubs

        ____ civic or community organizations

        ____ units of government or governmental agencies

        ____ research organizations

        ____ businesses or corporations

        ____ labor organizations

        ____ others (Please name):_____

1-7   A. Does your organization require membership dues? Yes ____ No ____

       B. If you charge dues, what is the annual dues amount? $_____

1-8   Which of the following best describes the scope of responsibility of your group?

       ____ national or regional   ____ provincial or state

       ____ sub-provincial or sub-state   ____ local level only

1-9   A. Is your organization an affiliate of a national organization? Yes ____ No ____

       B. If yes, please name this national organization:

       _____

1-10   Is your organization an affiliate of a provincial or state organization?

       Yes ____ No ____   If yes, please name this provincial/state organization:

       _____

1-11   Does your organization have sub-provincial/sub-state or local chapters?

       Yes ____ No ____   If yes, how many? _____

1-12   Please record a rough estimate of your organization's current annual budget:

                                                              $_____

1-13   Approximately what percentage of your annual budget comes from:

       ____ % member dues or contributions

       ____ % foundations

       ____ % government sources

       ____ % private corporations or businesses

       ____ % other funding sources (Please name): _____

       _____

1-14   A. Are contributions to your organization tax-exempt? Yes ____   No ____

      B. If your group is incorporated in the U.S., which type of tax status does it have?

                                          ____ 501c3   ____501c4

Part 2

In this section of the survey the focus shifts to the sources of information and types of information used by your organization.

2-1   What external sources does your organization use to compile information on environmental problems? Check all that apply:

    ____ affiliates or offices of this organization

    ____ other environmental organizations

    ____ scientists or experts in universities or research institutes

    ____ lawyers or legal experts

    ____ elected governmental officials or their staff

    ____ non-elected government personnel

    ____ others (Please name): _____

2-2   What type of research information is used by your organization? Please check all that apply and indicate whether each type of research used is SELF-GENERATED, PROVIDED BY OTHERS, OR A COMBINATION OF BOTH OF THESE:

    ____ research on the scientific/technical aspects of environmental problems

    ____ self-generated   ____ provided by others   ____ combination

    ____ research on the legal aspects of environmental problems

    ____ self-generated   ____ provided by others   ____ combination

    ____ research on the political aspects of environmental problems

    ____ self-generated   ____ provided by others   ____ combination

    ____ research on economic aspects of environmental problems

    ____ self-generated   ____ provided by others   ____ combination

---

Part 3

In this section, the focus is directed to the ways in which your organization informs members (or contributors) about environmental issues and informs them about your activities. In the following questions, the term 'members' will be used to represent both members of and contributors to an organization.

3-1 Does your organization have a regular means of written communication with your members?

Yes ____ No ____ If yes, check all forms of written communication used:

____ newsletter

____ magazine

____ other (Please name):_____

3-2 What other means do you use to inform members about group activities and environmental issues? Please check all of the following that apply:

____ periodic membership meetings

____ special reports or pamphlets

____ workshops or short courses

____ videotapes or films

____ community or regional newspapers

____ radio

____ television

____ others (Please name): _____

3-3 What percentage of total staff time is devoted to the following activities?

____ % fundraising   ____ % political activities

____ % educational activities   ____ % scientific or technical research

---

Part 4

In this section, we are interested in how you communicate and share information on environmental problems and issues with government officials.

4-1   When communicating or sharing information on environmental matters with government officials on the national level, how frequently do representatives of your organization interact with the types of officials listed below?

	Never		Occasionally		Often
National-level:					
Elected officials or their staff	1	2	3	4	5
Heads of department, divisions, agencies, or commissions	1	2	3	4	5
Mid-level personnel in departments, divisions, or agencies	1	2	3	4	5
Legal experts in government	1	2	3	4	5
Scientific experts in government	1	2	3	4	5

4-2   When communicating or sharing information on environmental matters with government officials on the provincial or state level, how frequently do representatives of your organization interact with the types of officials listed below?

	Never		Occasionally		Often
Provincial/State-level:					
Elected officials or their staff	1	2	3	4	5
Heads of department, divisions, agencies, or commissions	1	2	3	4	5
Mid-level personnel in departments, divisions, or agencies	1	2	3	4	5
Legal experts in government	1	2	3	4	5
Scientific experts in government	1	2	3	4	5

4-3   When communicating or sharing information on environmental matters with government officials on the local level, how frequently do representatives of your organization interact with the types of officials listed below?

Local-level:	Never		Occasionally		Often
Elected officials or their staff	1	2	3	4	5
Heads of departments, divisions, agencies, or commissions	1	2	3	4	5
Mid-level personnel in departments, divisions, or agencies	1	2	3	4	5
Legal experts in government	1	2	3	4	5
Scientific experts in government	1	2	3	4	5

4-4   Which (if any) of the following services does your organization typically provide for members of the provincial parliament or state legislators? Check all the services provided for these officials in the first column; in the second column, please rank the services you have checked in terms of their importance ("1" indicates the most important; "2" indicates the second most important, etc.)

**Methods
Used   Rank**

____   ( )   Testifying at hearings

____   ( )   Providing information on pending legislation

____   ( )   Building public support for legislative proposals

____   ( )   Campaign support (funds and/or time)

4-5   Which (if any) of the following services does your organization typically provide for provincial or state civil servants? Check all the services provided for these officials in the first column; in the second column, please rank the services you have checked in terms of their importance ("1" indicates the most important; "2" indicates the second most important, etc.).

**Methods
Used   Rank**

____   ( )   Participation in public advisory bodies

____   ( )   Providing information on public attitudes

____   ( )   Support for agency policies

____   ( )   Recommendations on appointees to high-level posts

4-6   Organizations like yours make use of a variety of methods to influence
       government actions or policies affecting the interests of their members. Next to
       the methods listed below, please check all those used by your organization in the
       first column. In the second column, rank the methods you checked in terms of
       their effectiveness ("1" indicates the most effective method, "2" indicates the
       second most effective method, etc.).

Methods
Used   Rank

____   ( )   Briefs to parliamentary committees (Ontario) OR testifying
                before legislative committees (Michigan)

____   ( )   Briefs to cabinet ministers (Ontario) OR submitting reports to
                the governor's office (Michigan)

____   ( )   Appeals to executive assistants of cabinet ministers (Ontario) OR
                appeals to agency personnel (Michigan)

____   ( )   Briefs or appeals by outside experts (lawyers, former government
                officials, scientists, etc.)

____   ( )   Contacts with governmental regulatory bodies

____   ( )   Filing court suits

____   ( )   Instigating a letter-writing campaign

____   ( )   Building coalitions with other groups

____   ( )   Releasing information through the mass media

____   ( )   Organizing political protests

4-7   What kind of information on environmental matters does your organization
       communicate to elected government officials in your provincial or state
       government? Please check all that apply:

____ scientific information (e.g., reports on scientific studies, etc.)

____ technical information (e.g., news on recent monitoring devices, etc.)

____ legal information (e.g., news on cases or administrative rulings, etc.)

____ political information (e.g., news on sources of policy support or opposition)

____ economic information (e.g., findings on cost-benefit studies, etc.)

4-8   What kind of information on environmental matters does your organization communicate to career service government officials in your provincial or state government? Please check all that apply:

_____ scientific information (e.g., reports on scientific studies, etc.)

_____ technical information (e.g., news on recent monitoring devices, etc.)

_____ legal information (e.g., news on cases or administrative rulings, etc.)

_____ political information (e.g., news on sources of policy support or opposition)

_____ economic information (e.g., findings on cost-benefit studies, etc.)

4-9   On matters affecting the environment, how successful is your organization in its attempts to inform provincial or state government officials, the members of the organization, and the general public?

	Not successful		Uncertain		Very successful
Provincial or state government officials	1	2	3	4	5
Members of the organization	1	2	3	4	5
General public	1	2	3	4	5

THANK YOU FOR YOUR KIND ATTENTION TO THIS ORGANIZATIONAL PROFILE. YOUR COOPERATION IS VERY MUCH APPRECIATED. WE WILL PROVIDE A COPY OF THE RESULTS OF THIS STUDY TO EACH ENVIRONMENTAL ORGANIZATION COMPLETING THIS PROFILE.

References

Abrahamson, Bengt (1977). *Bureaucracy or Participation: The Logic of Organization.* Beverly Hills: Sage Publications.

Aldrich, John H., and Forrest Nelson (1984). *Linear Probability, Logit, and Probit Models.* Beverly Hills: Sage Quantitative Applications in the Social Sciences.

Almond, Gabriel, and G. Bingham Powell (1966). *Comparative Politics: A Developmental Approach.* Boston: Little, Brown.

Almond, Gabriel, and Sidney Verba (1963). *The Civic Culture: Political Attitudes and Democracy in Five Nations.* Princeton: Princeton University Press.

Altheide, David L., and Robert P. Snow (1991). *Media Worlds in the Postjournalism Era.* New York: Walter de Gruyter.

Atwood, Margaret (1972). *Survival: A Thematic Guide to Canadian Literature.* Toronto: Anansi Press.

Atwood, Margaret (1984). *Second Words: Selected Critical Prose.* Toronto: Anansi Press.

Bachrach, Peter (1967). *The Theory of Democratic Elitism.* Boston: Little, Brown.

Bachrach, Peter, and Morton Baratz (1970). *Power and Poverty.* New York: Oxford University Press.

Baer, Douglas, Edward Grubb, and William Johnson (1991). "National Character, Regional Culture and the Values of Canadians and Americans." Paper delivered at the biennial meeting of the Association for Canadian Studies in the United States, Boston, November.

Bailey, Stephen K. (1950). *Congress Makes a Law.* New York: Columbia University Press.

Bakvis, Herman, and Neil Nevitte (1987). "In Pursuit of Postbourgeois Man: Postmaterialism and Intergenerational Change in Canada." *Comparative Political Studies* 20: 357–389.

Barber, Benjamin (1984). *Strong Democracy: Participatory Politics for a New Age.* Berkeley: California Press.

Barnes, Samuel, Max Kaase, and Klause R. Allerbeck (eds.) (1979). *Political Action: Mass Participation in Five Western Democracies.* Beverly Hills: Sage Publications.

Bauer, Raymond A., Ithiel de Sola Pool, and Lewis Dexter (1963). *American Business and Public Politics of Foreign Trade.* New York: Columbia University Press.

Beer, Samuel (1958). "Group Representation in Britain and the United States." *Annals of the American Academy of Political and Social Sciences* 319: 130–140.

Bennett, Douglas, and Kenneth E. Sharpe (1984). "Is There a Democracy 'Overload'?" *Dissent* 31: 319–326.

Bentley, Arthur (1908). *The Process of Government.* Chicago: University of Chicago Press.

Benveniste, Guy (1972). *The Politics of Expertise.* Berkeley: Glendessary Press.

Berry, Jeffrey M. (1981). "Maximum Feasible Dismantlement." *Citizen Participation* 3: 3–5.

Berry, Jeffrey M. (1984). *The Interest Group Society.* Boston: Little, Brown.

Berry, Jeffrey M. (1989). "Subgovernments, Issue Networks, and Political Conflict." In *Remaking American Politics,* edited by Richard Harris and Sidney Milkis. Boulder, CO: Westview Press.

Boorstin, Daniel (1971). *The Image: A Guide to Pseudo-Events in America.* New York: Atheneum.

Boorstin, Daniel (1973). *The Americans: The Democratic Experience.* New York: Random House.

Brooks, Harvey (1975). "Expertise and Politics: Problems and Tensions." *Proceedings of the American Philosophical Society* 119: 257–261.

Brooks, Harvey (1984). "The Resolution of Technically Intensive Public Policy Disputes." *Science, Technology and Human Values* 9: 14–25.

Bruce, Peter G. (1989). "Political Parties and Labor Legislation in Canada and the United States." *Industrial Relations* 28: 115–141.

Bruner, Jerome (1985). *Actual Minds, Possible Worlds.* Cambridge: Harvard University Press.

Bryce, James (1887). *The American Commonwealth.* New York: Macmillan.

Butler, David, and Austin Ranney (1981). *Referendums.* Washington, DC: American Enterprise Institute.

Canadian Study of Parliament Group (1989). "Interest Groups and Parliament." Ottawa: Canadian Parliament.

Carroll, James D. (1971). "Participatory Technology." *Science* 171: 647–653.

Caulfield, Henry P. (1989). "The Conservation and Environmental Movements: An Historical Analysis." In *Environmental Politics and Policy: Theories and Evidence,* edited by James P. Lester. Durham, NC: Duke University Press.

Chacko, James (1987). "Introduction." In *Cultural Sovereignty: Myth or Reality,* edited by James Chacko. Windsor: Centre for Canadian–American Studies, University of Windsor Press.

Clark, Peter B., and James Q. Wilson (1961). "Incentive Systems: A Theory of Organizations." *Administrative Science Quarterly* 6: 129–166.

Commager, Henry Steele (1950). *The American Mind: An Interpretation of American Thought and Character Since the 1880s.* New Haven: Yale University Press.

Commager, Henry Steele (1977). *The Empire of Reason.* New York: Anchor Press.

Cook, Constance E. (1984). "Participation in Public Interest Groups: Membership Motivations." *American Politics Quarterly* 12: 409–430.

Cook, Terrence (1985). "Commentary on the Blacksburg Manifesto: A Polemic in Defense of Administrative Elitism in American Government." Paper presented at the annual meeting of the American Society for Public Administration (Region 9), Spokane, Washington, March.

Cooper, Chester L. (1987). "The CO_2 Challenge." In *Science for Public Policy*, edited by Harvey Brooks and Chester L. Cooper. New York: Pergamon Press.

Cowling, E. (1982). "Acid Precipitation in Historical Perspective." *Environmental Science and Technology* 16: 115–122.

Crawford, Craig, and James Curtis (1979). "English Canadian–American Differences in Value Orientations: Survey Comparisons Bearing on Lipset's Thesis." *Studies in Comparative International Development* 14: 23–44.

Crick, Bernard (1959). *The American Science of Politics*. Berkeley: University of California Press.

Cronin-Cossette, Ann (1988). "Comments." In *Transboundary Air Quality: Proceedings of a Special Seminar*, edited by James Chacko and David Haffner. Windsor: University of Windsor Press.

Dahl, Robert A. (1967). *Pluralist Democracy in the United States: Conflict and Consent*. Chicago: Rand McNally.

Dahl, Robert A. (1985). *Controlling Nuclear Weapons: Democracy versus Guardianship*. Syracuse, NY: Syracuse University Press.

Dahl, Robert A. (1989). *Democracy and Its Critics*. New Haven: Yale University Press.

Dalton, Russell J. (1988). *Citizen Politics in Western Democracies: Public Opinion and Political Parties in the United States, Great Britain, West Germany and France*. Chatham, NJ: Chatham House Publishers.

Dawson, Helen Jones (1975). "National Pressure Groups and the Federal Government." In *Pressure Group Behavior in Canadian Politics*, edited by A. Paul Pross. Toronto: McGraw-Hill Ryerson.

De Sario, Jack, and Stuart Langton (1984). "Citizen Participation and Technocracy." *Policy Studies Review* 3: 223–233.

de Tocqueville, Alex (1948). *Democracy in America*. New York: Knopf.

DiMento, Joseph F. (1986). *Environmental Law and American Business: Dilemmas of Compliance*. New York: Plenum Press.

Dizard, Wilson P. (1985). *The Coming Information Age: An Overview of Technology, Economics, and Politics*, 2d ed. New York: Longman.

Dogan, Mattei, and Dominique Pelassy (1990). *How to Compare Nations: Strategies in Comparative Politics*, 2d ed. Chatham, NJ: Chatham House Publishers.

Dolbeare, Kenneth (1982). *American Public Policy: A Citizen's Guide*. New York: McGraw-Hill.

Dolbeare, Kenneth M., and Linda J. Medcalf (1988). *American Ideologies Today: From Neopolitics to New Ideas*. New York: Random House.

Douglas, Mary, and Aaron Wildavsky (1983). *Risk and Culture: An Essay on the Selection of Technological and Environmental Dangers*. Berkeley: University of California Press.

Dunlap, Riley E. (1989). "Public Opinion and Environmental Policy." In *Envi-

ronmental Politics and Policy: Theory and Evidence, edited by James P. Lester. Durham, NC: Duke University Press.

Dunlap, Riley E., and Kent D. VanLiere (1978). "The 'New Environmental Paradigm'." *Journal of Environmental Education* 9: 10–19.

Dunlap, Riley E., and Kent D. VanLiere (1984). "Commitment to the Dominant Social Paradigm and Concern for Environmental Quality." *Social Science Quarterly* 66: 1013–1027.

Easton, David (1965). *A Systems Analysis of Political Life*. New York: John Wiley and Sons.

Eckstein, Harry (1963). "Group Theory and the Comparative Study of Pressure Groups." In *Comparative Politics: A Reader*, edited by Harry Eckstein and David Apter. New York: Free Press of Glencoe.

Edelman, Murray (1964). *Politics as Symbolic Action*. Urbana: University of Illinois Press.

Edelman, Murray (1988). *Constructing the Political Spectacle*. Chicago: University of Chicago Press.

Ehrmann, Henry (1960). *Interest Groups in Four Continents*. Pittsburgh: University of Pittsburgh Press.

Enloe, Cynthia (1975). *The Politics of Pollution in a Comparative Perspective*. New York: McKay.

Farber, Daniel A., and Philip P. Frickey (1991). *Law and Public Choice: A Critical Introduction*. Chicago: University of Chicago Press.

Fiorino, Daniel J. (1990). "Institutional Responses to the Emerging Global Environment." In *Regulatory Federalism, Natural Resources and Environmental Management*, edited by Michael S. Hamilton. Washington, DC: American Society for Public Administration.

Flanagan, Scott (1982). "Measuring Value Change in Advanced Industrial Societies: A Rejoinder to Inglehart." *Comparative Political Studies* 14: 403–444.

Flanagan, Scott (1987). "Changing Values in Industrial Societies Revisited: Towards a Resolution of the Values Debate." *American Political Science Review* 81: 1303–1319.

Foucault, Michel (1980). *The History of Sexuality*. New York: Vintage Books.

Fry, Geoffrey C. (1985). *The Changing Civil Service*. London: George Allen and Unwin.

Galbraith, John Kenneth (1952). *American Capitalism: The Concept of Countervailing Power*. Boston: Houghton Mifflin.

Galbraith, John Kenneth (1958). *The Affluent Society*. Boston: Houghton Mifflin.

Galbraith, John Kenneth (1967). *The New Industrial State*. Boston: Houghton Mifflin.

Gappert, Gary (1979). *Post-Affluent America: The Social Economy of the Future*. New York: Franklin Watts.

Garceau, Oliver (1941). *The Political Life of the American Medical Association*. Cambridge: Harvard University Press.

Gibbins, Roger, and Neil Nevitte (1985). "Canadian Political Ideology: A Comparative Analysis." *Canadian Journal of Political Science* 18: 577–598.

Gifford, Bill (1990). "Inside the Environmental Groups." *Outside* (September): 69–84.

Globerman, Steven (1987). *Culture, Governments and Markets: Public Policy and the Culture Industries*. Vancouver: Fraser Institute.

Goodman, Nelson (1983). *Of Mind and Other Matters*. Cambridge: Harvard University Press.

Gorz, Andre (1980). *Ecology as Politics*. Boston: South End Press.

Graham, Loren (1987). "Lay Participation in Decision-Making Involving Science and Technology." In *Science for Public Policy*, edited by Harvey Brooks and Chester L. Cooper. New York: Pergamon Press.

Granberg, Donald, and Soren Holmberg (1988). *The Political System Matters: Social Psychology and Voting Behavior in Sweden and the United States*. Cambridge: Cambridge University Press.

Groth, Alexander J., Larry L. Wade, and Alvin D. Wiggins (1984). "Classifying the World's Political Systems: A Resource-Allocation Approach." In *Comparative Resource Allocation: Politics, Performance, and Policy Priorities*, edited by A. J. Groth and L. L. Wade. Beverly Hills: Sage Publications.

Gruber, Judith E. (1987). *Controlling Bureaucracies: Dilemmas in Democratic Governance*. Berkeley: University of California Press.

Grupp, Fred W. (1971). "Personal Satisfaction Derived from Membership in the John Birch Society." *Western Political Quarterly* 24: 79–84.

Gwyn, Richard (1987). "Socio-Political Differences Between Canada and the United States." In *Cultural Sovereignty: Myth or Reality*, edited by James Chacko. Windsor: Centre for Canadian–American Studies, University of Windsor.

Habermas, Jurgen (1971). *Knowledge and Human Interests*. Translated by Jeremy Shapiro. Boston: Beacon.

Hadden, Susan G. (1989). *A Citizen's Right to Know: Risk Communication and Public Policy*. Boulder, CO: Westview Press.

Hagan, Charles B. (1958). "The Group in a Political Science." In *Approaches to the Study of Politics*, edited by R. Young. Evanston, IL: Northwestern University Press.

Hargrove, Edwin C. (1967). "On Canadian and American Political Culture." *Canadian Journal of Political Science* 33: 107–111.

Hartz, Louis (1955). *The Liberal Tradition in America: An Interpretation of American Political Thought Since the Revolution*. New York: Harcourt Brace and World.

Hawkins, Brett, Mary Ann E. Steger, and Jean Trimble (1986). "Attributes of Community Organizations that Adapt to Fiscal Strain." *Research in Urban Policy* 2: 117–125.

Hays, Samuel P. (1987). *Beauty, Health and Permanence: Environmental Politics in the United States*. New York: Cambridge University Press.

Heinz, John, Edward O. Lauman, Robert Salisbury, and Robert Nelson (1990). "Inner Circles or Hollow Cores? Elite Networks in National Policy Systems." *Journal of Politics* 52: 356–390.

Heisler, Martin (ed.) (1974). *Politics in Europe: Structures and Processes in Some Postindustrial Democracies*. New York: McKay.

Herring, E. Pendleton (1940). *The Politics of Democracy*. New York: Rinehart.

Heyrman, John (1989). "Mobilizing Citizens: Citizens' Group Membership and Political Participation." Paper prepared for the annual meeting of the Midwest Political Science Association, Chicago, March.

Honadle, Beth Walter (1982). *Public Administration in Rural Areas and Small Jurisdictions: A Guide to the Literature*. New York: Garland.

Horowitz, Gad (1966). "Conservatism, Liberalism, and Socialism in Canada: An Interpretation." *Canadian Journal of Public Policy* 32: 143–171.

House, Verne W. (1981). *Shaping Public Policy: The Educator's Role*. Bozeman, MT: Westridge Publishing.

Huntington, Samuel (1974). "Postindustrial Politics: How Benign Will It Be?" *Comparative Politics* 6: 147–177.

Huntington, Samuel (1975). "The Democratic Distemper." *The Public Interest* 41: 9–38.

Huntington, Samuel (1981). *American Politics: The Promise of Disharmony*. Cambridge: Harvard University Press.

Inglehart, Ronald (1971). "The Silent Revolution in Europe: Intergenerational Change in Post-Industrial Societies." *American Political Science Review* 65: 991–1017.

Inglehart, Ronald (1977). *The Silent Revolution: Changing Values and Political Styles among Western Publics*. Princeton, NJ: Princeton University Press.

Inglehart, Ronald (1990). *Culture Shift in Advanced Industrial Society*. Princeton, NJ: Princeton University Press.

Inglehart, Ronald, Neil Nevitt, and M. Basanez (1991). *North American Dilemma*. Ann Arbor, MI: Institute for Social Research.

Ingram, Helen M., and Dean E. Mann (1989). "Interest Groups and Environmental Policy." In *Environmental Politics and Policy: Theories and Evidence*, edited by James P. Lester. Durham, NC: Duke University Press.

Jennings, M. Kent (1989). "The Crystallization of Orientations." In *Continuities in Political Action: A Longitudinal Study of Political Orientations in Three Western Democracies*, edited by M. K. Jennings and Jan W. van Deth. New York: Walter de Gruyter.

Johnson, Janet Buttolph (1985). "The Dynamics of Acid Rain Policy in the United States." In *Public Policy and the Natural Environment*, edited by Helen M. Ingram and R. Kenneth Godwin. Greenwich, CT: JAI Press.

Jones, Charles O. (1984). *An Introduction to the Study of Public Policy*, 3d ed. Monterey, CA: Brooks/Cole.

Kaplan, Norton A. (1976). *Alienation and Identification*. New York: The Free Press.

Kassiola, Joel Jay (1990). *The Death of Industrial Civilization: The Limits to Economic Growth and the Repoliticization of Advanced Industrial Society*. Albany: State University of New York Press.

Kellner, Douglas (1990). *Television and the Crisis of Democracy*. Boulder, CO: Westview Press.

Kelmen, Steven (1988). "Why Public Ideas Matter." In *The Power of Public Ideas*, edited by Robert B. Reich. Cambridge, MA: Ballinger.

Key, V. O. (1966). *The Responsible Electorate*. Cambridge, MA: Belknap Press.

King, David C., and Jack L. Walker (1989). "The Provision of Benefits by American Interest Groups." Paper prepared for the annual meeting of the Midwest Political Science Association, Chicago, March.

Kluegel, James R., and Eliot R. Smith (1986). *Beliefs About Inequality: Americans' Views of What Is and What Ought to Be*. New York: Aldine de Gruyter.

Knoke, David (1988). "Incentives in Collective Action Organizations." *American Sociological Review* 53: 311–329.

Knoke, David (1990). *Organizing for Collective Action: The Political Economics of Associations*. New York: Aldine.

Kobrak, Peter (1984). "Michigan." In *The Political Life of the American States,* edited by A. Rosenthal and M. Moakley. New York: Praeger.

Krimsky, Sheldon (1984). "Beyond Technocracy: New Routes for Citizen Involvement in Social Risk Assessment." In *Citizen Participation in Science Policy,* edited by James C. Peterson. Amherst: University of Massachusetts Press.

Kritzer, Herbert, William A. Bogart, and Neil Vidmar (1990). "The Aftermath of Injury: Compensation Seeking in Canada and the United States." *Working Paper: Disputes Processing Research Program.* Madison: University of Wisconsin Law School.

Kweit, Grisez, and Robert W. Kweit (1981). *Implementing Citizen Participation in a Bureaucratic Society: A Contingency Approach.* New York: Praeger.

Ladd, Everett Carl, and Charles D. Hadley (1978). *Transformations of the American Party System,* 2d ed. New York: Norton.

Lafferty, William, and O. Knutsen (1985). "Postmaterialism in a Social Democratic State" *Comparative Political Studies* 17: 411–430.

Lane, Robert E. (1969). *Political Thinking and Consciousness.* Chicago: Markham.

LaPalombara, Joseph (1960). "The Utility and Limitations of Interest Group Theory in Non-American Field Situations." *Journal of Politics* 22: 29–49.

Lasch, Christopher (1972). "Toward a Theory of Post-Industrial Society." In *Politics in the Post-Welfare State: Responses to the New Individualism,* edited by M. Donald Hancock and G. Sjoberg. New York: Columbia University Press.

Latham, Earl (1952). *The Group Basis of Politics.* Ithaca, NY: Cornell University Press.

Leman, Christopher (1980). *The Collapse of Welfare Reform: Political Institutions, Policy and the Poor in Canada and the United States.* Cambridge: MIT Press.

Lipset, Seymour Martin (1963). *The First New Nation: The United States in Historical and Comparative Perspective.* New York: Norton.

Lipset, Seymour Martin (1985). "Canada and the United States: The Cultural Dimension." In *Canada and the United States: Enduring Friendship, Persistent Stress,* edited by Charles F. Doran and John H. Sigler. Englewood Cliffs, NJ: Prentice-Hall.

Lipset, Seymour Martin (1990a). *Continental Divide: The Values and Institutions of the United States and Canada.* New York: Routledge, Chapman and Hall.

Lipset, Seymour Martin (1990b). *North American Cultures: Values and Institutions in Canada and the United States.* Orono, ME: Borderline Project.

Loomis, Burdett A. (1983). "A New Era: Groups and the Grass Roots." In *Interest Group Politics.* Washington, DC: Congressional Quarterly.

Lovrich, Nicholas P., and John C. Pierce (1984). "Knowledge Gap Phenomena: Effect of Situation-Specific and Transsituational Factors" *Communication Research* 11: 415–434.

Lovrich, Nicholas P., and John C. Pierce (1986). "The Good Guys and Bad Guys in Natural Resources Politics: Content and Structure of Perceptions of Interests Among General and Attentive Publics." *The Social Science Journal* 23: 309–326.

Lowe, Philip, and Jane Goyder (1983). *Environmental Groups in Politics.* London: George Allen and Unwin.

Lowi, Theodore (1969). *The End of Liberalism.* New York: Norton.

Lowi, Theodore (1976). *Incomplete Conquest: Governing America*. New York: Holt, Rinehart and Winston.

MacKuen, Michael (1990). "Speaking of Politics: Individual Conversational Choice, Public Opinion, and the Prospects for Deliberative Democracy." In *Information and Democratic Processes*, edited by John A. Ferejohn and James H. Kuklinski. Urbana, IL: University of Illinois Press.

Macridis, Roy C. (1961). "Interest Groups in Comparative Analysis." *Journal of Politics* 23: 25–46.

Manga, Pran, and Robert Broyles (1986). "Evaluating and Explaining U.S.–Canada Health Policy." In *Research in Public Policy Analysis and Management: A Research Annual*, vol. 3, edited by Stuart S. Nagel. Greenwich, CT: JAI Press.

Marcuse, Herbert (1970). *One-Dimensional Man: Studies in the Ideology of Advanced Industrial Society*. Boston: Beacon Press.

Maslow, Abraham K. (1954). *Motivation and Personality*. New York: Harper and Row.

Maslow, Abraham K. (1971). *The Farther Reaches of Human Nature*. New York: Viking Press.

Mazur, Allan (1981). *The Dynamics of Technical Controversy*. Washington, DC: Communications Press.

McClosky, Herbert, and John Zaller (1984). *The American Ethics: Public Attitudes Toward Capitalism and Democracy*. Cambridge: Harvard University Press.

McConnell, Grant (1966). *Private Power and American Democracy*. New York: Knopf.

McFarland, Andrew S. (1976). *Public Interest Lobbies: Decision Making on Energy*. Washington, DC: American Enterprise Institute.

McFarland, Andrew S. (1983). *Common Cause*. Chatham, NJ: Chatham House.

Medcalf, Linda J., and Kenneth M. Dolbeare (1985). *Neopolitics: American Political Ideas in the 1980s*. Philadelphia: Temple University Press.

Meisel, John (1979). "The Decline of Party in Canada." In *Party Politics in Canada*, 4th ed., edited by H. Thorburn. Scarborough, Ontario: Prentice-Hall.

Merelman, Richard M. (1991). *Partial Visions: Culture and Politics in Britain, Canada and the United States*. Madison, WI: University of Wisconsin Press.

Milbrath, Lester W. (1983). "Images of Scarcity in Four Nations." In *Scarce Natural Resources: The Challenge to Public Policymaking*, edited by Susan Welsh and Robert Miewald. Beverly Hills: Sage Publications.

Milbrath, Lester W. (1984). *Environmental Vanguard for a New Society*. Albany: State University of New York Press.

Milbrath, Lester W. (1989). *Envisioning a Sustainable Society: Learning Our Way Out*. Albany: State University of New York Press.

Miles, Ian and Jonathan Gershung (1986). "The Social Economics of Information Technology." In *New Communication Technologies and the Public Interest: Comparative Perspectives on Policy and Research*, edited by Marjorie Ferguson. Beverly Hills: Sage Publications.

Miller, Warren E., and Teresa E. Levitin (1976). *Leadership and Change*. Cambridge, MA: Winthrop.

Minkenberg, Michael, and Ronald Inglehart (1989). "Neoconservatism and

Value Change in the USA: Tendencies in the Mass Public of a Postindustrial Society.'' In *Contemporary Political Culture: Politics in a Postmodern Age*, edited by John R. Gibbons. London: Sage Publications.

Mitchell, Robert Cameron (1979). ''National Environmental Lobbies and the Apparent Illogic of Collective Action.'' In *Collective Decision Making: Applications from Public Choice Theory*, edited by Charles S. Russell. Baltimore: Johns Hopkins University Press.

Mitchell, Robert Cameron (1990). ''Public Opinion and the Green Lobby: Poised for the 1990s?'' In *Environmental Policy in the 1990s*, edited by Norman J. Vig and Michael E. Kraft. Washington, DC: Congressional Quarterly Press.

Mitchell, William C. (1971). *Why Vote?* Chicago: Markham.

Moe, Terry M. (1980). *The Organization of Interests*. Chicago: University of Chicago Press.

Mucciaroni, Gary (1991). ''Unclogging the Arteries: The Defeat of Client Politics and the Logic of Collective Action.'' *Policy Studies Journal* 19: 474–494.

Nash, Roderick Frazier (1989). *The Rights of Nature: A History of Environmental Ethics*. Madison, WI: University of Wisconsin Press.

National Academy of Sciences (1983). *Acid Deposition: Atmospheric Processes in Eastern North America – A Review of Current Scientific Understanding*. Washington, DC: National Academy Press.

Nelkin, Dorothy (1979). *Technological Decisions and Democracy*. Beverly Hills: Sage Publications.

Nelkin, Dorothy, and Laurence Tancredi (1989). *Dangerous Diagnostics: The Social Power of Biological Information*. New York: Basic Books.

Nevitte, Neil, Miguel Basanez, and Ronald Inglehart (1991). ''Directions of Value Change in North America: The Survey Evidence.'' Paper prepared for the Facing North/Facing South Conference, Calgary, May.

Nimmo, Dan, and David L. Swanson (1990). ''The Field of Political Communication: Beyond the Voter Persuasion Paradigm.'' In *New Directions in Political Communication: A Resource Book*, edited by David L. Swanson and Dan Nimmo. Newbury Park, CA: Sage Publications.

Noel, S. J. R. (1976). ''Patrons and Clients in Canadian Politics.'' Paper presented at the annual meeting of the Canadian Political Science Association, Quebec City, May.

Odegard, Peter H. (1928). *Pressure Politics: The Story of the Anti-Saloon League*. New York: Columbia University Press.

Olson, Mancur (1965). *The Logic of Collective Action*. Cambridge: Harvard University Press.

Olson, Mancur (1982). *The Rise and Decline of Nations: Economic Growth, Stagflation, and Social Rigidities*. New Haven: Yale University Press.

Paehlke, Robert (1991). ''Government Regulating Itself: A Canadian–American Comparison.'' *Administration and Society* 22: 424–450.

Paltiel, Khayyam (1982). ''The Changing Environment and Role of Special Interest Groups.'' *Canadian Public Administration* 25: 198–210.

Peterson, Paul E. (1990). ''The Rise and Fall of Special Interest Politics.'' *Political Science Quarterly* 105: 539–556.

Pierce, John C., Kathleen M. Beatty, and Paul R. Hagner (1982). *The Dynamics of*

American Public Opinion: Patterns and Processes. Glenview, IL: Scott Foresman.

Pierce, John C., Lynette Lee-Sammons, and Nicholas P. Lovrich (1988). "U.S. and Japanese Source Reliance for Environmental Information." *Journalism Quarterly* 65: 902–908.

Pierce, John C., and Nicholas P. Lovrich (1983). "Trust in the Technical Information Provided by Interest Groups: The Views of Legislators, Activists, Experts and the General Public." *Policy Studies Journal* 11: 626–639.

Pierce, John C., and Nicholas P. Lovrich (1986). *Water Resources, Democracy and the Technical Information Quandary.* Port Washington, NY: Associated Faculty Press.

Pierce, John C., Nicholas P. Lovrich, Taketsugu Tsurutani, and Takematsu Abe (1987). "Environmental Policy Elites: Trust of Information Sources in Japan and the United States." *American Behavioral Scientist* 30: 578–596.

Pierce, John C., Nicholas P. Lovrich, Taketsugu Tsurutani, and Taketmatsu Abe (1989). *Public Knowledge and Environmental Politics in Japan and the United States.* Boulder, CO: Westview Press.

Presthus, Robert (1973). *Elite Accommodation in Canadian Politics.* Toronto: Cambridge University Press.

Presthus, Robert (1974). *Elites in the Policy Process.* London: Cambridge University Press.

Pross, A. Paul (1975). "Pressure Groups: Adaptive Instruments of Political Communication." In *Pressure Group Behavior in Canadian Politics,* edited by A. Paul Pross. Toronto: McGraw-Hill Ryerson.

Pross, A. Paul (1985). "Parliamentary Influence and the Diffusion of Power." *Canadian Journal of Political Science* 18: 235–266.

Pross, A. Paul (1986). *Group Politics and Public Policy.* Toronto: Oxford University Press.

Przeworski, Adam, and Henry Teune (1970). *The Logic of Comparative Social Inquiry.* New York: Wiley Interscience.

Rohrschneider, Robert (1991). "Public Opinion Toward Environmental Groups in Western Europe: One Movement or Two?" *Social Science Quarterly* 72: 251–266.

Rosenbaum, Walter A. (1978). "Public Involvement as Reform and Ritual: The Department of Federal Participation Programs." In *Citizen Participation in America,* edited by Stuart Langton. Lexington, MA: Lexington Books.

Rossini, Frederick A., and Alan L. Porter (1984). "Public Participation and Professionalism in Impact Assessment." In *Citizen Participation in Science Policy,* edited by James C. Peterson. Amherst: University of Massachusetts Press.

Roszak, Theodore (1972). *Where the Wasteland Ends: Politics and Transcendence in Postindustrial Society.* New York: Doubleday.

Rothenberg, Lawrence C. (1988). "Organizational Maintenance and the Retention Decision in Groups." *American Political Science Review* 88: 1129–1152.

Rothman, Stanley (1960). "Systematic Political Theory: Observations on the Group Approach." *American Political Science Review* 54: 15–33.

Rummands, James S. (1970). "A Challenge to the Law." In *Ecotatics: The Sierra Club Handbook for Environmental Activists,* edited by John G. Mitchell and Constance L. Stallings. New York: Simon and Schuster.

Salisbury, Robert H. (1969). "An Exchange Theory of Interest Groups" *Midwest Journal of Political Science* 13: 1–32.

Savage, J. (1985). "Postmaterialism of the Left and Right." *Comparative Political Studies* 17: 431–451.

Scarce, Rik (1990). *Eco-Warriors: Understanding the Radical Environmental Movement*. Chicago: Noble Press.

Schattschneider, E. E. (1960). *The Semisovereign People*. New York: Holt, Rinehart and Winston.

Schlozman, Kay Lehman, and John T. Tierney (1986). *Organized Interests and American Democracy*. New York: Harper and Row.

Schmidtz, David (1991). *The Limits of Government: An Essay on the Public Goods Argument*. Boulder, CO: Westview Press.

Segsworth, R. V. (1990). "Policy and Program Evaluation in the Government of Canada." In *Program Evaluation and the Management of Government: Patterns and Prospects Across Eight Nations*, edited by Ray Rist. New Brunswick, NJ: Transaction Publishers.

Seroka, Jim (ed.) (1986). *Rural Public Administration: Problems and Prospects*. Westport, CT: Greenwood Press.

Stanfield, Rochelle L. (1985). "Environmental Lobby's Changing of the Guard is Part of Movement's Evolution." *National Journal* (June 18): 130–153.

Steel, Brent S., Mary Ann Steger, Nicholas P. Lovrich, and John C. Pierce (1990). "Consensus and Dissension Among Contemporary Environmental Activists: Preservationists and Conservationists in the American and Canadian Context." *Government and Policy* 8: 379–393.

Steel, Brent S., Rebecca L. Warner, Nicholas P. Lovrich, and John C. Pierce (1992). "The Inglehart–Flanagan Debate Over Postmaterialist Values: Some Evidence From a Canadian–American Case Study." *Political Psychology* 13: 61–77.

Steger, Mary Ann E., John C. Pierce, Brent S. Steel, and Nicholas P. Lovrich (1988). "Information Source Reliance and Knowledge Acquisition: Canadian/U.S. Comparisons Regarding Acid Rain." *Western Political Quarterly* 41: 747–764.

Tatalovich, Raymond, and Byron W. Daynes (1988). *Social Regulatory Policy: Moral Controversies in American Politics*. Boulder, CO: Westview Press.

Thurow, Lester C. (1983). *Dangerous Currents: The State of Economics*. New York: Random House.

Touraine, Alain (1971). *The Post-Industrial Society: Tomorrow's Social History*. New York: Random House.

Truman, David B. (1951). *The Governmental Process*. New York: Knopf.

Tsurutani, Taketsugu (1977). *Political Change in Japan*. New York: McKay.

Vasu, Michael L., Debra W. Steward, and G. David Garson (1990). *Organizational Behavior and Public Management*, 2d ed. New York: Marcel Dekker.

Verba, Sidney (1965). "Organizational Membership and Democratic Consensus." *Journal of Politics* 27: 467–497.

Vogel, David (1981). "The Public-Interest Movement and the American Reform Tradition." *Political Science Quarterly* 95: 607–627.

von Hippel, Frank, and Joel Primack (1972). "Public Interest Science." *Science* 177: 1166–1171.

Wamsley, Gary L., Charles T. Goodsell, John A. Rohr, Camilla M. Stivers,

Orion F. White, and James F. Wolf (1987). ''The Public Administration and the Governance Process: Refocusing the American Dialogue.'' In *A Centennial History of the American Administrative State*, edited by Ralph Clark Chandler. New York: Collier Macmillan.

Waterman, Nan (1978). ''The League of Women Voters: Exploring American and Organizational Futures.'' In *Anticipating Democracy: People in the Politics of the Future*, edited by Clement Bezold. New York: Random House.

Weisskopf, Michael (1990). ''Environmental Groups Sail the Mainstream.'' *Washington Post National Weekly Edition*. (April 30–May 6): 10–11.

Wenk, Edward (1986). *Tradeoffs: Imperatives of Choice in a High-Tech World*. Baltimore: The Johns Hopkins University Press.

Wenner, Lettie McSpudden (1990). *U.S. Energy and Environmental Interest Groups: Institutional Profiles*. Westport, CT: Greenwood Press.

Westell, Anthony (1991). ''The Weakening of Canadian Culture.'' *The American Review of Canadian Studies* 21: 263–268.

Wetstone, Gregory S. (1987). ''A History of the Acid Rain Issue.'' In *Science for Public Policy*, edited by Harvey Brooks and Chester L. Cooper. New York: Pergamon Press.

White, Graham (1989). *The Ontario Legislature. A Political Analysis*. Toronto: University of Toronto Press.

White, John Kenneth (1988). *The New Politics of Old Values*, 2d ed. Hanover, NH: University Press of New England.

White, Orion, and Gideon Sjoberg (1972). ''The Emerging 'New Politics' in America.'' In *Politics in the Post-Welfare State: Responses to the New Individualism*, edited by M. D. Hancock and G. Sjoberg. New York: Columbia University Press.

Wills, Gary (1972). ''Working Within the System Won't Change Anything.'' *The Center Magazine* (July–August): 34.

Wilson, James Q. (1962). *The Amateur Democrat*. Chicago: University of Chicago Press.

Wilson, James Q. (1973). *Political Organizations*. New York: Basic Books.

Yang, Kuo-sho (1988). ''Will Societal Modernization Eventually Eliminate Cross-Cultural Psychological Differences?'' In *The Cross-Cultural Challenges to Social Psychology*, edited by Michael H. Bond. Beverly Hills: Sage Publications.

Yankelovich, Daniel (1982). *New Rules: Searching for Self-Fulfillment in a World Turned Upside Down*. New York: Bantam Books.

Yankelovich, Daniel (1991). *Coming to Public Judgment: Making Democracy Work in a Complex World*. Syracuse: Syracuse University Press.

Zald, Mayer N., and John D. McCarthy (1987). *Social Movements in an Organizational Society*. New Brunswick, NJ: Transaction Publishers.

Ziegler, Harmon (1964). *Interest Groups in American Society*. Englewood Cliffs, NJ: Prentice-Hall.

Zolberg, Aristide R. (1966). *Creating Political Order: The Party-States of West Africa*. Chicago: Rand McNally.

Index

ABOUT THE AUTHORS

The four authors have collaborated for eight years in the research of issues in environmental politics involving Canadians and Americans. They have co-authored over a dozen articles in refereed journals, and they have received two separate grants from the Canadian government (U.S. Canadian Embassy Faculty Research Grant Program) to support their research.

JOHN C. PIERCE is Professor of Political Science and Dean of the College of Sciences and Arts, Washington State University.

MARY ANN E. STEGER is Associate Professor of Political Science, Northern Arizona University.

BRENT S. STEEL is Assistant Professor of Political Science, Washington State University at Vancouver.

NICHOLAS P. LOVRICH is Professor of Political Science and Director of the Division of Governmental Studies and Services, Washington State University.